DOGMA ➤ *Volume 2: God and Creation*

A PROJECT OF JOHN XXIII INSTITUTE
Saint Xavier College, Chicago

DOGMA

by Michael Schmaus

Under the theological supervision of T. Patrick Burke

2 *God and Creation*

The Foundations of Christology

SHEED AND WARD : KANSAS CITY AND LONDON

Translated by Ann Laeuchli, William McKenna, S.J., and T. Patrick Burke

Third printing, February 1976

© Sheed and Ward, Inc., 1969
6700 Squibb Road
Mission, Ks. 66202

Library of Congress Catalog Card Number 68-26033
ISBN: 0-8362-0282-1

Printed in the United States of America

Contents

Contents   vii

Preface

The first volume of this series was concerned with the foundations on which Christian doctrinal theology must rest. With the present volume we begin a presentation of the subject matter of theology. Since the time of Peter Lombard in the twelfth century it has been customary to begin with the doctrine of God, as One and Three. However, if we are to bring out the Christocentric structure of the Christian faith we need to take as our point of departure the event of Christ. And yet it is impossible to speak of Jesus without speaking of his relationship to God and to the world, since these are essential preconditions for understanding what he said and did and was. Therefore although the basis of this work is Christological, we must begin with some consideration of God and the world. But it is intended that this should take place in the light of the fact of Jesus Christ. We shall treat of God here, then, only insofar as is necessary for comprehension of Jesus Christ the Son of God. So we shall speak of the conceptions of God in the Old Testament, adding only a few observations from the New Testament for the sake of completeness. In particular there is no intention of offering an entire doctrine of the Trinity at this point. An attempt will be made in that direction in the course of the treatment of the salvific words of Jesus in Volume 3. No doubt this procedure involves certain methodological difficulties, but some problems of this sort are unavoidable no matter where we begin. In view of the value of bringing out clearly the Christological center of Christian theology, the present arrangement seems to involve the lesser evil. This volume is to be understood, therefore, not so much as a treatment of God and creation in themselves, but Christologically, that is, as a prelude to Christology in the strict sense.

‹ I

The Old Testament Concept of God as the Presupposition for an Understanding of Christ

‹1

The One God

Scripture does not provide us with a systematic doctrine of God. What it does instead is bear witness to the experience which certain people had of God in certain situations. In what follows Scripture will be taken as the point of departure and the doctrine of the Church will be considered subsequently as a development of what is to be found in Scripture. The reason for treating the matter in this way is the question of order. Out of the mass of material which Scripture provides, the determinative elements have to be selected and the rest arranged in relationship to them; and then, as far as possible, we must follow their development through various stages, so that we see how the doctrinal formulas of the Church arose.

THE MONOTHEISM OF THE OLD TESTAMENT

The foundation of the faith of the Old Testament is the conviction of the uniqueness of that universal, living, personal power, transcending the world and in no way subject to human manipulation, yet active in human history, which is called by the name "God." This belief that there is only one God who transcends the world, a belief which grew up in the midst of a general polytheism, is the basic achievement of the Old Testament. Genesis traces the

5

conviction of the uniqueness of the God Yahweh back to the beginnings of mankind. The research done in the history of religion
confirms this scriptural account in that there is no evidence that
this belief in the one true God was the product of evolution from
primitive conceptions of divine forces (Mircea Eliade). Nevertheless, according to Exodus 6:3 the name Yahweh was not yet
known to Abraham, Isaac or Jacob. They spoke of God as the
"highest Lord," El Shaddai. According to Exodus 3:13 the name
Yahweh was not revealed until the time of Moses. We have to
assume, then, that in all probability the period of the patriarchs
was characterized rather by an elevated form of monolatry (heno-
theism). The God known to the patriarchs as the high and most
powerful Lord gradually came to be identified with Yahweh (Gen.
14:18–22). In this way the monolatry of the early period developed into monotheism in the strict sense. For Moses and the period
which followed him Yahweh alone is God, not only the God of
Israel but God as such.

Yahweh is not a national God. In his nature he is superior to
the world; his power is not limited, it reaches out beyond the
boundaries of his own people. He has dominion over nature also.
As the one and only true God Yahweh does not tolerate strange
gods. "I am the Lord your God, who brought you out of the land
of Egypt, out of the house of bondage. You shall have no other
gods before me" (Ex. 20:2f.; Deut. 5:6f., *RSV*).[1] There are no
other gods. Yahweh unites in himself everything that is divine, all
the qualities which those who believed in myths attributed to their
gods. It is of fundamental significance that monotheism seems to
have arisen not as the result of speculative reflection but through
experience, the experience of the one, all-powerful God. The liberation from slavery in Egypt and the event on Sinai involved the
experience of Someone, a Power—unique, superior to the world,
and irresistible: it is he who is God. This development of monotheism out of historical experience gave it a practical or ethical
character. Again and again the people are called—by the Yahwist,
Samuel, David, Elias and Elijah—to declare for the one and only
God (see especially 1 Kgs. 18:21–40).

As the story of Elias shows, we find the idea still widespread among the people that a certain power has to be attributed to the divinities of other nations. Hence there is a constant danger of their falling away, and we find elements of uncertainty in these passages where the superiority of the God of Israel over other gods is praised. Perhaps this is simply poetical language. However, it is really only in the time of the prophets that the existence of other divinities besides Yahweh is totally rejected and that of the one true God fully affirmed. Examples of this strong and emphatic monotheism of the prophets are Is. 2:8–18; 6:1–3; 10:12; 19:1–3; Jer. 2:11; 5:7; 14:22; 10:9f.; Deut. 4:39; 6:4; 32:39; Is. 40:21–28; 41:29; 43:10f.; 44:8; 45:5,14,21f.; 46:9.

The strict monotheism which characterizes the time of the prophets was a natural development of beliefs already present at the time of Moses. If it took centuries before the Jewish people clearly grasped the fact that there is only one true God, we nevertheless find from the beginning that the one God is praised: for his power, greater than that of the world, irresistible; for his ontic and ethical holiness, his justice and his faithfulness to the covenant. This sense of God's unique dynamism is of greater weight than any speculative theses about his nature. The prophets establish the fact that there is only one God in terms of a judicial process involving him and the divinities worshipped by the tribes surrounding Israel. The issue is that these divinities are simply nothing. The disciples of Isaiah, for example, attribute the following words to God: "Thus says the Lord, the King of Israel and his Redeemer, the Lord of Hosts: 'I am the first and I am the last; besides me there is no God. Who is like me? Let him proclaim it, let him declare and set it forth before me. Who has announced from of old the things to come? Let them tell us what is yet to be. Fear not, nor be afraid; have I not told you from of old and declared it? And you are my witnesses! Is there a God besides me? There is no Rock; I know not any.' " (Is. 44:6–8; similarly Is. 45:5f.; 45:18–24; Jer. 10:10–16). The question will be discussed further in the treatment of the names of God.

Monotheism formed the central dogma of late Judaism. Every male Israelite was expected to confess his belief in it twice daily in what was called the Shema. The doctrine is also stressed in

Hellenistic Judaism, in its attempt to preserve the traditional faith in the midst of a polytheistic world (see Wisdom 13). Philo's doctrine of a divine Logos is not a deviation from strict monotheism. In view of the later development of monotheism in the New Testament it should be emphasized that the God of the Old Testament was considered to be one person.

The New Testament adopts the monotheism of the Old Testament as an established part of its tradition (Mk. 12:29; 1 Cor. 8:4; Jas. 2:19; 1 Tim. 2:5). The God of the New Testament is the God of the patriarchs (Acts 3:13; 5:30; 22:14), the God of Israel (Mt. 15:31; Lk. 1:68; Jn. 8:41f.; Acts 13:17; Heb. 11:16) and so also of the Church (Acts 15:14f.; Heb. 4:9; 11:16; 1 Pet. 2:10). For the early Jewish Christians, then, polytheism was not a serious danger. For those who came to Christianity from paganism, Jesus was the way from the gods to the one God (Gal. 4:3; 1 Thess. 1:9; 1 Cor. 10:14; 12:2; Col. 2:8; Acts 14:15ff.; 2 Cor. 6:16). All the same, the heathen Christian communities of the early Church were faced with a constant temptation to fall into some sort of polytheism, and for this reason the apostles and their companions attempted to counter polytheism not only in their mission speeches to the heathen but also in their catechetical instructions and sermons to the converted heathen Christians. Again and again the preachers of the Christian gospel came up against polytheism—in Athens, in Lystra, in Ephesus (Acts 17:24f.; 14:15; 19:26). They equate the worship of idols with godlessness. These gods have no real existence (Gal. 4:8f.); they are nothing (1 Cor. 8:4; 10:19). Here we see the New Testament taking its concept directly from the Old Testament. To worship idols is to despise the one true God and necessarily leads to subjection to demonic powers (1 Cor. 10:7; Gal. 4:8; Rom. 1:28–32; 1 Cor. 10:20f.). It was the work of Christ to free us from the gods, from slavery to the elemental powers of the world. If polytheism remained a danger for early Christianity (2 Cor. 4:4), the lords and gods who abound on all sides are nevertheless not lords and gods for the Christian. For him there is only the one true God (1 Cor. 8:4f.), the God of the Old Testament revelation (Mt. 15:31; Lk. 1:68; Mk. 12:35f.; Acts 3:13; 5:30; 22:14; 2 Cor.

6:16f., etc.). The Christian may not worship or profess belief in any other god but the one true God—neither mammon nor his own belly nor idols nor the powers of the world nor the deified emperor in Rome (Mt. 6:24; Lk. 12:19ff.; Phil. 3:19; 2 Cor. 6:16; Gal. 4:8–11; Mk. 12:17). It is emphasized in these texts that all economic and cultural life and the world of politics as well is subject to the one Lord God. It is a question of serving God and of giving him what belongs to him, of obeying him alone and relying on him alone, of remaining faithful to him even in the most difficult situations, even unto death. For Jesus and for the early Church this is the real meaning of the *Eis Theos*.[2]

For early Christianity this belief in the one true God is not in the category of a piece of interesting information or of philosophical insight; it is the object of unconditional profession and commitment. The power it exercises may be seen perhaps most clearly in the Acts of the martyrs. There we find joy and gratitude for the revelation of the one God and a full grasp of the implications of true faith in God as opposed to the polytheistic conception of divinity which prevailed in the surrounding culture. The fact that there is only one God—that is, his uniqueness—implies his universality. The early Church rejected all national divinities uncompromisingly.

Polytheism was frequently defended by the writers of the ancient world on political grounds. In the second century, for example, Celsius speaks of belief in one God as a revolt in the political order. He views the various national cults as expressions of the distinctions between nations. Whoever attacks them attacks the Roman empire, whose great achievement is was to bring together many nations into a kind of political unity in which they did not lose their own individuality, and the fitting theological expression of this is the Pantheon. The attempt to do away with the national divinities therefore is an attack on the character and constitution of the Roman Imperium. A monotheistic conception of God would be possible only if it were possible for Asians, Europeans and Libyans, Greeks and barbarians to adopt one uniform "law." But only a total ignorance of human nature could make such a view tenable. So the question whether there is one God became a political matter, and politics claimed primacy in deciding religious questions.

In point of fact, belief in one God is not without political consequences. The early Christian writers maintained, in reply to the objections of the pagans, that it was precisely the one God who had made, and makes, it possible for such a variety of human qualities and such a multitude of human groups to exist; that it is precisely he who summons the multiplicity of creatures to that definitive future in which all created individuals and communities will reach their consummation without losing their individuality. From the standpoint of strict monotheism the gods are to be understood as the adversaries of the one God or as misinterpretations of that numinous power which we find in the world. In polytheism this power simply takes on a multiplicity of forms.

What we encounter in Scripture has been expressed by the Church in many professions of faith; these have always been made in reply to some threat against monotheism, whether from polytheism, Gnosticism, Manicheism or some form of dualism (DS 40ff.; 457ff.; 685; 790; 800; 854; 1330; 1333; 1336; 1731; 2902; 3021).[3]

Associated with the experience of the oneness of God in the sense we have been discussing is the experience of his total power over the world. It is questionable whether justice is done to the weight which Scripture gives to this power if it is considered simply as a quality of the divine will, and especially if it is considered as simply one quality among others. For the Old Testament it represents in a certain sense precisely that which is divine in God. It is his unlimited power which distinguishes God from the gods: it is this which shows that the gods are nothing, are merely human inventions. In judging the statements of Scripture about the omnipotence of God, it must be emphasized that this conviction is not the result of philosophical reflections but of immediate experience. The power of God is experienced first of all in his salvific interventions in history, and secondly in his work of creation in the world which he has made (Gen. 18:14; 49:24; Deut. 32:4,30; 33:29; Ex. 15; Job 34:10–18; 26:5–14; 38:4–12). His manner of acting is often mysterious to men, and even frightening (Job

34:22–33). The Psalms especially contain many passages referring to the experience of God's almighty power. The oldest names
for God—El Shaddai, Elohim—also express this experience of
God as the living and all-powerful one whom no one can effectively
resist (Gen. 17:1; 35:11; 43:14; 49:25). There are of course
numerous statements of a more doctrinal nature in the Old Testament about the power of God. It can be ascertained without
difficulty that these are reflections on experiences of God (Jer.
32:17,27; Job 42:2; Ps. 113; 135:5).[4] God needs no help (Is.
44:24) and knows no obstacle (43:13). A special expression
of his omnipotence is to be found in his "wonderful deeds" (Gen.
18:14; Ps. 77:15; 35:15).

In the Septuagint the unlimited power of God is frequently referred to by the use of the word *Pantokrator,* in the Vulgate with
the word *Omnipotens.* The sense of the first is dynamic, that of
the second static. The first refers to unlimitedly powerful action,
the second to the divine power as one quality among others. In
this sense it must be understood as the infinite perfection of the
active power of God in the non-divine sphere, extending to everything that is not intrinsically impossible. It must, however, be emphasized that God himself is the measure of possibility. Because
he surpasses our comprehension we are not in a position to draw
a clear boundary between what is possible and what is impossible
(Karl Rahner).

In the New Testament God's power is shown in physical healing and in the forgiveness of sinners (Mt. 19:26; Mk. 14:36;
10:27; Lk. 1:37; Eph. 3:20). The power it takes to make a justified man out of a sinner is no less than that required to create
the world of nature (Mk. 2:1–12). Christ, in carrying out his
work of redemption, is wielding the unlimited power of God (Mt.
28:18; Mk. 16:17f.; Jn. 1:3). He has received all his power from
his Father (Jn. 5:19–22). He has the divine commission to work
saving deeds of power, thus bringing the history of man's salvation towards its fulfillment. His deeds of power are anticipations
—images, as it were—of the way the world will be when God has
brought it to its maturity: the pattern of this life to come is the
glorified life of Christ. The revelation of God's power in the New

Testament has considerably more of a hidden character than it has in the Old Testament. In fact here the power of God looks more like weakness. When God entered human history to make himself present to men in the person of Jesus, he laid his power down at the door (Romano Guardini), he emptied himself, assuming the helplessness of the human condition (Phil. 2:7). In Jesus, God has become so helpless that men can bring to trial this One he has sent, condemn and execute him. However, the power of God will not remain hidden forever. A time will come when history is brought to completion, and the divine power will then assert itself definitively throughout the whole cosmos as the fullness of love and truth. Ultimately the testimony which Scripture bears to the unlimited power of God must be understood in eschatological terms if it is not to seem unrealistic and incredible.

The doctrinal statements of the Church on this matter are to be found in the forms of professions of faith (DS 11; 44; 45; 75; 125; 163; 683; 800; 851; 1338; 3001). The Church's faith in God's power can also be seen in its official prayers. It is interesting to see that here the Eastern Church continues to stress the all-powerful acts of God (Pantokrator) and the Western Church, by contrast, the all-powerful being of God (Deus Omnipotens).

THE FATHER OF JESUS

The Old Testament people of God experienced their God as living and gracious, as one who by his intervention in human affairs created history. The New Testament message confirms the experience of God expressed in the Old. But in the New Testament we learn that the God who intervened so powerfully to establish the ancient covenant is the Father of Jesus Christ. In the language of the early Church councils and of the theology which prepared the way for them beforehand and interpreted them afterwards, the God of the Old Testament, the Father of Jesus Christ, is the first divine person in a divine life which is one and yet triune. In this manner of speaking the word "God" does not refer to the trinitarian God as such but to this first divine person. The one God of the Old Testament is referred to in the New Testament also simply as God, as *the* God. The word "God" is rarely used of Jesus (see, however, Rom. 9:5; Jn. 1:1; 20:28; 1 Jn. 5:20; Tit. 1:3). The expression is never used of the Holy Spirit. Of the one God who was proclaimed as the living God and the only God, the New Testament assures us that he sent his son, that Jesus comes from him, that after his death he was raised again by God. Thus for the New Testament also it is this God who brings about the history of man's salvation (Acts 3:12–26; 4:24f.; Eph. 3:9f.; Heb. 1:2). The meaning of the term "son of God" will be discussed later.

This witness of both the Old and the New Testaments to the fact that there is only one God and the witness of the New Testament, on the other hand, that Jesus is the son of God, was precisely what created a most difficult theological problem for the post-apostolic period. For a long time it seemed impossible to reconcile monotheism with a metaphysical conception of Jesus' sonship of God. The one seemed to exclude the other. An immense effort of thought was needed to reconcile the apparent contradiction. The principal milestones in this long search were the Councils of Nicea (325 A.D.), Ephesus (331 A.D.[333]) and Chalcedon (451 A.D.).

Notes

[1] *RSV: Revised Standard Version*. Except where otherwise indicated all Old Testament quotations in this book are from the *Revised Standard Version and the Apocrypha*, copyrighted 1957 by the Division of Christian Education, National Council of the Churches of Christ in the U.S.A., and used by permission.

[2] E. Stauffer in *Theologisches Wörterbuch zum Neuen Testament*, ed. G. Kittel, Stuttgart (1930–   ), III, 102.

[3] DS: H. Denzinger, *Enchiridion Symbolorum*, ed. Adolf Schönmetzer (Freiburg: Herder, 1965 [33]). Quotations from this work are in the English translation contained in *The Church Teaches*, trans. the Jesuit Fathers of St. Mary's College, Kansas, with a preface by Gerald Van Ackeren, S.J. (St. Louis: Herder, 1955).

[4] The numbering of the psalms is that of *The Revised Standard Version*.

◄ 2

The Mystery of the Revealed God: His Names

We do not see God directly anywhere, but history and nature give us an experience of his hidden, dynamic presence. The real experience of God was given in those events in which Israel was constituted as a people, but this very experience shows how little God allows himself to be seen directly and understood even by his closest friends; even they depend on mediating signs. This is an experience inescapable as it is painful. It is not without significance that we find that in those books of the Old Testament which belong to the Hellenistic period the dynamism of the living experience of God is transformed into a static doctrine.

When Moses asked God to travel with him and to teach him his ways if he had really found grace in his eyes, he received the answer:

"I myself will go with you, and I will give you rest." Moses said, "If you are not going with us yourself, do not make us leave this place. By what means can it be known that I, I and my people, have won your favor, if not by your going with us? By this we shall be marked out, I and my people, from all the peoples on the face of the earth." Yahweh said to Moses: "Again I will do what you have asked, because you have won my favor and because I know you by name."

Moses said: "Show me your glory, I beg you." And he said: "I will let all my splendor pass in front of you, and I will pronounce before you the name Yahweh. I have compassion on whom I will, and I show pity to whom I please. You cannot see my face," he said, "for man cannot see me and live." And Yahweh said, "Here is a place beside me. You must stand on the rock, and when my glory passes by, I will put you in a cleft of the rock and shield you with my hand while I pass by. Then I will take my hand away and you shall see the back of me; but my face is not to be seen." (Ex. 33:14–23,*J*).[1]

This text makes it clear that to know God means to experience his grace but that the experience can never develop into seeing him. Ontologism, in its several varieties, was mistaken in its thesis that God can be seen directly by the human mind (A. Rosmini, V. Gioberti; see DS 3201–3241).

Knowledge of God requires knowledge of God's name. In our experience the nameless is the unknown, the stranger, and so also the nameless God is unknown and strange. When God appeared to Moses near Mt. Horeb from the midst of the burning bush while Moses was herding the sheep of his father-in-law, Jethro, a priest of Midian, God announced that he had come down in order to free the people, the descendants of the patriarchs, from their bondage in Egypt. He gave Moses the task of putting his plan into operation. Moses expressed doubts of his own adequacy, but he was reassured: "I shall be with you." Moses was still not wholly content with this promise, for he anticipated that when he communicated God's plan to his compatriots, they were sure to ask: Who was this God? After all, they had known many gods in Egypt. Moses asked this God who had appeared to him what reply he was to give to such a question. Here follows God's definitive self-revelation, reported in the third chapter of the book of Exodus:

God said to Moses, "I AM WHO I AM." And he said, "Say this to the people of Israel, 'I AM has sent me to you.' " God also said to Moses, "Say this to the people of Israel, 'The LORD, the God of your fathers, the God of Abraham, the God of Isaac, and the God of Jacob, has sent me to you'; this is my name for ever, and thus I am to be remembered throughout all generations." (Ex. 3:14–16)

This text has frequently been interpreted in terms of Greek metaphysics, as if it permitted God to be defined as absolute existence, but the interpretation is possible only on the basis of Greek ontology. Greek metaphysics in fact is already reflected in the translation of the Septuagint, for here the word in question is rendered by the formula "I am the one who is," an interpretation which cannot be directly justified from the Hebrew text itself. The latter is not without metaphysics, but its metaphysics is not the Greek metaphysics of being. It is, if we want to put it that way, the I-Thou metaphysics of the whole Old Testament. There will always be a question as to whether or how this I-Thou metaphysics can be expressed in terms of a Greek metaphysics of being. To be sure, this was done in western theology and might even be said to be characteristic of it. Yet the problem remains of whether the gain—which cannot be denied—did not also entail a loss; the clarity sought by the western mind was at least partially attained, but at the risk of the original fullness in the grasp of reality. The expression means that God is he who possesses reality. By his reality he is distinguished from all the other gods. The latter are nothing—so devoid of reality that the living God Yahweh, at least from the time of the prophets, became known not only as the highest among the Gods but as the only one—as *the* God. The people of Israel are forbidden to revere other gods besides him, even as inferior gods. Yahweh's uniqueness is such that, in contrast with all other gods, he does not even have a female god as a consort. Although all that belongs to sex is based upon his creative will, he himself is not sexed. This one and only real God is present not only as an unchangeable being but as a God who acts in the midst of his people as the gracious creator of human history. He desires to conclude a covenant with his people, and he will always be a faithful partner in the covenant (Deut. 7:6ff.; 23:6; Is. 49:15f.; 54:5–8; 63:9; Jer. 3:12; Hos. 14:15f.).

The covenant which he makes with his people will not be rendered void even by the infidelity of his human partners. It will last eternally, owing to the unchangeable faithfulness of God. In the word Yahweh, therefore, is expressed God's activity, his active and gracious relationship to the people he has chosen. The characteristic thing that we can say of God is that he remains always among his people as savior and helper, and goes with them through all the vicissitudes of history. He is Immanuel, "God with us" (Is. 7:14). Nothing more or greater can be said of him. The proof of his unchanging fidelity is in the fact that he already had been with the patriarchs, and that he remains with his people, showing the same mercy and the same fidelity with which he called and led Abraham, with which he guided Isaac and Jacob. Now he desires to lead his people towards a future which will be their ultimate salvation. What God calls himself is thus an expression belonging to the history of salvation, not a formula in the sense of Greek metaphysics. If a man had given the answer which God gave to Moses, we should probably have to say that an answer had been refused. One would have to interpret it as: I am myself. And that would mean that the speaker was cutting off communication between himself and the questioner. But from God the reply expresses exactly the opposite: it is stressed that God is one on whom we can always rely, because he remains among his people with a constant fidelity. He is present for his people, so that they can always call to him when they need him. His power is one with his faithfulness. In view of this richness of meaning in the word "Yahweh" it is understandable that he was often addressed by this name, and according to Ezekiel he uses it of himself in speaking to the people: "You will learn that I am Yahweh, when I bring you back to the soil of Israel" (Ez. 20:42, J). Both the prophetic literature and the psalms are imbued with the idea that God can be characterized as "the God who is with his people" (cf. Is. 7:14f.).

The fact that there is only one God, and that he is unparalleled, as well as the fullness of his divine being, are also expressed in another name, "Elohim." We can consider the word "Yahweh" as God's own name. The word "Elohim," however, is a generic name. The fact that the plural form is used means that all that is divine is summed up in Yahweh. There are no elements of divinity which are not gathered into a unity in him. The word "Elohim" thus serves the need which piety has to express itself in worship. It expresses more than does "Yahweh" the sublimity of God's greatness and man's awe before it. The singular "El," also used for God, emphasizes his power, but this word is also used for the heathen gods. When the true God is meant, this is usually made clear by additional expressions. The frequently found "Adonai" as a name for God also points to the aspect of sovereignty. God is the highest Lord, Kyrios. The same is true, with a certain difference in emphasis, of the expression "Shaddai," Powerful One. All these formulations show that the Old Testament experience of God was not that of Plato's Supreme Good or Aristotle's Unmoved Mover: the God of the Old Testament is known as the Lord who creates and controls human history. The idea of transcendence is not lacking from the word "Yahweh," although the idea of immanence in the sense of effective presence is predominant; in this respect it is supplemented by the designation "Kadosh," the Holy One. God is felt to be holy insofar as he is unapproachable.

The names of God employed in the Old Testament, therefore, characterize God as near, even present, and at the same time as unapproachable and remote. He is experienced as inaccessible not in the metaphysical sense of separation from his creatures—the difference in kind between his being and theirs—but in his freedom from sin and in the judgment which he passes on his people in order to call them back to faithfulness after their infidelities; that is to say, to call them back to grace. We may say, all in all, that the biblical books which originated before the Hellenistic period speak more of the dynamism of God, while those that originated in the Hellenistic period tend simply to express his presence. Scripture conveys this unity of transcendence and immanence by saying that God is present as "the hidden God" (1 Cor. 2:7,9,10; Mt. 11:25; Is. 45:15). Again and again the mysterious character of their God was brought home to the people of Israel. Despite the closeness of the bond between them (particularly their leaders) and this God who had made them into one people, they still found his designs unpredictable and impenetrable. God's mystery was experienced in the most disheartening way when he allowed the heathen to triumph and his own people to be defeated, and the heathen could mock them, saying, Where is your God? (Ps. 115:2). But more than that, the people themselves were struck by the same question: Where is our God? (Ex. 17:7). Isaiah expresses a deep sense of God's mystery, and his anonymous disciples of the sixth century elaborate it still more in a grandiose image when they describe the seraphim crying, "Holy, holy, holy is Yahweh Sabaoth" (Is. 6:3,*J*).

In spite of his presence in history God is wholly other than the rest of reality (Is. 5:19; 12:6; 40:25; 45:15). In the end we cannot say who he is. Even in affliction we experience his care and his grace, always he is the "Immanuel"; but what he is in himself is unknown to us, and so also is his name. He tells us his name; yet there is a dialectic which requires us to understand him as the Nameless One (Judg. 13:17f.). On the one hand he can be addressed by name; on the other, what he is cannot be uttered in any name. It is possible for man to experience God's incomprehensibility, his awesome mystery, to the point of despair in the agonies which assault him without warning and depart from him without apparent reason; all too often he can find no certain cause for these "nights," they are wrapped in impenetrable darkness. Such an experience of God is described in the book of Job, and we see how no human reasoning is of any avail here; only submission to the mystery gives liberation.

In the New Testament the mysterious character of God manifests itself even more powerfully, for here he is revealed to us as triune. The First Vatican Council formulated the mystery of the tri-personal life of God in this fashion: the mystery could not be discovered by human reason without divine revelation, nor can it be transformed into a rational truth even when it has been revealed (DS 3015ff.).

It is all the more striking then, and all the greater cause for joy, that this mysterious God allows himself to be called "Father" —even in the Old Testament, but more emphatically in the new (Eph. 2:18; Rom. 8:15–17, 23–30). Jesus even proclaims that "Father" is the principal title of God. Nevertheless this title is still full of mystery. How tremendous the Church feels this to be is shown in the Mass, her central ceremony, where she prefaces the use of it by saying: "Urged by Our Savior's bidding, we *dare* to say, Our Father. . . ."

The men of the Old Testament did not see any danger to God's transcendence in their efforts to describe him in a human way. The innumerable anthropomorphisms of the Old Testament do not mean that God was thought to be of the same kind as the rest of reality, but only that he is to be thought of as a living Thou. They were not thinking about making God into an image of man, but simply of praising him as the One who is truly living and powerful, and they could only do this by speaking of him as we speak of a man. It did not occur to them to localize God. In spite of the old concept of the earth as a flat dish placed on the waters beneath, with the sky as a dome holding back the waters above, God is never thought of as the God of a particular locality. He is present everywhere and always: man can never escape him, though he should fly to the ends of the earth. He is present in the depths of the human heart and present as sovereign Lord in the furthest reaches of heaven and earth. (2 Chron. 6:18; Job 11:7–9; 26:5f.; Ps. 139:1–16.)

Although in this section we are treating the concept of God in the Old Testament only as a prerequisite for understanding Jesus, we should note that the New Testament concept of God not only does not contradict that of the Old, but confirms and develops it. This is particularly true of the creative love which God shows in carrying on his plan of salvation to a further stage by sending his Son, with the effect that it becomes irrevocable and universal in scope and that the absolute future is now guaranteed not only by God's power and fidelity but also by the openness and receptivity of man.

Later on, in the analysis of Jesus Christ's salvific speech, we shall deal with those elements which lead essentially beyond the Old Testament. Here we shall confine ourselves to pointing out briefly how the revelation of God in the Old Testament is confirmed in the New. Jesus presupposed the earlier understanding and brought out its real meaning in an interpretation which was authoritative. Jesus' audience was acquainted with the divine self-revelation up to that time, so that he could use it as a basis for his preaching. In his Sermon on the Mount, and especially by his constant struggle against externalization, he freed the Old Testament idea of God from the many accretions and distortions to which it had become subject in the course of time, owing to an interpretation and practice which had become superficial, and restored its original beauty and vitality. In the New Testament the exaltation of God over the world, his sovereignty over both nature and history, and so his transcendence, are stressed. This means that in spite of his closeness to man, by the fact that he sent his Son, God is still the distant one, the inscrutable one, the Other. Perhaps a few examples will illustrate this. In the Book of Revelation (1:4,7f., *RSV*) we find it said: "Grace to you and peace from him who is and who was and who is to come. . . . Behold, he is coming with the clouds, and every eye will see him, everyone who pierced him; and all tribes of the earth will wail on account of him. Even so. Amen. 'I am the Alpha and the Omega,' says the Lord God, who is and who was and who is to come, the Almighty." At the end God speaks to John (22:12f., *RSV*): 'Behold, I am coming soon, bringing my recompense, to repay everyone for what he has done. I am the Alpha and the Omega, the first and the last, the beginning and the end." The apostle Paul is deeply shaken in face of the inscrutable majesty of God who is free to choose or reject as he will (Rom. 11:33–35). He sees that everything has its origin in God, lives from him and for him. We cannot take issue with God (Rom. 9:20–24). God's will is sovereign in nature and in human history (1 Cor. 15:28; 2 Cor. 12:8; Rev. 4–11). In the New Testament God is the Holy One whom man can only approach in awe. The "Holy" cry of Isaiah (Is. 6:3) resounds in the uninterrupted praise of the guardians of the throne in John's vision (Rev. 4:8f.). This takes place, as John sees it in his vision, in "heaven," in the space above creation which is reserved for God and belongs itself to the sphere of holiness. Almightiness and eternity are characteristic features of God's holiness. The Holy One will avenge the blood of his martyrs. If in the meantime he is silent and lets things take their course, he does so only in order to allow the number of the chosen witnesses to be completed (Rev. 6:10).

Mary inserts into her praise of God's power and greatness, of his justice and his judgments, and of his eternal fidelity (Ps. 111:9) the confession of faith: Holy is his name (Lk. 1:49). In Christ God's holiness has been disclosed to men, so that they can participate in it, once they are liberated from "the world." In consequence of his transcendence God is an eternal mystery to man. No human mind could ever have foretold what God has prepared for those who love him (1 Cor. 2:7–10). But even the manner in which God reveals his mystery is again wrapped in mystery. For the mystery which is God did not appear before men in radiant glory but in the form of a servant sharing the life of common humanity, suffering and dying. It could not appear in the unveiled splendor of its richness and profundity because, in order to show itself to man, it had to empty itself, entering into human forms, into human words and actions. Beyond the lowering of himself which necessarily accompanied his self-revelation in Jesus, God submitted to the weakness and vulnerability of our human condition, and it is precisely in this that he seems incomprehensible. In Jesus' everyday life, in his speech and his silences, his goings and comings, his anger and forgiveness, his suffering and dying, God's mystery is being unveiled. But this does not mean that we have been told something which we did not understand before and which, now that we know it, "explains" the mystery: God's self-revelation only makes the depth of the mystery more evident. The consequence of this revelation-in-concealment is that the masses of the people were on the one hand amazed at Jesus' words and actions and on the other totally unable to comprehend his message. Even the disciples failed to understand Jesus and his work until the coming of the Spirit. So steeped in mystery is God's hiddenness in his public revelation, the otherness of the divinity revealed in Jesus, that the divine wisdom can be mocked and rejected as folly by the man who relies simply on the power of his own knowledge and insight and is prepared to accept only what can be shown to be reasonable. By such a man the imponderable mystery of God will be regarded as meaningless nonsense. This is shown with greater force in that event in which Jesus was charged with declaring himself to be the son of God and was put to death. We must have light from God if we are to see this mystery which baffles the mind as indeed the mystery of God. Only the person who is enlightened by the Holy Spirit is capable of recognizing the gift God has given us (1 Cor. 2:12).

This survey of the doctrine of the New Testament concerning God's transcendence must be supplemented by a consideration of those passages in which his gracious and salvific presence is proclaimed and praised, in the New Testament as well as in the Old. "Yet he is not far from each one of us, for 'in him we live and move and have our being' " (Acts 17:27f., *RSV:* Paul's sermon). According to the New Testament God takes man into the care of his love. Even knowing God is nothing but the acceptance of God's grace by man. God knows his own (2 Tim. 2:19). Whoever loves God is known by him. Otherwise he could not turn to God in love (1 Cor. 8:3). Here God is viewed as our comforter. To be sure, the God who is near is also the God who judges; for everything is clear and open to him (Heb. 4:13). But it is the "Father in heaven" who sees into what is hidden (Mt. 6:4,6). We have explicit testimony of the healing and comforting power of God's knowledge (1 Jn. 3:19–22, *RSV*): "By this we shall know that we are of the truth, and reassure our hearts before him whenever our hearts condemn us; for God is greater than our hearts, and he knows everything. Beloved, if our hearts do not condemn us, we have confidence before God; and we receive from him whatever we ask, because we keep his commandments and do what pleases him." Newman once expressed this thought as follows:

God beholds thee individually, whoever thou art. He "calls thee by thy name." He sees thee, and understands thee, as He made thee. He knows what is in thee, all thy own peculiar feelings and thoughts, thy dispositions and likings, thy strength and thy weakness. He views thee in thy day of rejoicing, and thy day of sorrow. He sympathizes in thy hopes and thy temptations. He interests Himself in all thy anxieties and remembrances, all the risings and fallings of thy spirit. He has numbered the very hairs of thy head and the cubits of thy stature. He compasses thee round and bears thee in His arms; He takes thee up and sets thee down. He notes thy very countenance, whether smiling or in tears, whether healthful or sickly. He looks tenderly upon thy hands and thy feet; He hears thy voice, the beating of thy heart, and thy very breathing. Thou dost not love thyself better than He loves thee. Thou canst not shrink from pain more than He dislikes thy bearing it; and if He puts it on thee, it is as thou wilt put it on thyself, if thou art wise, for a greater good afterwards.[2]

In the ancient Church Augustine said something similar:

You try to fathom the depth of the ocean—what is more unfathomable than the human heart?[3] If what is imponderable is an abyss, do we not think that man's heart is an abyss? . . . Men can speak, reveal themselves in gestures and in what they can be heard to say: but whose thoughts can we penetrate, into whose heart can we look? What impulses are within a man, what he is capable of doing, and does and prepares for inwardly; what he wills or does not will in the depths of his heart—who can grasp this? . . . So secret are the recesses of a man's soul that his thoughts are hidden even from himself.[4]

The Fathers passionately rejected Eunomius's thesis that God can be comprehended from the aspect of uncreated being. Chrysostom calls this godlessness.[5] "What you understand is not God," said Augustine.[6] This ignorance is not the ignorance of the person who knows little, but of him who knows much, it is a *docta ignorantia*. According to Augustine, God is better known through ignorance than through knowledge.[7]

The nearness of God to man is actualized in a decisive way in Jesus Christ. Like the Old Testament, the New Testament too tells us that we have reason for confidence in God, who is both immanent in the world and transcends it because of his immutability, his eternity, his fidelity and his love. According to James 1:17 there is no change, not even a shadow of variation, in God our Father. The unchanging fidelity of God is described in detail by Paul in his Epistle to the Romans. As God is eternal, because he outlasts all ages, we who live in this mortal life, subject to decay, may hope for "eternal" life. Eternal life consists in participation in the life of God. God's eternal life is not extension into the past beyond the beginning of time and extension into the future beyond the end of time, but fullness of life and existence, a fullness which created time from out of itself and which always remains present as the foundation of events which take place in time. With the coming of Jesus Christ all these transcendent statements about God were confirmed. At the same time, however, the God to whom the Old Testament bears witness drew near to men in Christ to a degree which cannot be surpassed in its own order. This implies that what the Old Testament told us about God has been surpassed in the New Testament. But it has even greater import in that God, by entering human history as an active and historical subject, calls men to participate in his divine fullness of life.

God's manner of existence is described in theology in terms of the analogy of our knowledge of God. Our knowledge of God is not univocal but analogous in character, that is, our statements about God are never true in the same sense as those which we make about the data of experience. If we call God "Father" we say something about him which is true. At the same time the reality of what we state of him exists in him in an altogether different way from that in which we experience human fatherhood, and thus in a way altogether unknown to us. The Fourth Lateran Council (DS 806) declared in 1215 that there is no similarity between creature and creator which is not intrinsically pervaded by an even greater dissimilarity. This sentence emphasizes that similarity does not occupy a certain area and then dissimilarity begins, but that wherever similarity of God and creature begins, dissimilarity, too, and a greater one, is present. Because of the dissimilarity between creature and creator we cannot say in the last analysis what God is really like.

Augustine suffered immensely from his consciousness of this fact. He tried to overcome it spiritually by declaring on the one hand that we can only be silent before God, because we do not know what he is, while on the other hand this very ignorance of God is a dark knowledge, so that we nevertheless can and must speak of him. However, all speaking of him must be born and formed out of silence, out of ignorance, and must return again into ignorance. The consequence is that we can give God many names, that in fact we must give him many. Every name expresses a different aspect or activity of God, but God must be understood at the same time as the nameless one, because no name can express his true nature.

We shall not solve this problem if we assume too much with regard to our knowledge of God, but we shall also fail if, in an agnostic or skeptical attitude, we deny to man any capacity for knowing God. Ancient Christian theology tried to come to grips with the paradox by means of a method which can be summed up as the three ways of theological knowledge: the way of affirmation, the way of negation, and the way of supereminence *(via eminentiae)*. In the way of affirmation an activity or a characteristic of God such as his kindness or salvific action or his existence is stated; in the way of negation it is then denied insofar as what is stated is not true of God in the same way in which we state it of creatures. For example, if we say of creatures that their existence is real, the word "real" has quite a definite meaning which we gain from the data of experience. If we apply what we know of reality from our experience to God, then he cannot be said either to exist or to be real, so that in an amazing dialectic his existence, his being real or even his being a person must simultaneously be affirmed and denied if we are to avoid the danger of ascribing existence, reality or personality to God in the same sense in which we ascribe them to a creature. It is insofar as we comprehend what God is not that we comprehend who he is. With this dialectic of affirmation and negation the mode of our knowledge by way of supereminence must be combined. When we deny a quality of God, what we are denying is that quality not absolutely but as it is found in creatures. On the contrary, in the third stage we raise to the mode of the absolute the quality which was ascribed to God but was denied of him so far as the mode in which this quality exists in creatures is concerned. This way of supereminence states not only that there is a correspondence between the perfections which we know in creatures and the perfections which exist in God but that in God these perfections exist in a different and an absolute way. St. Thomas writes: "In the terms which we predicate of God there are two things to consider, namely, the actual perfections signified, like goodness, life and so forth, and the mode of signification. As regards the former, these belong properly to God, indeed more properly than to creatures; and the terms are predicated primarily of God. But as regards the mode of signification, they are not properly predicated of God. For they have a mode of signification which belongs to creatures." [8]

Notes

[1] *J: The Jerusalem Bible.* Excerpts from *The Jerusalem Bible,* copyright © 1966 by Darton, Longman & Todd, Ltd. and Doubleday & Company, Inc. Used by permission of the publishers.

[2] *Parochial and Plain Sermons,* Vol. III, No. 9 (1891), pp. 124–125.

[3] *On Psalm 76,* 80.

[4] *On Psalm 41,* 13.

[5] "On the Incomprehensible," Migne, *Patres Graeci,* 48, 711ff.

[6] *Sermon,* 52, 61; 117,37.

[7] *De Ordine,* I, II, 16.

[8] *Summa Theologica* Ia, 13, 3. Trans. F. C. Copleston in *Aquinas* (Baltimore: Pelican Books, 1961).

‹ 3

The God Who Is Life

Life and death are the primary motifs and motives at work in the entire history of salvation. That man moves towards a future in which there is no more death but only abundant life is God's promise and our hope. The promise and the hope have their guarantee in the fact that God is a living God: in that he lives the true God is distinguished from idols (Jer. 10:10–16). The question of what is meant by "life" is not a matter for speculation in the Old Testament: God is grasped and experienced as a living God, present and effective. Thus it belongs to the oldest and most definite convictions of the Old Testament Jews that God lives (see Gen. 16:13). His voice is heard speaking loudly out of the fire and the thundercloud (Deut. 5:23); more particularly, he is a present help in time of danger. Because we are confident that he is the living one, we can pray to him and our heart thirsts for him (Ps. 43:1f.): he is invoked again and again in the psalms as the one who lives (Pss. 18:46; 42:2; 84:2). The inexhaustible power which God exhibits in history shows that his life is inexhaustible, without any end or indeed any beginning: it cannot be cut off or endangered by anything. In this it is distinguished from all human life with its fragility. God is deathless: he is not subject to the transience of mortality (Deut. 8:3). On the contrary, he is the creator of everything which lives (Gen. 2:7; Ps. 104:29f.; Ps. 36:9); men become living beings through the breath of God (Gen.

2:7). When he withdraws his breath they pass away (Ps. 104:29; Is. 42:5). God, and he alone, is Lord over life and death (Deut. 32:39f.; 1 Sam. 2:6). Ezekiel (37:1–10) offers the most impressive testimony to God's power of creating life.

God's life is a life of the spirit. It is not easy to say what we mean by "spirit." The Old Testament itself does not use the concept in our sense. "Spirit" in the Old Testament means a power emanating from God. As the revelation of the Old Testament progresses, a certain clarification is attained by connecting the expressions "word" and "wisdom" with spirit. Thus the term gradually approaches the ideas which we associate with it. Let us point out here that the distinction of body and soul, of matter and mind, which has been fundamental for the Christian understanding of man, was for long not clearly elaborated in the Old Testament. It was only in the time of the Hellenistic writings that body and soul came to be considered as two separable principles, one of which can perish without involving the other in destruction. We shall return to this question later.

Augustine confesses that he owes his understanding of spirit to Platonic or neo-Platonic philosophy. Following Aquinas, we can sketch the difference between material and spiritual being in terms of the capacity of being for "turning back upon itself," for self-reflection. Aquinas holds that the degree of reality a thing has depends upon (or is proportioned to) the degree to which it can "turn back upon itself." [1] The objective reality which is known therefore is not simply material things as they actually are; objective reality in its full sense includes the element which the intellect in its operations gives to the data of the senses—the element of subjectivity. Since, according to Aquinas, not only the intellect but also will turns back upon itself (the will reverting to the point at which the intellect set out), the subjectivity of spirit must find completion in the will. Thus subjectivity becomes self-possession, "standing-in-oneself." Self-reflection is the mark of spirit: spirit is in itself by constantly returning to itself ("in quantum in seipsa habet esse, in seipsam redit" [2]). Spirit possesses itself by grasping, laying hold of, itself continuously: the static element is the continuously produced effect of the dynamic. We can say, therefore, that a differentiation occurs in its being because a dialogical element is present in it. Subjectivity, which is characteristic of spiritual being, does not, for Aquinas, represent merely a higher level of being: it is different in kind; through it alone does material being come to itself. Non-spiritual things attain their true being only in and through the human spirit. Because God is absolutely independent, not subject to any coercion from outside, we must say that he possesses himself to an absolute extent, not in an immovable and rigid state but in the activity of constantly "turning back upon himself." Thomas Aquinas declares that God is he who "turns back" most completely to his own being.[3] God is present to himself in an absolute manner in that he possesses himself unconditionally. We shall see later how fruitful this dialogical character of being is for the doctrine of the Trinity.

THE PERSONHOOD OF GOD
(HIS KNOWLEDGE AND WILL)

We encounter the living God in Scripture as a personal reality. The expression "person" itself is by no means biblical but is of Latin origin (a translation of the Greek *prosopon*). Its introduction into theology occurred in relation to Christology and the doctrine of the Trinity. As far as the thing itself is concerned, God's personhood (and even personal being in general) was recognized through the experience of the God of revelation and not as a result of philosophical endeavors. In the encounter with the God who acted powerfully in human history, he was experienced as that reality which we designate with the Latin expression "person." The word "person" is fitting, at least to a certain degree, to characterize the reality of God from the point of view of his aliveness, his powerful deeds in history, his self-possession, and his freedom. Greek philosophy itself did not develop the content which we understand by the concept "prosopon"—"person." Great effort was required on the part of Christian theologians to give content, on the basis of the experience of God narrated in Scripture, to the word "prosopon"—"person" and its counterpart, the word "ousia" (Latin *natura*). The main work here was done by Tertullian and Augustine. The first definition of the concept "person" was given by Boethius (died c. 526), who, in relation with Christology, defined "person" as "an individual substance of a rational nature." In the twelfth century Richard of St. Victor corrected this definition in connection with the doctrine of the Trinity, since the three divine persons are not "individual substances," and defined person as "the immediate existence of an intellectual being." (According to this God would be one intellectual being with three distinct acts of existence—a view which has its own difficulties.)

However valuable the concept of "person" is for theology and however indispensable it has become, we should not underestimate the difficulties it involves. In view of the resistance (especially of the oriental mind) to the concept of person, we may ask whether it would not be better to imitate Scripture in using it as little as possible, letting the content of the idea instead speak for itself. It will no doubt be scarcely possible to dispense with the concept of person entirely if we are to be able to make clear statements regarding the Trinity and Christology, and we should therefore keep in mind that the objections which have been and are raised against this term are the product of our experience of human persons. A certain delimitation is connected with it in its human context which inevitably destroys the idea of infinity. Hence not only to the oriental mind but to some Christian thinkers also—the mystics above all—the application of the concept of person to God has seemed dangerous and even impossible.

The very fact that God is not one person but three makes it impossible to apply the concept of person to him in the sense it has for our daily experience. Indeed the threefold personhood of God makes the use of the concept of person extraordinarily difficult in theology; yet, as we have indicated, it is precisely theology which gives it the appearance of being indispensable. It was owing to such difficulties that Richard of St. Victor made his attempt to revise the definition. The idea of analogy is particularly important here. That is to say, God is personal in a sense different from that in which human beings are personal, and personhood as it applies to human beings must be denied when we speak of God. But at the same time we must affirm that he is personal—in a sense different from the human. This dialectic can lead either to the total rejection of God's personhood, on the one hand, or on the other to the application of the concept of personhood to God in too naive or unreflective a manner.

In applying the concept of person to God we must consider both the element of self-possession, which occurs in his "turning back to self" (Aquinas's *reditio ad seipsum*), and the element of openness to which existential philosophy has drawn attention. Absolute being will be personal to the extent that it is open. In God personhood means absolute consciousness and absolute power of self-disposal, and so it is personhood in its highest perfection. God's openness of being has its most powerful expression in the exchange of life between the three persons which takes place within the godhead. It manifests itself also in the creation, the incarnation and the consummation of the world, the "Last Things."

Scripture describes the form of life which we mean by the word "person" when it testifies to God's acts of power, in which he sets a beginning and an end to things (Gen. 1:1-2; 2:4; Mk. 13:32f.; Heb. 1:2; 11:3); when it speaks of him as knowing and loving; when it ascribes to him decision, anger, justice, mercy and fidelity, promises and threats; when it presents the divine will as the assertion of a self. It denies that God has needs like those of eating, drinking or sleeping. God does not get tired (Pss. 121; 120:4; Is. 40:28), and for that very reason he can be the ever reliable partner of the people whom he chose for the covenant. In Scripture, God never appears as an "it," but always as an "I." He establishes the covenant with Israel (Ex. 19:1-6). His "I" character appears particularly in the emphatically monotheistic statements in Isaiah 40 to 49. The characterization of man as an image of God (Gen. 1:26f.; 9:6) also indicates God's personhood. Of course it is precisely here that the Old Testament author must use anthropomorphic language in order to give adequate emphasis to the personal nature of the divinity. It becomes evident in the prohibition of images (Deut. 4:9-24) how little he pictures God as a kind of man. The reserve in describing theophanies (Ex. 24:10f.; Is. 6) points in the same direction. We find no actual description of how this mysterious event occurs. The otherness of

God is as clearly stressed as his personhood (Num. 23:19; 1 Sam. 15:29).

When Scripture emphasizes God's personality in the manner described above, without using the word itself, it is intent not on elaborating metaphysical structures but on bringing out the religious and ethical significance of the divine. God is the contradiction of sin. Thus he is clearly different from all human persons (Hos. 11:9); yet he is the archetype of human behavior (Lev. 19:21f.; 20:8).

This way of speaking about God's person pervades the whole of Scripture. In the New Testament it is led to its climax in the testimony concerning the coming of Christ.

The personhood of God expresses itself in two basic activities, knowing and willing. It is a conviction of faith, expressed in Scripture in the most varied ways on the basis of historical experience of God, that God is conscious of himself, that he knows himself fully. That God should be conscious of himself belongs with his transcendence of the world and his personhood. The outward expression of God's self-awareness is revelation, in which he addresses his word to man—warning, commanding, judging, comforting, and granting grace. God's self-consciousness includes consciousness of being different from and exalted above the world (Jn. 8:42–47; 15:18–21; 18:36). The expression of the divine self-consciousness has its most vital form in the "I" statements which the Old Testament ascribes to Yahweh, and the New to Jesus sent by Yahweh. God's comprehension of himself, which cannot be formally equated with self-awareness and is yet identical with it, can be seen expressed in Mt. 11:27; Jn. 10:15; 1 Cor. 2:10ff. Only God knows himself (Mt. 11:27). In contrast to pantheism and the materialism of the nineteenth century the Catholic Church's First Vatican Council professed faith in God's self-consciousness and self-comprehension (DS 3001–3003).

God's knowledge not only embraces the whole of reality, it also has creative force. It does not derive from the created things he knows. He does not know creation by observing it as a *fait accompli*. Scripture stresses particularly that God's vision penetrates into the future as well as embracing the past. Isaiah reports him as saying: "My name is Yahweh, I will not yield my glory to another, nor my honor to idols. See how former predictions have come true. Fresh things I now foretell; before they appear I tell you of them." (Is. 42:8f., *J*) God's knowledge is in the first place turned towards man. In this process God never knows merely theoretically, his knowing is always at the same time action. Scripture emphasizes especially that God sees into the depths of man's soul (Ps. 7:9; Prov. 16:2; Jer. 11:20; Mt. 6:4,18; Acts 1:24; 15:8, Rom 8:26). There is no abyss in man which God cannot reach and penetrate with his knowledge. Man cannot hide from him (Ps. 139). In the psalms in particular, the all-embracing knowledge of God is presented as a motive for faith and as a foundation for hope. "Yahweh looks down from heaven, he sees the whole human race, from where he sits he watches all who live on the earth, he who moulds every heart and takes note of what all men do" (Ps. 33:13–15, *J*). In Psalm 44:21f. (*J*) there is the prayer: "Had we forgotten the name of our own God and stretched out our hands to a foreign one, would not God have found this out, he who knows the secret of the heart?" Psalm 90:8 (*J*): "Having summoned up our sins you inspect our secrets by your own light." In Proverbs 16:1f. (*J*): "Man's heart makes the plans, Yahweh gives the answer. A man's conduct may strike him as pure, Yahweh, however, weighs the motives." Ecclesiastes 17:1–13 (*J*) reads:

The Lord fashioned man from the earth, to consign him back to it. He gave them so many days' determined time, he gave them authority over everything on earth. He clothed them with strength like his own, and made them in his own image. He filled all living things with dread of man, making him master over beasts and birds. He shaped for them a mouth and tongue, eyes and ears, and gave them a heart to think with. He filled them with knowledge and understanding, and revealed to them good and evil. He put his own light in their hearts to show them the magnificence of his works. They will praise his holy name as they tell of his magnificent works. He set knowledge before them, he endowed them with the law of life. He established an eternal covenant with them, and revealed his judgments to them. Their eyes saw his glorious majesty, and their ears heard the glory of his voice. He said to them, "Beware of all wrong-doing"; he gave each a commandment concerning his neighbor. Their ways are always under his eye, they cannot be hidden from his sight.

(See also 39:19f.; Jer. 11:20; 17:10; Mt. 6:4,6; Lk. 16:15; Acts 1:24,15:8; Rom. 8:17; 1 Jn. 3:20; Heb. 4:13.)

God's knowledge has existential significance both for us human beings and for the whole of creation. This may be explicated in the following manner: God's life consists in the fact that, to use the language of Aquinas, he "turns back upon himself." God possesses himself in an unfailing dynamism. In this "turning back upon himself" he perceives himself so completely that his self-consciousness, self-knowledge and self-comprehension form one and the same spiritual act of life. For himself God contains no mystery. By the fact that in full and dynamic self-possession and in absolute freedom of decision he pours himself out into that which he himself is not, and so brings forth things distinct from himself, he takes up into his own knowledge that which is distinct from himself; or rather, this draws its existence from his knowledge, in virtue of a free act of his will. In this way it is taken up into God's knowledge of himself in the act by which he "turns back to himself," and so it too "returns" to God. The idea of this cyclic movement, deriving from neo-Platonic thought, runs through the whole work of Aquinas—when not explicitly, at least as a consistent undercurrent.

These considerations show that God's relation to the world is not like that of a knowing subject with the object of its knowledge nor like that of an interested observer; on the contrary, he is directly involved, in care and love. According to Scripture the fact that the world is known by God means that it is acknowledged as his own, loved, cared for, and indeed chosen by him (Gen. 1:31; 18:19; Ex. 33:12; Deut. 11:13–15; Amos 3:2; Hos. 13:5; Jer. 1:5; Job 31:6; Prov. 31:23; 2 Tim. 2:19; 1 Cor. 8:3; 13:12; Gal. 4:9f.). God's gaze on his creation is not indifferent; it is a look of creative love (Ex. 32:12; Gal. 4:9; 2 Tim. 2:19). Correspondingly, not to be "known" by God means not to be acknowledged by him—that is, to stand under his judgment (Job 34:21ff.; Ps. 139; Mt. 25:12).

To stand in the sight of God means for the creature that he does not stand alone in the immensity of a universe which has no knowledge of him (cf. Pascal) and is indifferent to his fate; which, despite his progress in controlling it, will always threaten him with its awesome powers. God's gaze is a look of love; it assures every creature that it has a home with him, that its life has meaning and value. As God's knowledge of himself is the foundation of his creative activity, all creatures are analogous realizations of his thought and knowledge. This is the basis of the "ontological truth" of creatures—that is, their objective reality. On the other hand, the objective reality of the world is the prerequisite for it to be knowable, for the establishment of the subject-object relationship in creation.

As far as divine knowledge of non-divine reality is concerned, the attention of theologians in the sixteenth and seventeenth centuries was given chiefly to a particular question which attained great significance for the development of the so-called "Molinistic" and "Thomistic" schools. In view of the importance of this problem for the question of divine predestination, which will be treated later, the main points need to be mentioned here briefly. The question was how God knows free human potential actions—that is, those free human decisions which *would* be made if certain conditions were fulfilled but which will not actually be made in point of fact. The question was not seen as a problem until the late sixteenth century. Luis de Molina answered that God knows the potential actions of men by means of *scientia media*. Molina uses this expression to designate that divine knowledge which lies "in the middle" between the knowledge of pure possibilities *(scientia simplicia intelligentiae)* and the knowledge of what is real *(scientia libera)*. The latter presupposes the decisions of God's will, since there is nothing real in the realm of the non-divine which is not an effect of God's free decision. Molina sees the basis for his theory of *scientia media* in the fact that God is present to the entire being of man, which includes all his potentialities, however remote; that is, God knows each man so well that he knows what he would do, freely, in any given situation. Molina terms this total knowledge which God has of every free man *supercompre-hensio*. With this thesis Molina became the founder of a school which was soon divided by a variety of interpretations (e.g., Suarez, Alfonsus Liguori). On the other hand the Thomists located God's knowledge of men's free potential actions in his *scientia libera*. That is, they explained God's knowledge of these acts by conditional decrees of the divine will. The main representative of this group was Bañez. While Molinists have to wrestle with the problem of the *scientia media*, Thomists are faced with the problem of preserving human freedom.

The other form in which God's life manifests itself, according to the testimony of Scripture, is that of will. In fact this receives stronger emphasis than his knowledge. The assertion that God has knowledge is an assertion that his will is not a blind force but purposive activity. It is described in the forms of power, holiness, justice, kindness; as the will to save, to create—in short, as love. God possesses himself in the act of turning back on himself not only in knowledge but in love, as Aquinas emphasizes. In this absolute self-possession which cannot be threatened by anything, the distinction of the divinity from all that is not himself is manifested. We must say of the divine will what we have said of the divine knowledge: by pouring himself out, in his dynamic self-possession, into that which is not himself God both creates the non-divine and takes it up into the preserving power and activity of his will. Thus non-divine reality is taken up through a free decision of God into the divine act of self-possession and existence. It is from this that creatures derive their ontological goodness.

It has frequently been maintained that God's attitude towards creation is seen in the Old Testament more from the aspect of severity than of love, and in the New Testament more from the aspect of love. Such a distinction does not reach the heart of the matter, for in the Old Testament too we find God's will interpreted as love for the world. It is true that this reached a height in the New Testament which, though it had been foretold by the Old Testament as the promise of the future, was never attained there. The New Testament states explicitly that God is love itself (1 Jn.

4:7f.). There is no such formulation in the Old; nevertheless the Old Testament is one continuous testimony to God's concern for man.

We can see on two levels the love which, even according to the Old Testament, is God: first, God is the bringer of salvation for man; second, there is explicit testimony, in an almost anthropomorphic way, to God's actual love for man, both the community of men and the individual. As far as the first level is concerned there is nothing God does which does not serve man's salvation. God's creative act itself is a work of salvation. It is the beginning, the first step, in the way which was continued according to plan in the calling of Abraham. In the liberation of the people of Israel from Egyptian bondage and their guidance into the promised land the salvific action of God reached a preliminary climax. The people of Israel had such a tremendous experience of the saving God that their whole existence as a people must be ascribed to God's salvific power. God is the savior. He himself is grace. Not only are his gifts joy but he is himself joy. He is the center of the whole of salvation. All the more amazing, then, is the intensity with which the people of Israel experienced the transcendence, the otherness, the strangeness of God—"the man who sees the face of God must die." But the distant God, he who inspires this sense of the *mysterium tremendum,* is at the same time the God who is near. The dialectics of divine love is expressed with special clarity in the following passage in the book of Exodus:

He called on the name of Yahweh. Yahweh passed before him and proclaimed, "Yahweh, Yahweh, a god of tenderness and compassion, slow to anger, rich in kindness and faithfulness; for thousands he maintains his kindness, forgives faults, transgression, sin; yet he lets nothing go unchecked, punishing the father's fault in the sons and in the grandsons to the third and fourth generation." And Moses bowed down to the ground at once and worshipped. "If I have indeed won your favor, Lord," he said, "let my Lord come with us, I beg. True, they are a headstrong people, but forgive us our faults and our sins, and adopt us as your heritage." (Ex. 34:6–9, *J*)

(See also Ex. 6:1–8; 3:13–15.) The choice and the covenant give expression to this divine will of salvation. The people chosen by God knew that it had been granted special grace but that the other peoples of the world were also the object of God's concern. It knew that, being chosen, it was a representative for all the others and recognized that its task was to proclaim to all men God's greatness and love. God's will to save is not particular—that is, limited in scope—but universal. Nevertheless it intervenes in history at definite points from which its power radiates, becoming effective throughout the whole of creation. That is what is meant when it is said in Exodus 19:4f. (*J*).

You yourself have seen what I did with the Egyptians, how I carried you on eagle's wings and brought you to myself. From this you know that now, if you obey my voice and hold fast to my Covenant, you of all the nations shall be my very own, for all the earth is mine. I will count you a kingdom of priests, a consecrated nation. Those are the words you are to speak to the sons of Israel.

The people is aware that it lies under a particular obligation because it has been chosen. This realization is expressed especially in Deuteronomy 4:6–9 and 23–24 (*J*):

Keep them [the precepts of the Law], observe them, and they will demonstrate to the peoples your wisdom and understanding. When they come to know of all these laws they will exclaim, "No other people is as wise and prudent as this great nation." And indeed, what great nation is there that has its gods so near as Yahweh our God is to us whenever we call to him? And what great nation is there that has laws and customs to match this whole Law that I put before you today? But take care what you do and be on your guard. Do not forget the things your eyes have seen, nor let them slip from your heart all the days of your life; rather, tell them to your children and to your children's children. . . . Take care therefore not to forget the covenant which Yahweh your God has made with you, by making a carved image of anything that Yahweh your God has forbidden you; for Yahweh your God is a consuming fire, a jealous God.

How universally salvation is understood is shown by the statement that in Abraham all generations shall be blessed (Gen. 12:3). This same paradox of a mediated salvation, of choosing the one and not the others, but in order to grant salvation to them through the chosen ones, is testified to by Isaiah and his disciples (Is. 2:2–5; 42:1–7; 49:1–6). The intimacy of the bond of the covenant which Yahweh concluded with Israel is represented by the prophets—Hosea above all—by the image of a wedding and the communal life of marriage (Hos. 1–3; Jer. 3; Ez. 16:23; Is. 50:1; 54:5–8). The foundation of God's will to save is love (Ex. 33:19; 34). This thesis is not contradicted by the fact that the covenant is carefully hedged about with exact legal decrees: they serve order, but the covenant in its entirety derives from God's creative love. God promised a future to the people which would mean fullness of life for them. We know from the New Testament that this future is not, as the people of the Old Testament supposed, within history; on the contrary, it is beyond history and transcends it and therefore brings it to fulfillment. The prophet Moses describes with the utmost vigor and clarity the intense and even passionate quality of God's love. Hosea 11:9 (*J*) contains a sentence which points to the depths of the divine love: "I will not give rein to my fierce anger . . . for I am God, not man: I am the Holy One in your midst and I have no wish to destroy." God loves in a different manner from human beings. He loves because he is God and not a man. His love is not limited by emotions and doubts. It is not a reaction to the love of others and is therefore not dependent on it. By acting out of an unconditional love God shows himself to be God (see Jer. 12:31). In Isaiah (49:15) God's love is compared to that of a mother (see also 54:5–8). In 41:10 he encourages them: "Do not be afraid, for I am with you; stop being anxious and watchful, for I am your God. I give you strength, I bring you help, I uphold you with my victorious right hand." The book of Wisdom, which originated in the Hellenistic period, bears witness (11:24—12:2, *J*), deriving from the notion of creation, that God's love does not recognize national frontiers, even though he chose out one people:

Yet you are merciful to all, because you can do all things and over-look men's sins so that they can repent. Yes, you love all that exists, you hold nothing of what you have made in abhorrence, for had you hated anything, you would not have formed it. And how, had you not willed it, could a thing persist, how be conserved if not called forth by you? You spare all things because all things are yours, Lord, lover of life, you whose imperishable spirit is in all. Little by little, therefore, you correct those who offend, you admonish and remind them of how they have sinned, so that they may abstain from evil and trust in you, Lord.

God's love is given in the first place to the community, the people (Deut. 7:6–8; 23:6f.); accordingly, God waits for their love (Deut. 6:4f.; 11:13; see also Lev. 19:18; Mt. 22:37ff.; Mk. 12:29–34; Lk. 10:26ff.). However, the individual also finds acceptance in God's creative and saving love (Ps. 8; Prov. 15:9). Because of God's love his enduring fidelity and care are guaranteed (Is. 49:15; 54:5–8; 41:10; 63:9). Therefore every individual, as is said innumerable times in the psalms, can surrender himself to God in hope and confidence (Pss. 23; 27:1–3, 10; 34:9; 31; 33; 35; 42; 46; 54; 62; 71:1–11; 91; 86; 111; 102; 103; 121; 123). God's love is likewise present to man in the night of suffering. For he who surrenders unconditionally to God and bears up for his sake under the torments which life can bring succumbs to hostile powers only externally and in appearance. In reality he experiences God's love all the more profoundly: he will receive eternal life (Wis. 3:4–12). God's love is demonstrated in its sincerity and creative fertility also by the fact that it stimulates and awakens man's love for God. In the last analysis all human love is the work of God (Deut. 30:6).

With regard to the poor and the sinful God's love assumes the form of mercy. Although the Old Testament often emphasizes God's severity and justice for pedagogical reasons, nevertheless his concern and love remain in the foreground to the eyes of the believer. Isaiah (25:4) says: "For thou hast been a stronghold to the poor, a stronghold to the needy in his distress, a shelter from the storm and a shade from the heat." The worshipper in Psalm

9:19 is able to say: "For the needy shall not always be forgotten, and the hope of the poor shall not perish for ever." (See also Pss. 12:6; 35:10; 46:6-9.) The poor, the widows, and the orphans are God's wards. God gives many commandments for their protection (i.e., Ex. 22:21-27; Jer. 7:5-7). Their oppressors are threatened with severe punishment (Jer. 5:26-29; Ez. 16:49; Amos 8).

God's love towards sinners takes the form of compassion, mercy, patience, consideration for weakness, pardon, mitigation of wrath (Jon. 4:2; Soph. 2:1f.; 2 Chron. 30:6-9; Jer. 18:5-11; Mich. 7:18-20). The last passage says: "Who is a God like thee, pardoning iniquity and passing over transgression for the remnant of his inheritance? He does not retain his anger for ever because he delights in steadfast love. He will again have compassion upon us, he will tread our iniquities under foot. Thou wilt cast all our sins into the depths of the sea." The strength of God's inclination to forgive sins is described thus in Isaiah (1:18): "Though your sins are like scarlet, they shall be as white as snow; though they are red like crimson, they shall become like wool." Forgiveness on the part of God presupposes that the sinner turns from his ways (Jer. 3; 4; 35:15; Mal. 3:7; Zach. 1:3; Is. 44:21f.; 55:6-9; Hos. 14). It must be borne in mind that the forgiveness which God grants the sinner always reopens the way into that joyous future promised by God. Despite the defection of nations and individuals God does not retract his promise: he wants to remain in dialogue with his people. When they break off the dialogue, God does not withdraw, but finds new means of resuming the salvific conversation. The covenant concluded by God, directed towards the future, is always preserved, for the divine partner remains faithful to his promise. This is, in the last analysis, the meaning of God's forgiveness of sin.

The exacting nature of God's love is summed up in a word which, though it receives its real and final meaning only in the New Testament, is nevertheless characteristic of God's relationship to his chosen people in the Old—namely, the word "Father." Israel is Yahweh's son. The word "son" has in this instance a collective meaning (Ex. 4:22; Deut. 14:1; 32:18; Hos. 11:1; 31:20). Yahweh is Israel's father (Deut. 32:6; Ps. 89:27; Tob. 13:4; Ps. 2:7;

Jer. 31:9). As father, he shows solicitude for his people; at the same time he is their Lord (Is. 63:15f.). The estrangement is all the more serious, then, when Israel turns away from God; it is forsaking its father. God himself wants his people to call upon him as a father (Sir. 23:1–4). The basis for the father-son relationship is frequently seen by the writers of the Old Testament in the election of the people, and occasionally also in the fact of creation (Deut. 32:6; 64:7f.; Mal. 2:10). Not only love but respect also is due to the father. This concept combines the proximity and the remoteness of God, the loving immanence and the awe-inspiring transcendence (Mal. 1:6).

God's justice, so much stressed in the Old Testament, often seems to stand in a relationship of tension to his love. It is nonetheless praised as that conduct whereby God provides justice for the righteous—a hope expressed vividly in the psalms (Pss. 7:12; 10:7; 145:17ff.). Elsewhere the Old Testament depicts God's justice as a reward or a punishment. Difficult problems arise here. The question is whether justice must not be viewed as the opposite of divine love, whether love must not be seen as undermining divine justice. Do not these two realities cancel each other out? Such a notion would place contradiction in God. It is better to understand justice as the form in which love must express itself when the creature is in a certain condition. If God bestows his love upon a man and the latter rejects it, love remains effective, but in this situation it can only function as justice. The person who refuses God's love is repulsed by that same love. God's love is fair to the situation; or rather, because it bestows itself upon persons, it is fair to the person in his situation.

We can make a distinction with regard to the divine justice as to whether it is creative, legislative or retributive. It appears as creative justice to the extent that God, in the creation of the nondivine, confers on it in a limited way the absolute value which he himself represents. It manifests itself as legislative justice when he establishes certain immanent laws in creatures, and in particular when he imposes commands upon men. These commands do not constitute duties foreign to man's nature but are aids to the individual creature's attainment of its own being. They serve self-realization. Obedience to God's commands means that man is simply acting according to his nature—that is, in a truly human way. This becomes all the more apparent when we consider that all God's commands are intended as forms of expression of his love. Viewed in this way they are not, and are not meant to be, restrictive and oppressive; they liberate man from the confining pressures of life. If it seems otherwise, the cause is our short-sighted self-centeredness, our failure to see what it means to live in a genuinely human fashion. Retributive justice consists in the fact that God rewards what is good and punishes what is evil. For a more detailed explanation of the concepts of reward and punishment, the reader is referred to the treatment, later on, of grace and of the "Last Things."

We shall consider briefly two further questions. First, should God's punishment of evil be designated as intrinsic or extrinsic? By intrinsic punishment is meant such punishment as results through sin from man's contradiction of his own nature (*ab intrinseco*). Extrinsic punishment means one imposed by God on the sinner in a free and particular decision, from outside, as it were (*ab extrinseco*). Ultimately the difference between the two can be reduced to a minimum, since any extrinsic punishment, if there were such, would be conceivable only as the consistent development of a contravention of human nature already in being. We shall examine this problem, too, more closely when we come to the "Last Things"—namely, the conditions which are referred to as "heaven" and "hell."

A final question concerns the contradiction which exists between our experience of life and the biblical doctrine of the justice of God. It is often precisely the good who suffer, while those who disregard the rights of their fellow men lead a comfortable life. This problem has long weighed heavily on the minds of men. We must acknowledge as a matter of fact that it often seems as if God were not concerned about men, as if he quite arbitrarily showered some with misery and others with happiness. This can lead to doubt not only of God's justice but even of his very existence. No satisfactory answer to the problem can be seen if we look only at a particular moment in the present. The question must be ap-

proached from the perspective of the evolutionary process of creation and from the perspective of the development of the individual
within the course of this evolution. Only the consummation which
is to come in the absolute future will show us in retrospect what
the real function was of the events we experienced within history
as salvific or death-dealing. We must return to this question also.

Just as experience speaks, or seems to speak, against God's
justice, so also it seems to speak against God's love. The path of
mankind is so drenched with blood and tears that the question
inevitably arises whether a demonic, godless purpose has not ruled
throughout the entire history of the world. The perpetual suffering, the constant prevalence of crime, the torture of men and animals, the senseless destruction and death which we experience,
seem to cry out against the idea that God is good, or even that he
exists. But if God is cruel, then certainly the Christian God does
not exist at all. This question simply cannot be answered satisfactorily, and it is a heavy burden on any belief in God, but a few
things point in the direction of a solution. It may clarify the question if we distinguish between natural pain and the evil which is
inherent in sin: the two cannot be completely separated, but for
the sake of elucidation we can make a distinction. Pain in nature
can be understood only in the context of the total order of things,
which must be understood as dynamic, not static—that is to say,
by looking at the evolution of the whole of reality, of the whole
creation. It is a consequence of evolution that one being serves
another, one creature must be used and consumed by another.
This function of mutual service, of the subordination of the individual to the totality, cannot by any means answer our question
completely, but it shows at least that pain is not wholly meaningless, that the pain of the individual may find its meaning in the
totality.

There are, of course, real difficulties here. What is involved is
the sacrifice of the individual to the whole, and this theory is most
fully tenable when it is a question of the lowest forms of life. As
soon as we turn our attention to the world of animals it becomes
less convincing. Every animal has a certain center of consciousness and therefore undeniably an individuality, even if this is essen-

tially different from that of man. It seems hardly conceivable that
an animal should be sacrificed in this way, that it should have no
claim to happiness. The problem becomes even more difficult
when we consider human reality. The evolutionary perspective
helps us to some extent—we realize that before we can understand his fate each individual must be seen from the viewpoint of
that absolute future as it affects him within the total movement of
history. Only in retrospect from the absolute future will the meaning of each individual be revealed. For this the cross of Jesus
Christ is decisive. Jesus Christ, as the representative of mankind,
of all creation, took death upon himself as a transition to a full
and complete life. The Revelation of John brings out clearly this
meaning of the death of Jesus when it proclaims (Rev. 5) that
no man is capable of opening the scroll of history which is sealed
with seven seals and that therefore no one can answer these questions of why and wherefore. Only the Lamb which was slain yet
is alive, which not only conquered death but gained through death
true life, can open the scroll with its seven seals. This scene which
is described in the Book of Revelation shows that the opening of
the scroll—showing history's true meaning—is of such great consequence that the heavenly hosts rejoice. The cross itself, it is true,
still stands in impenetrable mystery, the mystery of sin. And this
brings us to the final question: why does God allow sin? Without
denying man his freedom God could have produced a creation in
which it would not have been possible for him to sin. There is no
certain answer to this question, but one can assume that human
freedom, even in its most radical form, is seen by God as such a
noble good that it was granted to man at any risk, even the risk
of abuse. By it man participates in God's own sovereignty.

To conclude, let us say something about divine freedom. The
love which God bestows upon man, or rather in which he bestows
himself upon man, is given in absolute freedom. God is not forced
into any action either because of an inner necessity to realize his
own nature or because of external coercion. In this of course he
is essentially different from man. For his self-realization man is
in need of a continual decision—which is forced upon him from
within even though it is freely carried out—to transcend himself,

because he comes to possession of himself only in coexistence with his fellow beings. Man does not possess himself completely but only comes to possess himself gradually, and only through a continual, ever newly achieved return to himself. The perfect freedom of God, though it stands in contrast to that of men, is not to be confused with arbitrariness. It is not freedom in the sense of caprice, but freedom to create the true and the good, a freedom to create salvation. The question arises in this connection of what is good and what is evil, what is salvation and what is damnation. As we know, the first men wanted to determine for themselves what was good and what was true (Gen. 3:5). Therein lay their offense: only God can decree what is true and what is good. Nevertheless this answer does not really solve the problem: it could be understood in the sense that something was good only because God said so, and evil only because God said it was evil. If that were so, the answer would not come from the inherent problematic of the situation but from an external and arbitrary decision by God, whereas in fact God declares what is good and true on the basis of his own being, which is both good and true. We cannot see this with certainty from Greek philosophy: it is clear only from the I-Thou metaphysics which, as we have seen, lies at the root of the Old Testament. According to this metaphysics all being is constructed dialogically, whether one wants to call the differences in being purely logical or formal or virtual. To say, with Aquinas, that God turns back upon himself in a continuous act and in an altogether different, more intensive, manner than man means that he knows and loves himself. This presupposes that he is knowable and lovable, that he possesses the properties of transcendental truth-in-being and goodness-in-being. It is because God is an impenetrable mystery to us that we are often incapable of deciding with certainty what in the concrete is good and what evil. (It is well-known that Duns Scotus differed from Thomas Aquinas regarding this conception of God.) We shall attempt a few clarifications of the concept of God in the chapter which follows.

Notes

[1] *Summa Theologica,* I, q. 14, a. 2, ad 1; *In Quattuor Sententiarum,* I, 17, 5, ad 3. Citations of the *Summa Theologica* (abbreviated *ST*) hereafter in this book are from *Summa Theologiae,* ed. Blackfriars in co-operation with Eyre and Spottiswoode, London, and McGraw-Hill, New York.

[2] *ST,* I, q. 14, a. 2, ad 1.

[3] *ST,* I, q, 14, art 2.

‹4

The Structure
of the
Divine Life

We turn now to some aspects of the structure of the divine life, in particular to the question of divine eternity, universal presence, immutability, and unity as simplicity.

The eternity of God means, at the least, beginninglessness and endlessness. More than this, it means that God stands above the flow of time altogether. The flow of time is measured on the basis of our experience and observation in the categories of before, now and after. Such a measurement is possible only if man carries the categories of time within himself, if time is built into his structure. Every human idea of time is a synthesis of "objective" happenings and "subjective" experience. This means that a certain synthesis of the objectivistic scholastic view and the subjectivistic view of modern times (Kant) is necessary.

Scripture emphasizes duration—immeasurable length of time— rather than timelessness, which would involve the absence of a temporal before or after. The reason is that God's eternity was arrived at by Israel not through abstract speculation, as in the philosophy of the Greeks, but out of a living experience of God. Old Testament expressions for eternity are ambiguous, but from the time of Deutero-Isaiah at the latest eternal life was clearly recognized as a distinguishing characteristic of God. By his eternity God is differentiated from creatures—especially men—with their fragile, declining, transitory existence. The proclamation of his eternity is an appeal for belief in the otherness and uniqueness of God as compared with the pagan gods; for patience and confidence in face of the afflictions he sends. God exists before and after all else: he has no beginning and no end: he is the first and last in history (Is. 41:4; 43:12). In Moses' hymn of victory we find (Ex. 15:18): "The Lord will reign for ever and ever." In Tobias' hymn of praise (31:1, *J*): "Blessed be God who lives for ever, for his reign endures throughout all ages." The psalms in particular praise God's eternity. In Psalm 9:8 we find: ". . . the Lord sits enthroned for ever, he has established his throne for judgment." (See also Pss. 10:16; 33:11; 90:1f.). Psalm 90 begins: "Lord, thou hast been our dwelling place in all generations. Before the mountains were brought forth or ever thou hadst formed the earth and the world, from everlasting to everlasting thou art God." The writer of Psalm 93:1f. prays: "The Lord reigns; he is robed in majesty; the Lord is robed, he is girded with strength. Yes, the world is established; it shall never be moved; thy throne is established from of old; thou art from everlasting." (See Ps. 102:12f., 25–28; Ps. 135:13; Ps. 146:10; Sir. 18:1; 39:20). So exalted is God above the flow of time that a thousand years in his sight are but as a day (Pss. 90:4; 102:26ff.).

God's existence outside time means that he is not subject to the process of coming into existence. He has no past or future, only the present. In himself he has no history. (Later we shall investigate the question of whether God received a history when he became man.) Consequently God can neither look back to a past nor reach out in hope towards a future. Boethius gave the classical definition of eternity: "interminabilis vitae tota simul et perfecta possessio"—"the complete possession of unending life in a single act without duration." [1] This definition states that God is the absolute fullness of being; hence he can receive no increment from any process of becoming nor suffer any loss deriving from transitoriness. If we emphasize the fact stressed by Aquinas that God possesses himself in an act of turning back upon himself which is total self-reflection (as opposed to the partial self-reflection of other beings)—that is, if we understand his being as dynamic—then we could say that the divine eternity is an unending event, and in this sense "endless time," but yet without the connotation of change. It would then be possible to conceive of the eternity of God as primal history (*Urgeschicte*) and primal time (*Urzeit*). Such an interpretation runs the risk of obscuring God's fullness of being—that is, his absolute possession of himself. On the other hand it must be emphasized that God's eternity is to be understood not merely negatively, as the absence of time, but positively, as absolute fullness. This absolute fullness of God has an inner, vital relation to creaturely time which is indispensable: creaturely time derives from eternity, and hence God is the Lord of time and also of history.

What we call time had its origin in the fact that God poured himself out into the non-divine in a self-emptying which reached its climax in the incarnation of the eternal Logos. The consequence of the divine self-emptying was that God entered into time and history without surrendering his eternity (Augustine). God's "temporalization" has the meaning and function of allowing temporal creatures to share in eternity, in God's absolute fullness of being. "Eternal" life consists precisely in participation in God's absolute fullness of being.

The omnipresence of God must be understood in a similar fashion. It means that the category of space does not apply to God and, at the same time, that God is the Lord of spatial creatures. Spatiality was created by God in that he poured himself into the non-divine; at the same time he retains his sovereignty over space.

As we have already emphasized, Scripture seems to localize God when it reports his appearance in particular places—the burning bush, Mt. Sinai—or speaks of God "in heaven"; yet in Scripture every part of the creation bears witness to his presence. This dialectic must be interpreted to mean that Scripture wishes to express both God's nearness and his hiddenness; that he is truly a living God, both immanent in the world and transcendent to it. In our human way of knowing, a reality which is truly alive for us is present to us here and now. Since the biblical writers can communicate only in human terms, they cannot speak of the living God otherwise than by describing him as speaking in the here and now. In truth one must say that according to Scripture, God is with Jacob in Mesopotamia (Gen. 28:13f.), that there he becomes the invisible witness of human dealings (Gen. 31:3), that he stays with Joseph in a foreign country (Gen. 39:2) and moves to Egypt with Jacob (Gen. 46:4). Neither the heavenly spheres nor the temple in Jerusalem can contain him (1 Kgs. 8:27), nor can the whole earth. Conversely, he fills the entire earth (Jer. 23:24). Heaven is his throne and the earth is his footstool (Is. 66:1). One cannot escape him even in the realm of the dead (Ps. 139:8). He is at the same time close at hand and far off (Jer. 23:23), and his eyes are upon every place (Sir. 5:3; see also Sir. 16:17–19; Wis. 1:7; 8:1; Is. 3:8f.; Amos 9:2–4; Mt. 5:34ff.; Acts 17:28). We should be contradicting the intention of Scripture completely if we assumed that it supposes God to be localized in any way, whether in heaven above or in a sacred place. This does not eliminate the possibility that God can show himself as merciful in a special way when he chooses to turn to man, or that his ever-lasting grace exerts its effects upon men in certain places with special power. Scripture speaks of God's immanence in and transcendence to the world in terms of the ancient conception of the world. There is no great difficulty in disentangling the meaning of these statements from what they literally say. Precisely the contradictions within the scriptural texts force us to inquire into their intention: only thus can we determine what they really mean.

Since Gregory the Great it has become customary to distinguish different modes of God's presence to creatures in order to obtain a more comprehensive idea of it. The first form of presence is as supporting being (*per essentiam*), insofar as God grants things their being and sustains it in an uninterrupted act of creation. The second is as universally acting power (*per potentiam*), in that he, as sovereign creator, pervades all things, especially the actions of men; in that he gives men and things the power to act; in that he creates earthly power and sets it in motion by the power whose origin is himself. Finally, he is present as all-embracing knowledge (*per praesentiam*) insofar as he sees completely into the being and activity of creatures. In these statements the dynamic and onto-logical elements of God's presence are viewed together. We should understand God's spacelessness too negatively if we did not con-sider at the same time its positive qualities of fullness of being and meaning. As we have said, material beings can be distinguished from spiritual beings in terms of the power of self-reflection. It is not a sufficient distinction to ascribe to spirit unextended being and to material being extension in space and to see that as the difference between them. This conception, which goes back to Descartes, is too much caught up with the appearance of things. Spiritual being reflects upon itself, possesses its own being by and in itself, as material being does not. When we say that God is not in space we are saying that he is immaterial in an absolute way. This means that he "turns back upon" himself unconditionally and hence unconditionally possesses himself. From this point of view we must say that standing beyond temporality and standing beyond spatiality are so closely related that one cannot exist with-out the other: both derive from God's total reflection upon himself and his total possession of himself in a single act of which there is no "before" or "after." Only when God freely wills to pour himself out into the non-divine do the realities of time and space come into being. If reality is temporal it must also be spatial, since time is the measure of change in space.

God's sovereignty over space and time means that since "be-coming" is essential to spatial and temporal creatures, God leads human history into the final, absolute future. Only because of his sovereignty over time, on the one hand, and his presence in time, on the other hand, can God plan and carry to fulfillment that salvific future which is testified to in the Old and New Testaments and which represents the meaning of all divine self-emptying.

The immutability of God is closely connected with his eternity and spacelessness. In Scripture the basis of belief in it is the ex-perience of God and not speculative reflection. Because God is steadfast, we can rely on him. In Malachi God says: "For I, the Lord, do not change" (3:6). This is also expressed in Numbers (23:19): "God is not a man that he should lie, or a son of man that he should repent. Has he said, and will he not do it? Or has he spoken and will he not fulfill it?" Or in Psalm 102:24–29 we find: " 'O my God,' I say, 'take me not hence in the midst of my days, thou whose years endure throughout all generations!' Of old thou didst lay the foundation of the earth, and the heavens are the work of thy hands. They will perish but thou dost endure; they will all wear out like a garment. Thou changest them like raiment, and they pass away; but thou art the same, and thy years have no end." Psalm 33:10f. says: "The Lord brings the counsel of the nations to nought; he frustrates the plans of the peoples. The counsel of the Lord stands for ever, the thoughts of his heart to all generations."

The early Church Fathers defended God's unchangeableness, together with his eternity and spacelessness, against the pantheistic and dualistic conceptions of God which are to be found in the Gnostics, Stoics, and Manichaeans. The following text by Augustine can add clarification to this point:

In a word, they claim, God can be saved from the charge either of an unbegun past of long-drawn-out and slothful leisure or of a rash and haphazard creation, only if one accepts the cyclic hypothesis of endlessly repeated patterns of change—whether the same world remains intact throughout or whether it keeps setting into disintegration and rising into newness with each rotation of the wheel of time. Whereas, if one rejects the periodicity of identical patterns, one is left with an infinite diversity of events which no knowledge or pre-knowledge could possibly comprehend.

By such arguments do the pagans try to turn us from the straight path of simple faith and keep us walking around with them in circles. Even if reason could not refute them, faith should laugh at them. But it so happens that, with the help of the Lord our God, clear reasoning breaks the revolving wheels that sophistry makes.

The fundamental fallacy of these men, who prefer to walk in roundabout error rather than keep to the straight path of truth, is that they have nothing but their own tiny, changing, human minds to measure the divine mind, infinitely capacious and utterly immutable, a mind that can count uncountable things without passing from one to the next.

Such men, to use the words of the Apostle, "comparing themselves with themselves" end by understanding nothing. Of course, every time such philosophers decide to do something, they have to form a new mental resolution because their minds are mutable, and they imagine it is the same with God. Without having a notion of God, they mistake themselves for Him, and, instead of measuring God by God, they compare themselves to themselves.

To us, however, it is simply incredible that God should be affected in one way when He is inactive and in another way when He works, for the simple reason that God cannot be said to be affected at all, in the sense that something can occur in a divine nature which was not already occurring.

What is affected suffers a change and whatever suffers a change is mutable. Hence, one can no more think of God in His leisure suffering fom indolence, inactivity, or inertia than we can think of Him suffering from labor, effort, or eagerness in His work. For He knows how to rest while He acts and to act while He rests. To every new work whatsoever He applies not a new but an eternal design. Nor does regret for any former inactivity prompt Him to create what had not been created before.

When his "former" leisure and "subsequent" activity is mentioned—and I do not know how man can understand this—surely, the time reference is not to Him, but to things which "formerly" did not exist but "subsequently" did, for in Him there is no "subsequent" choice which modifies or rejects a "former" resolution. It is by one and the same, eternal, and unchangeable will that He brought it about that His created works should "formerly" not exist so long as they had no existence and should "subsequently" exist from the moment they began to be.[2]

In the religious priority of faith, the truth that God is unchangeable causes no slight difficulty, owing to its apparent implication of rigidity and lifelessness. But in the Book of Wisdom we read (7:24,27): "For wisdom is more mobile than any motion; because of her pureness she pervades and penetrates all things. . . . Though she is but one, she can do all things, and while remaining in herself, she renews all things; in every generation she passes into holy souls and makes them friends of God, and prophets."

Another text of Augustine's is instructive and revealing at this point:

What then is my God, what but the Lord God? *For Who is Lord but the Lord, or Who is God but our God?* O Thou, the greatest and the best, mightiest, almighty, most merciful and most just, utterly hidden and utterly present, most beautiful and most strong, abiding yet mysterious, suffering no change and changing all things: never new, never old, making all things new, *bringing age upon the proud and they know it not;* even in action, ever at rest, gathering all things to Thee and needing none; sustaining and fulfilling and protecting, creating and nourishing and making perfect; ever seeking though lacking nothing. Thou lovest without subjection to passion, Thou art jealous but not with fear; Thou canst know repentance but no sorrow, be angry yet unperturbed by anger. Thou canst change the works Thou hast made but Thy mind stands changeless. Thou dost find and receive back what Thou didst never lose; art never in need but dost rejoice in Thy gains, art not greedy but dost exact interest manifold. Men pay Thee more than is of obligation to win return from Thee, yet who has anything that is not already Thine? Thou owest nothing yet dost pay as if in debt to Thy creature, forgivest what is owed to Thee yet dost not lose thereby. And with all this, what have I said, my God and my Life and my sacred Delight? What can anyone say when he speaks of Thee? Yet woe to them that speak not of Thee at all, since those who say most are but dumb.[3]

The fact that God is immutable does not mean that he does not respond to man or enter in any way into human history. On the contrary, Scripture often speaks of God's approaching or withdrawing, addressing words of consolation to man, acting in history with deeds of love and chastisement. In so doing, God is turning to the creature in that total freedom which is founded in his possession of himself. Ever since the creation of the world God has been directed towards the creature according to his changeless will: he is continuously engaged in giving himself to the creature. It is on the creature's side that the question arises: how God fares with the creature—whether he is received at all, whether the creature opens up to him. The receptivity of the creature to the divine love was most intense in Jesus Christ and in his acts of obedience which were summed up in his death on the cross. Therefore God could give himself to Christ, dying on the cross, with a power which demonstrated its salvific dynamism in the resurrection. Because Jesus Christ was the representative of mankind, God gave himself to all mankind in giving himself to Christ. By means of the cross on Golgotha mankind was reconciled to God. Augustine's words concerning God in Sermon 22, 6 are most apposite here: "When you change, he changes."

Man does not change God's mind by means of his religious acts; rather, he himself becomes capable of accepting God's gifts. In prayer, especially in the supplication which is an undertone in every prayer, man confesses his limitations, his weakness, and his sinfulness. At the same time he acknowledges God's merciful kindness and the abundance from which he expects those benefits which he is incapable of obtaining for himself. Supplication does not become a means whereby man gains power over God or magic through which he has God at his disposal. Instead it is an instrument in God's hands putting man at his disposal in the sense that it permits him to give himself to man. No situation in human history takes God by surprise: so far as his saving power is concerned, no one situation is more favorable than another. But man is not equally capable at all times or in the same way of freely giving himself to God's saving activity. Human acts of freedom are in the last analysis, of course, the gift of God, since everything which is not divine is an expression of the divine freedom. Nevertheless, in a mysterious interaction between the Creator and the creature, man himself is responsibly engaged in free human activities.

Since, from the human point of view, the fact remains that man is not in every situation and in the same way capable of accepting God's gifts, the encounters between God and man are of unequal value. The alteration in value always derives from the creature's side; yet it is not without significance from the divine viewpoint in that God is sometimes able to reach man and sometimes not. Since it is God's loving will to create, not to destroy, freedom, he respects the freedom of man and does not intrude when the door is not open to him. Hence it can be said that whereas God does not change himself in himself, he does to a certain degree change himself in man insofar as his saving action, which remains steadfastly turned towards man at all times, is successful at one time but not at another.

By way of footnote let us remark that we must distinguish between the concepts of the immutability of God's nature and the immutability of his decisions. God can in no way alter his nature, but he is free so far as his plan for the world is concerned. To be sure, if he has once decided upon a definite plan for the world, then it also is immutable (see the doctrine of creation). We must hold that God is both immutable and free, paradoxical though this is.

These reflections come to a climax in the final structural element, the divine simplicity. If we emphasize this characteristic, it means that we reduce the plurality of polarities, which is typical for being, to a unity.

By denying that which divides we affirm that fullness which unites all contradictions in God. Precisely by this means God both surpasses all our comprehension and becomes comprehensible to us as inscrutable mystery.[4] We must not overlook the fact that God's simplicity becomes less rigid within the divine tri-personhood. The Church maintains that there is complete unity (*unum*) in God, insofar as the distinction of the persons is not opposed to this (DS 1330). God's simplicity is founded in his absolute fullness of being. According to the principle of divine simplicity God is totally identical with himself. We must inquire more closely into the type of this identity. Thomas Aquinas was of the opinion that in God all characteristics and actions are identical with one another and that one could speak only of a "virtual" distinction. He sees this distinction in the fact that the fullness of God has such power that we can only describe God's works and properties in different concepts and words. Duns Scotus held that such a real identity would eliminate the various characteristics of God in their true form in favor of an undifferentiated monotony. If we teach the doctrine of a virtual distinction, we can only assume that the characteristics attributed to God are rooted in him, and are such that God is able to act justly, faithfully, or mercifully but that God's activity and properties do not exist in him in their true form.

Scotus believed that he could solve the problem by assuming a "formal" distinction. By formal distinction he means that individual divine properties and activities are to be found in God in their pure form as they are understood in their proper definition. They are prevented from descending into a real distinction by the power of divine infinity. Scotus likewise assumes a certain differentiation in God. He believes that he can do justice to the substantial fullness of divine life only in that way, and that he can avoid the risk of supposing division within God by pointing to the divine infinity.

However we may explain the divine simplicity, it in no case leads to the assumption that God is merely a fixed and static essence. This is out of the question because, to cite once more a frequently quoted statement of Aquinas's, in both ourselves and in God a certain "circuit" takes place in the activities of the intellect and the will. As we have already noted, the will, according to Aquinas,[5] returns to the point from which the mind set out. In a certain sense one can assume that in God there is also a distinction between that which knows and that which is known. This applies even if we accept, with Aquinas, the notion of real identity: it becomes all the more comprehensible if, with Scotus, we admit a formal distinction.

THE "METAPHYSICAL ESSENCE" OF GOD

In the course of history the question arose of whether there was a basic definition of God which would sum up all other statements about him. Such a definition would immediately reveal God in his being as God and hence would show him as different from the rest of reality. If there is such a fundamental definition, we must understand it as we would the characterization of a man, a landscape or an historical epoch by a single word. Since the Middle Ages this basic definition has been expressed in what is termed the "metaphysical essence of God." The sum of the divine attributes was, by contrast, called the "physical essence" of God. The most important divine attributes have already been mentioned. We have seen that owing to the analogous character of our knowledge of God, they are often conceived as in such tension with one another that we can speak of a *coincidentia oppositorum,* a union of opposing qualities and activities in God.

Since the time of Augustine, and especially since Aquinas, systematic formulation differing only in details has termed God the truth, absolute being, being itself, subsistent being, pure act, and has seen in these definitions the metaphysical essence of God. Other attempts to determine the metaphysical essence of God, such as Duns Scotus' idea that it consists in radical infinity or absolute spirituality have not been very successful, although they have their own significance. The concept of "being itself" must itself be understood in terms of an ontological difference between God and man. In every non-divine reality there is a difference between essence and existence, as we have already noted. In God there is no such difference. He is not *something* which is but is pure being itself: he does not *have* his existence, he *is* his own existence.

The question is whether this definition of the metaphysical essence of God, coming from the Greek mode of thought, can achieve what is required of it. Is it capable of summing up our remaining statements about God? Can it be understood as the basis from which all other statements about God may be derived? Does it distinguish adequately between God and the creature? There is no doubt that while this definition can fulfill the last requirement, it fails to satisfy the first two. Even if we use contemporary existential philosophy, and point out that "openness" is an attribute of absolute being, it is nevertheless difficult to derive from such an openness what Scripture asserts about God. Nor can we deduce from it what decisions God has made in his free salvific will. The concept can only serve to make theological statements already derived from divine revelation subsequently comprehensible and to show the appropriateness of God's salvific activity.

The Aristotelian philosophy of being cannot help us to any great extent towards a deeper understanding of the biblical statements concerning the nature of God. Any profit which may be gained from the use of Greek ontology must be paid for with considerable loss. Actually we do find in Scripture another conception of being besides the Greek, one which assumes a dialogical difference within being itself and constitutes the background of the I-Thou statements in Scripture. It can legitimately be said that an I-Thou metaphysics is implicit in Scripture. Its development, however, is outside the scope of the present work; we can merely draw attention to it. We should not be harsh, nonetheless, in our judgment of the use of the Greek conception of being, for even if it grants only a limited understanding of the biblical statements its value is surely exceptional. We must acknowledge with gratitude the achievement of theology from Augustine to Aquinas. To define God as pure being is to make the fact of his creative activity and the historical event of the incarnation all the more amazing. Aquinas answers the question of who it is who gives himself to us in Christ by interpreting God as absolute being. This answer expresses with the utmost clarity God's difference from all the realities of our experience. Thus we comprehend on a deeper level the freedom and graciousness of God's gift of himself to his creatures—something which becomes all the more incomprehensible the more perfect that being is which we understand as God. The definition accepted thus far by almost all theologians of the metaphysical essence of God should not be simply dismissed but should be incorporated into the I-Thou metaphysics proffered by Scripture.

THE CHURCH'S DOCTRINE

In a series of official statements the Church has set forth the idea of God which has been developed here. In order to give a general idea of the faith of the Church we wish to examine only the two most important assertions out of the many in which she has professed her faith in the one God. The first was made at the Fourth Lateran Council (the twelfth general council) in 1215 and the other at the First Vatican Council in 1870. The first statement says (in opposition to such dualistic conceptions as those of the Waldensians: DS 800):

We firmly believe and profess with sincere heart that there is only one true God, eternal, immense, unchangeable, incomprehensible, omnipotent, and indescribable: the Father, the Son, and the Holy Spirit: three persons but one essence and a substance or nature that is wholly simple.

The second statement asserts (DS 3001):

The holy, Catholic, apostolic Roman Church believes and professes that there is one true and living God, the creator and lord of heaven and earth. He is all-powerful, eternal, immeasurable, incomprehensible, and limitless in intellect and will and in every perfection. Since he is one unique spiritual substance, entirely simple and unchangeable, he must be declared really and essentially distinct from the world, perfectly happy in himself and by his very nature, and inexpressibly exalted over all things that exist or can be conceived other than himself.

(See also DS 3021–3025.)

There is a great difference between these two statements. At the Lateran Council in 1215 the important issue was the doctrine of the Trinity. The Council speaks of the one God and of the tri-personal God. In the declaration of the First Vatican Council the doctrine of the Trinity is not treated. Consequently, this statement treats God's reality in a rather abstract fashion. The Vatican Council took a stand against errors of the nineteenth century: materialism and pantheism. In the face of these two movements, it emphasized the fact that God is spirit, his absolute perfection, and his distinctness from the world. The Fourth Lateran Council, on the other hand, was concerned to secure faith in the tri-personhood of God. Nevertheless, neither of the councils confine themselves to making merely metaphysical statements; even though the wording sounds purely metaphysical, it is nonetheless related to salvation history. Metaphysics is the background for salvation history, and the statements made about salvation history have metaphysical statements implicit in them.

Notes

[1] *De consolatione philosophiae,* v.6.

[2] From *Saint Augustine, The City of God,* Books VIII–XVI, trans. Gerald G. Walsh, S.J., and Grace Monahan, O.S.U. (New York: Fathers of the Church, Inc., 1952), pp. 277–279.

[3] *The Confessions of St. Augustine,* trans. F. J. Sheed (New York: Sheed and Ward, 1943), p. 5.

⁴ Aquinas, *ST*, I, a. 12, 1 and 3; Nicholas of Cusa, "coincidentia oppositorum"; F. Lotz.
⁵ *De potentia*, 9, 9.

Readings for Part I

Eichrodt, W. *Theology of the Old Testament*, I. Philadelphia, Westminster, 1961.

Mouroux, J. *The Mystery of Time*. New York, Desclée, 1964. Part I, ch. 1.

Rowley, H. H. *The Faith of Israel*. Philadelphia, Westminster, 1957. Ch. 2; see also Macquarrie, J. *Principles of Christian Theology*. New York, Scribner's. Ch. 5.

Tillich, P. *Systematic Theology*, I. Chicago, University of Chicago Press, 1951.

‹II

God as Creator

‹ 5

God as Creator

THE SCRIPTURAL DATA AND THEIR THEOLOGICAL DEVELOPMENT

The second prerequisite for the understanding of Jesus as Savior is belief in God as the creator. The primary interest of the people of Israel was not in the origin of the world; their interest was centered on Yahweh's actions in salvation history, and those biblical texts which deal with the origin of the world from God and with God's sovereignty are to be placed in the context of salvation history. They show that God, who called Abraham and the other patriarchs; who at the time of Moses freed the people from slavery in Egypt, thus making them into one people; who sent his own son in Jesus Christ—God, who opened the way into the absolute future through these events—is Lord over the world. This mighty God is full of loving-kindness; yet he is the judge of his people. It is he who can be trusted unconditionally when he promises them that he will walk mercifully at their side into the future which will be the fulfillment of all their hopes. It is possible to put the matter simply by saying that the Old Testament story of creation serves to support the scriptural account of the divine plan of salvation (von Rad). The manifold statements about creation which occur in the prophets, the psalms, and the historical books call on the people to declare for the one true and living God as against the gods; they are meant to strengthen confidence and faith in spite of the people's experience of disaster, sin and destruction. The

67

longest passages which bear this out are the texts of the unknown author of Deutero-Isaiah, chapters 40–66 (cf. 1 Chron. 16:30ff.; Amos 5:8; 9:5; Jer. 10:1–16; Hab. 3:3–19; Mic. 2:2ff.; Gen. 14:19–22; 24:3; 1 Kgs. 8:12, 53; Pss. 19:1–7; 33:6f.; 146:6; 104; Sir. 42:15–26; 43). The expressions in these texts which describe God's creative activity are varied in character; the verbs used mean to shape, to form, to fashion, to bring forth.

The first two chapters of Genesis present a particularly detailed account of the world's derivation from God. First of all we must investigate how these chapters originated; their *Sitz im Leben* is of decisive significance. The texts rose out of the faith of the people in their covenant with God. They are the products of different authors and are components of one of the two great compilations of the history of the people of Israel. The general modern consensus is that these compilations were combined in the Pentateuch by an editor at the time of the Babylonian exile or shortly thereafter. The first text includes Genesis 1:1 to 2:4a; the second begins with 3:4b. The first text is called the Priestly Code and the second the Yahwistic Document, "Yahwistic" because the name used for God in this text is almost exclusively "Yahweh." In addition to these two texts, the so-called Elohistic text and Deuteronomy have been inserted into the Pentateuch.

The Yahwistic text probably dates from the time of Solomon, whereas the Priestly Code is likely to have originated in the Babylonian exile, or shortly afterwards, in priestly circles—perhaps in the milieu of the prophet Ezekiel. We may assume that the core of the Pentateuch goes back to the time of Moses or perhaps even to Moses himself. We also accept that this core was handed down in two principal traditions which were continually elaborated and augmented until the Yahwistic text reached its final form about 350 years after Moses in the time of Solomon, and the other text about 950 years after Moses at the time of the Babylonian exile. We must, or may, imagine the origin of these texts in the following manner. It was unheard of that a people should worship only one God and reject all the other gods worshipped in the area, and the people of Israel were tempted again and again to defect to the nature gods of the surrounding cultures. The temptation was greater because the living God, who the people knew had called them, appeared to keep none of his promises. The "promised land" did not materialize. Moreover, even at the time of the covenant with God, sin, crime, disaster, and affliction came upon the people. Doubts arose as to whether this God was really as mighty as Moses had asserted. Did not the heathen gods seem to be more powerful? This conjecture exerted all the greater influence because the heathen gods achieved victory, while the God of Israel seemed unable to protect his people from the violence of their neighbors. In this harassing situation thoughtful men, under the impulse of the Spirit of God, asked themselves how faith in the one God might be preserved. Questions arose as to where the evil and destruction in the world came from; whether the God of Israel was in truth the mighty Lord he claimed to be when he called upon his people to worship him; whether there was any point in taking seriously that command of his: Thou shalt have no other gods beside me. Just as the prophets and the psalmist glorified God as Lord of heaven and earth, the first two chapters of Genesis sing his praises.

The two Genesis texts are characteristically different, not only in their external structure but also in their purpose. The Yahwistic text seeks to answer the question, Where does evil come from? Does it come from a primal evil principle or from God himself? The Priestly Code, which is used for the first chapter, tries to answer the question of whether God, who wishes to be worshipped as the omnipotent Lord, is really this mighty ruler. Both texts give a doctrine of the origin of evil and of the sovereignty of God.

For the Priestly Code, teaching is of primary importance. However, it is teaching not only in the sense of instruction but also in the sense of an appeal—that is, it has an existential character. In the second text the appeal is in the foreground. It is made under one form of a didactic story. We might say that the first text is speculatively existential and the second existentially doctrinal. Properly speaking, the first text alone witnesses to creation, the second mentions the world's origin only casually; its primary interest centers on the origin of evil in a good world created by God. Even the first text is not intended as a report of the creation of the world, so much as a testimony of faith that it was from God that

the world originated. The author, using all the scientific and cultural knowledge he possessed, is explaining, on the basis of his
faith in God, how the world must have come into being. But his
point is not really "how" but "that" the world comes from God,
and he stresses that because of this, God has complete sovereignty
over it.

So if we ask how the author or authors could have known about
the origin of the world, we cannot—and need not—refer to an
original revelation "handed down from generation to generation."
It was simply through meditation on man and his relationship to
God that the writer arrived at the conclusion presented in our text.
He attempts—on the basis of the idea of God obtained from the
experience of the people on Mt. Sinai—to grope his way back, far
beyond the time of Abraham, beyond any possibility of written
evidence, back to the beginnings of mankind and whatever millions
of years came before that.

He investigates causes, which is the aetiological method of research. Although the scriptural text is very important, it is so
familiar that we need not quote it here. When the author states
that in the beginning God created heaven and earth it is obvious
that he means the absolute beginning—that beginning before which
nothing existed except God: God himself posited the beginning.
Because God uttered his creative word, the non-divine, which had
not existed until then, came into being. By the phrase "heaven and
earth" the writer means the universe. The word he uses for
"created" is *barah,* which does not in itself convey the meaning
that creation came directly out of nothing; yet the idea of creation
out of nothing is implicit in it if we give it its fuller sense. It is a
technical term in the theological language of the priests, and it is
used exclusively of divine operations. In the Old Testament it occurs forty-seven times, twenty of which are in chapters 40–46 of
Deutero-Isaiah. Only later, in the Hellenistic period, is the creation
of the world by God interpreted in Scripture as meaning strictly
"creation out of nothing": in 2 Maccabees 7:28 the expression
appears in connection with a warning which a Maccabean mother
gives her youngest son with regard to the omnipotence of God. We
must not give the term a strictly philosophical meaning in this con-

text, it is rather a matter of imagery; hence the term "out of nothing" does not imply that nothingness is conceived as an elemental substance out of which God fashioned the world. What it does convey is that no non-divine cause or exemplary cause or final cause exists distinct from God: the creation of the world has no precondition other than God's all-powerful will.

When the text asserts that God created the world by his word, it is expressing the fact that dialogue constitutes the basis of the relationship between God and the world. God did not create the world simply to have it on hand, but because he wanted to enter into communication and conversation with it. This has meaning only if we see man as the essential element in creation. It implies that creation without man would be senseless. Here we find the beginnings of that personal ontology, that I-Thou metaphysics of personality already mentioned, which distinguishes Old Testament thought from that of the Greeks. If we receive the impression from the second verse that God had to struggle with the powers of chaos, we must recognize in this a remnant of mythological conceptions. It indicates a knowledge of the dangers of chaos, which is continually being restrained by the creator who forms and sets things in order. The emphasis given to God's creation of the sun, moon, and stars is of special significance; it is doubtless a polemic against astrology, which was prevalent among the neighboring tribes.

If the author has God declare after each act of creation that it was good, he means "good" not in a metaphysical sense but in a functional sense—that is, it was capable of achieving what God wanted it to achieve. This emphasis on the goodness of the world is necessary. Those who are under the covenant need to hear that the evil in the world does not come from God; only good comes from God. The authors of this account do not explore the question of the origin of sin as does the author of the Yahwistic Document. Yet from Chapter 6 on it becomes evident that this question interests them and that they are not superficial optimists—this chapter suddenly and unexpectedly comments on the depravity and sin of the world. The author of the Priestly Code was obviously familiar with the Yahwistic Document; we have the impression that he attempted to correct its anthropomorphic terminology theologically. He seemed to consider it unnecessary to add anything himself about the origin of sin, since it had been exhaustively discussed in the Yahwistic Document.

When we survey the text in the first chapter of Genesis we must say that it presents an introduction to the history of salvation. It shows that God is Lord over the universe. He is praised not as a local Israelitic god but as the God of the entire cosmos. Everything is subject to him and must serve him. The mystery as to why he allows precisely his chosen to suffer affliction nevertheless remains.

The reason that the author uses the "week" for his imagery and ends it with the Sabbath is probably connected with his idea of salvation history. In the year of disaster (589), when all the leaders of the nation, the well-to-do and well-educated, were taken into the Babylonian captivity, services in the Temple ceased. Those left behind, like those in Babylon, had no liturgy: they could only turn in personal prayer to the God of their fathers. The allusion to the Sabbath in our text was a reminder that even in captivity the ancient laws of God were not to be forgotten or disregarded. That the account of creation is intended to be an introduction to salvation history had important consequences. The authors looked back from the present to the distant past in order to make men look forward to what, on the basis of that past, is to come in the future. Concerned with history as Genesis is, its orientation is towards what the future holds. We may conjecture that the authors of the account belonged to the groups around Ezekiel and the Deutero-Isaiah. If so, then what they wrote must be understood as having directly eschatological significance. Both Deutero-Isaiah and Ezekiel were trying to turn the attention of the despairing people towards a salvific future.

Isaiah prophesied a new heaven and a new earth, a whole new creation which is to arise. Here we see protology, the description of the beginnings of things, closely allied with eschatology. When God first created the world, he set its course for that ultimate future, still not realized, the prospect of which the prophets used to console the captives. We can even say that the author searched into the past only in order to find there the joyful future God had promised them, a future which will not forever remain unfulfilled, but will indeed become a reality.

The text from Genesis, with those indicated from the psalms and the prophets, expresses faith in God and in his continuing creative activity. Although it is true that God created in a single act by which the world was begun, his creative activity did not then cease. It is he who continues to bring about all that occurs in nature and history (*creatio continua*). Considered in this way, the dynamic character of creation becomes much more evident. Faith in creation must always hold itself in readiness for the new, for what is to come, for the future. The Deistic idea that God created the world in a single act billions of years ago and then withdrew his influence from it is unbiblical. His act of creation continues in a twofold sense: every creature exists at any given moment only because of the continuing creative act of God, and the creative act of God is constantly producing something new out of what is already in existence. The world is continuously in motion insofar as it arises vertically, so to speak, from the depths of God and moves horizontally towards an ever greater fullness of reality. However, there are passages in the wisdom books which stress static existence rather than this continual process of becoming. Such texts show the influence of Hellenistic thought. They, too, testify that God is the Lord of the world, though they focus on its present beauty and grandeur. But if the creation texts in the wisdom literature emphasize cosmology, they do not disregard salvation history. They are polemics against the Hellenistic tendency to worship the order and beauty of the world itself: their gods are only ways of expressing this adoration of the world. In opposition to this, the wisdom literature, while it bears witness to the world's splendor and beauty, stresses the fact that the world was created: that is to say, it testifies to the world's origin in God and the numinous element experienced in it (cf. Sir. 42:15ff.; 43; 37; 2:5ff.; Prov. 8:22ff.; Wis. 9:1–9; Job 37:14f.; 10:8–9ff.; 9:5ff.; 26:7ff.; 28:22ff.). These passages are an attempt at demythologization in a milieu of myth: that is their *Sitz im Leben*.

The New Testament first of all confirms what is said in the Old: we see this in the synoptic gospels and in the Acts of the Apostles as well. Here too the creation of the world is understood as the beginning of salvation history (cf. Acts 4:23–30; 14:15; Mt. 11:25; Lk. 10:21; Acts 17:24; Mt. 6:26–34; 5:45). The whole New Testament stresses the eschatological orientation of the divine act of creation. This is especially true of Revelation, in which Isaiah's words about a "new heaven and a new earth" are reiterated (Rev. 21:1). Paul uses a variety of prepositions to make it clear that the divine act of creation had absolutely no precondition: " 'For who has known the mind of the Lord, or who has been his counselor?' . . . For from him and through him and to him are all things. To him be glory for ever" (Rom. 11:34f.).

According to the author of Acts, Paul on the Areopagus spoke like an Old Testament prophet about the creation of the world; yet he added a completely new element to the idea of creation—namely, the Christological or Christocentric. We have already spoken of this and need only refer to that discussion. The first allusion to the Christocentric nature of divine creative activity is made in 1 Corinthians (8:6), but it is especially in Colossians, Ephesians, and Hebrews that the Christ-centeredness of the whole of creation is proclaimed. This Christ-centeredness of creation to which Paul bore witness is the application to his contemporary situation of Old Testament thought concerning salvation history. God's action in salvation history, which began at the creation, reached its culmination in the coming of Christ; hence creation is really the beginning of the Christ-event. The Christ-event is not something added to the divine plan for creation: it was the core of the divine plan from the very beginning. God's decision to pour himself into non-divine reality attained in Jesus Christ its objective, its ultimate meaning and its apex. Everything else is either a prerequisite or an effect of this divine self-donation. Thus Paul's way of viewing reality Christologically falls within the scope of salvation history as it is presented in the Old Testament as well as in the New.

In this Christological view it becomes concretely evident what is meant by a new heaven and a new earth. It means that form of the cosmos and of human history which manifested itself in the risen Christ. The new heaven and the new earth are heaven and earth transformed according to the archetype of the risen Christ. In order to understand what we mean by this new heaven and new earth, we must first consider the "old" heaven and the "old" earth: beginning and end are bound together, forming a unity in process of development. We shall understand the description of creation in Scripture only if we view it in this light.

In the post-apostolic period the biblical doctrine of creation was developed further as it came to grips with dualistic, pantheistic, and materialistic conceptions of the world. In the concrete, this arose from encounters with Stoic, Aristotelian, and neo-Platonic modes of thought. As this continued, the idea of the Christocentricity of creation lost more and more of its vitality, and on the other hand the Stoic idea of the purpose and order in everything gained ground, though the factor of salvation was never entirely forgotten. Special attention was paid to the concept of creation out of nothing: it is characteristic of the second century that the biblical doctrine of the pre-existence of the Logos was transformed into speculations concerning the origin of the world, and this led to serious Christological debates within Christianity itself. In developing a theory about the place of the Logos within the framework of creation, the Fathers sought to defend monotheism by rejecting both polytheism and any pantheistic fusion of God with the world: this was done chiefly by Apologists such as Athenagoras and Justin. In Irenaeus, on the other hand, we encounter a very original doctrine of creation which is completely Christocentric. He emphasizes so strongly the Christ-centeredness of the divine plan for man's salvation and for the world that hardly any room remains for the negative aspects of the cosmos—not even human sin—but to his merit, he, more than any other Church Father, showed the unity of the creator and the redeemer-God, the unity of the beginning and the end, and the summing-up of all of creation in Jesus Christ. Tertullian of Africa in his realistic way of thinking criticized this all too idealistic conception. We find other original conceptions of creation in the representatives of Alexandrian theology. According to Clement of Alexandria, God brought forth the entire creation simultaneously in one act: individual figures then appear in the course of history not in the sense of an evolution, but of an unfolding of what has always fully existed. Origen of Alexandria assumed a pre-world of spiritual substances. Matter was created in order to punish and educate the fallen spirits. The world process is understood as the unfolding of divine unity into multiplicity, and this then returns to God and is subsumed again into his unity.

In the West, Augustine's idea of creation became authoritative. Influenced by neo-Platonic thought, he assumed that there were a number of levels of being, from the spiritual to the material. He avoided the neo-Platonic tendency towards pantheism by ascribing the world to God's will to love. Against Manichean dualism he maintained that the personal divine principle of the world was one. His idea that time was created with the world, as opposed to the idea that God put the world into time as into a pre-existent framework, is especially important. Moreover, his doctrine of divine ideas was epoch-making in that he synthesized the Old Testament wisdom doctrine and the Platonic doctrine of ideas. Salvation history does not play a significant role in Augustine's thought, owing to the influence on him of neo-Platonism. An idea Augustine adopted from neo-Platonism which had significant consequences in the Middle Ages was that of the participation of created being in divine being.

In the theology of the thirteenth century we must mention Thomas Aquinas's and Bonaventure's conceptions of creation, the former in the Aristotelian neo-Platonic line of thought and the latter in the Augustinian neo-Platonic line. Thomas Aquinas sees creation in the categories of cause and effect; yet he did not entirely disregard the Platonic idea of participation. There are two elements in his conception of creation which are of special significance. The first is his doctrine of the temporal beginning of the world, which he, unlike Augustine, holds to be a truth of faith and not of philosophy. The second is his concept of the autonomy of the world. According to him the world is dependent upon God, yet at the same time possesses its own being and activity. This idea was to prove extremely fruitful. Franciscan theology emphasized the world's dependence upon God rather than its autonomy. On the other hand, this theology elaborated more than had Thomas the idea of salvation history implicit in the ontological theology of creation. We must insist, however, that Thomas does not ignore the idea of salvation history. For he is occupied with the neo-Platonic view that all things have their origin in God as a result of his free and creative will to love, and that they return to him. This idea of the cyclic movement of the world (coming out from God and returning to him) is just as important to Thomas as it is to Bonaventure, even if he does not stress it so markedly. Mention should be made of Duns Scotus because of his stress on the absolute freedom of the divine plan for creation. No other medieval theologian succeeded in emphasizing the freedom of God to the extent that he did without lapsing into the notion of an arbitrary God.

At the time of the Reformation the doctrine of creation was not a particularly controversial issue.

THE CHURCH'S PROCLAMATION

It is striking how frequently the Christian Church, as the community of faith established by Christ and animated by his Spirit, has professed its belief that God created the world. Already in the early Church of the apostolic age there were Christological formulas of faith which represented the world as being derived from God through Christ. (We may mention 1 Cor. 8:6 again.) Gradually these formulas of faith, as well as theology in general, came to disregard the Christological element within the doctrine of creation. The reason for this may lie in the fact that the Christians were trying to counter the pagan reproach of godlessness by a doctrine of creation which pointed to the creative activity of the one God, the Father.

One formula in particular, to which we have already referred, is significant for the development of the early Christian creeds: whereas the Greek text usually speaks of God as the Pantokrator who created the world and reigns over it, the Latin articles of faith refer to the Omnipotens deus, the former expressing the actualistic-dynamic element, the latter introducing the static one. Furthermore, the word "Father" has been appended to the word "God"

in the creeds, so that in all of them, including the "Apostles'
Creed" and the Nicene Creed, we have the salvific creativity of the
three divine persons as the most important element. The structure
is formed by the presence of these three persons. We do not have
first a statement about the three persons in God and then one
about their common work of creation in the manner which became
typical for theology after the time of Fulgentius of Ruspe and John
Damascene. Instead, individual divine works are attributed to each
person: creation to the Father; redemption to the Son, sent by the
Father; consummation to the Holy Spirit. The creeds picture God's
activity in the course of salvation history in this fashion. Creation
appears as the first step in the history of God's dealings with men.
Thus we see that there is continuity between creation, redemption,
and consummation. Furthermore, we can observe a certain process
of actualization. God's works are not treated separately from him
in their autonomous being but seen in their continuing derivation
from God. Here there is some evidence of biblical influence. As
we have seen, the word "God" in Scripture usually refers to the
first divine person, and the Church's confessions of faith continue
this usage. They do not first speak of God in general terms and
then draw from this concept the idea of Father, Son, and Holy
Spirit. The one God of whom they speak is identified with the
Father. There is still another factor. All confessions of faith express a doctrine; they are rules of faith. Nevertheless, they are not
merely didactic but are also the dramatic re-enactment of the faith.
Belief in the one God means the self-surrender of the believer to
the God in whom he believes (DS 1–15; DS 54).

In the course of her history the Church has found means other
than the creeds to profess her faith in God the creator (DS 800;
3001–3005). It is a constant temptation of the human intellect to
identify the world with God and God with the world and to attribute the evil in the world to an evil principle. Since the days of the
Renaissance and the rise of humanism, man has been increasingly
inclined to regard the world as something so self-explanatory that
it cannot be traced back beyond itself: he no longer raises the
question of the origin of the world because he is no longer con-

scious of this as a problem. Modern scientific discoveries and inventions, combined with a revival of Greek naturalism, have contributed essentially to this new attitude towards the world and towards life. As a counterbalance to this mentality the Church has unceasingly proclaimed that God is remote from the world and yet near at hand; she has united in her concept of the one God the idea of his being at work in creation and of his nevertheless transcending it; she has declared that the Father who governs the universe through his creative will is the maker of all things, both visible and invisible.

Because faith in God's creation of the world has significance for the total understanding of Christianity, and especially of Jesus Christ, some doctrinal statements of the Church should be mentioned at this point.

The teaching office of the Church has rejected all forms of ontological dualism, which posits two principles, one good and the other evil. In reply to the Origenists (whose beliefs are not necessarily to be traced back to those of Origen), a synod of the province of Constantinople, which was held in 543 under the auspices of the Patriarch Maenna and whose decisions seem to have been endorsed by Pope Vigilius, rejected a philosophical-theological system, nurtured by Platonic-Stoic forms of thought, according to which all events in the world follow their own inner law exclusively; and hence no room is left for the free creative activity of God. The statement of the synod is important: "Whoever asserts or believes that the power of God is finite or that God has created only as much as he can understand, let him be anathema" (DS 411). Shortly afterwards, the Synod of Braga in Portugal (561) condemned the particular Manichean-Gnostic system of thought which originated with Priscillian but was developed fully only after his death (385). In many ways this system is related to that of the above-mentioned Origenists, and may have been its source. It views the devil as the creator of matter and the substance of evil. The soul is divine; it existed before the body and was cast into it as punishment for sins. These errors, which were reflections of the times, gave the Church an opportunity to reject decisively the de-

preciation of matter, particularly of the human body, and to emphasize that everything that is, is good because it comes from the
one creator (DS 455–457; 462f.).

In the Middle Ages the Albigensians revived Manicheism, long
smoldering out of sight, and allowed heathendom, which had been
growing secretly, to emerge again. In response, the Profession of
Faith of Innocent III in 1208 refuted the teaching that matter was
evil and created by Satan out of nothing; that therefore Christ had
no true body but only an illusory one; and that the material world
should be rejected. The refutation also applied to the related hereti-
cal teachings of the Catharists and the Waldensians who, because
of their rigorous opposition to the display of power and the secularization of the Church, rejected all physical and material things
as evil. The wording of the refutation shows that a great change
had taken place since the original confessions of faith. The *Professio
fidei* of Innocent III designates the whole Trinity as the creator of
the world. The main text reads:

We believe in our heart and proclaim with our lips that the Father,
Son, and Holy Ghost is the one God, creator, maker, governor, and
ruler of all corporeal and spiritual things visible and invisible. We
believe that both the Old and the New Testament have one and the
same author: God, who, remaining in the Trinity, created all things
from nothing. (DS 790)

The Fourth Lateran Council used the truths of revelation as a
means to oppose the opinion of the Albigensians and the Waldensians that a god of darkness stands over against a god of light and
that the former is responsible for the realm of matter and evil:

God is the progenitor, the creator of all things visible and invisible,
spiritual and corporeal, who by his almighty power from the very
beginning of time has created both orders of creatures in the same
way, out of nothing, the spiritual or angelic world and the corporeal
or visible universe. And afterwards he formed the creature man, who
in a way belongs to both orders, as he is composed of spirit and body.
(DS 800)

The Council of Lyons expressed itself similarly. The Council of Florence (1439–1442) declared in its Instruction of Faith for the Jacobites, *Cantate Domino* of February 2, 1442 (DS 1333):

The holy Roman Church firmly believes, professes, and preaches that the one true God, Father, Son, and Holy Spirit, is the creator of all things visible and invisible. When God willed, in his goodness he created all creatures, both spiritual and corporeal. These creatures are good because they were made by the Supreme Good, but they are changeable because they were made from nothing. The Church asserts that there is no such thing as a nature of evil, because every nature, insofar as it is a nature, is good.

In 1870, at the third session of the First Vatican Council, the Church made its final, concluding statement against the materialism and pantheism of the nineteenth century:

The one true God, out of his goodness and almighty power, not in order to increase his own happiness or perfection but in order to reveal his perfection through the goodness which he confers on creatures, in a free decision of his will at the beginning of time created in the same fashion out of nothing both orders of creation, the spiritual and the corporeal—that is, the world of angels and the earth, and the world of men which in a certain sense embraces both, since man consists of body and spirit. (DS 3002)

The canons of the council state:

If anyone denies that there is one true God, creator and Lord of all things visible and invisible: let him be anathema. If anyone dares to assert that nothing exists except matter: let him be anathema. If anyone says that God and all things possess one and the same substance and essence: let him be anathema. If anyone says that finite things, both corporeal and spiritual, or at least spiritual, emanated from the divine substance; or that the divine essence becomes all things by a manifestation or evolution of itself; or, finally, that God is universal or indefinite being which by determining itself makes up the universe which is diversified into genera, species, and individuals: let him be anathema.

If anyone does not admit that the world and everything in it, both spiritual and material, have been produced in their entire substance by God out of nothing; or says that God did not create with a will free from all necessity, but that he created necessarily, just as he necessarily loves himself; or denies that the world was made for the glory of God; let him be anathema. (DS 3021–3025)

These ecclesiastical texts go beyond what is said directly in Scripture and explain the fact of creation as well as the motive and purpose behind it. It is significant that the Church's doctrinal statements from the Fourth Lateran Council to the First Vatican Council, like the *Professio fidei* of Innocent III, ascribe the act of creating the world to the Trinity as such. In this formulation, the trinitarian God is the one and only principle responsible for the creation of the world; we are no longer aware of the individual functions of the three divine persons. The idea of salvation history plays a less important role in this view, but it is, of course, not completely forgotten. The use of the Apostles' creed as well as the Nicene in the liturgy of the Church bears this out.

The Church has been repeatedly concerned with the meaning of the six- or seven-day week, over and above its interest in the fact of creation. The question took on special significance when the Ptolemaic and mythical idea of the world was replaced by the Copernican conception. Because the biblical witness to the derivation of the world from God was originally given expression in accordance with the ancient idea of the world, the question arose of whether a modern conception (say the Copernican or an even more recent one) could be compatible with the biblical one. Can the idea of the world be separated from a statement of faith or do we have to choose between the scriptural witness and the claims of one of the modern conceptions of the world? This problem became particularly acute in the case of Galileo. A long theological development was necessary before theology and Church proclamation recognized that a difference exists between the mode of expression of Scripture and its content. The Pontifical Biblical Commission began to acknowledge this distinction when, on June 13, 1901, it released a statement emphasizing those doctrinal elements which are obligatory for the Christian from the standpoint of content.

Here, indirectly, the mode of a statement of faith is distinguished from its content (DS 3512–3518). The answer which the Secretary of the Biblical Commission gave Cardinal Suhard of Paris on January 1, 1948, is especially important (DS 3862):

With regard to the authorship of the Pentateuch the Biblical Commission already recognized in its decree of June 27th, 1906, that the opinion is lawful that Moses used written documents and oral traditions in the composition of his work, and that subsequently. alterations and additions have taken place. There is no longer anyone today who doubts the existence of these sources and does not admit that the Mosaic law continually acquired accretions under the influence of later social and religious conditions, even with regard to its historical parts. Catholic scholars should investigate these problems without prejudgments, in the light of a positive, critical method and the results of the relevant sciences. Such an investigation will doubtless make clear how much of the work and what a deep influence on it must be attributed to Moses as author and legislator. The question of the literary form of the first twelve chapters of Genesis is much more obscure and complicated. These literary forms do not correspond to any of our customary categories and cannot be judged from the point of view of the Greco-Latin or modern literary genres. The historical character of the narrative can be neither denied nor maintained as a whole, without unjustifiably applying to it the standards of a literary form to which it does not belong. If it is said *a priori* simply that the account contains no history in the modern sense of the word, the impression could be easily given that it is not historical in any sense whatever, whereas what it does is convey in simple and picturesque language adapted to the intelligence of a less-developed period the truths which lie at the basis of the economy of salvation, and at the same time offers a popular description of the origin of the human race and of the chosen people.

Pius XII took a stand on this question in two documents: first in the encyclical *Divino afflante Spiritu* of September 30, 1943, which dealt with the literary genres of Scripture, and then in the encyclical *Humani generis* of 1950. To understand these assertions of the Church we must be aware of its fundamental concern for the salvation of man and for truth. The forms in which this expresses itself, however, are capable of change.

‹ 6

The Idea of Creation

The belief that God created the world illuminates our understanding of God and of man: it is of fundamental importance because of the light it throws on the relationship of God to the world and of God to man. Only through a true doctrine of creation can we understand grace, the supernatural, the promise of the ultimate consummation of things. The doctrine of creation requires to be analyzed with an eye to a diversity of contemporary issues. Science, as well as philosophy and history, is posing questions which have never been asked before, questions concerning the relation of a world-view to faith; matter; the relation of man to matter; the evolution of the world, especially of man; the age of the universe and man; the meaning of secular culture and of political and social struggle. Theology, too, is questioning science as never before: that a constructive relationship exists between science and theology is implicit in the belief that God created the world. Theology of course cannot and must not claim to have answers to all the questions which perplex or interest modern man—should theology make such a claim, it would have abandoned its own task and passed the bounds of the field assigned to it.

Belief in God's creation of the world implies a certain concept of God as well as a particular idea of the world and man.

THE IDEA OF A CREATOR GOD

The doctrine of creation presupposes a God separate from the world, transcendent, free, unique, omnipotent, other. To say that the world is created means that all non-divine reality comes into being without any non-divine preconditions: God is the author of everything other than himself. Non-divine being is characterized by an ontological difference from the divine in that a finite entity only has being and participates in being; it is not itself being. The being of an entity is distinct from the entity itself. Only in subsistent being does being attain complete identity with itself. Non-being is excluded absolutely from subsistent being. Nevertheless a particular entity has being insofar as it participates in subsistent being: its being is conferred on it by subsistent being. On the one hand, the being of an entity denotes the existence of God and points the way to him; on the other hand, it is the gift of God to the entity.[1]

God is not moved to create the world by anything outside himself. His activity has its basis exclusively in himself. God's existence is necessary—that is, it is impossible for him not to exist; he exists by reason of the fact that he is God. He is absolute being, being itself. His God-being is his existence; his existence is his God-being. Because, as we explained earlier on, his being is spirit, he is by the necessity of existence at the same time free: in him freedom and necessity coincide. God's freedom does not involve his existence, as if he could abolish that existence. It refers to his inner self-affirmation and to his decisions with regard to that which is not identical with himself, whether he wants to produce anything at all that is different from himself and what he wants to do with it. Why God should have decided to produce something distinct from himself is a profound mystery. He is perfect in himself and has no need which calls for satisfaction by means of creative activity. God lives his own divine life in a tri-personal intercommunication and needs no complement, supplement or fulfillment from a reality distinct from himself. He is infinite. Is it possible for something finite to exist alongside the infinite? Can the finite coexist with the infinite, or will it not of necessity be absorbed by the dynamism of the infinite? Must we not say that either *only* the infinite or *only* the finite exists—even if the finite is capable of being increased indefinitely? If God is infinite and if his creation is finite reality, then an insoluble problem lies at the root of created existence and of the Christian doctrine of creation.

The life of God is dialogical. It takes place in an exchange of love between the three persons of the Trinity. Later on we shall see that God, whom·St. John calls love (1 Jn. 4:8), penetrates his own reality in an act, of loving self-perception, and in an act of loving self-understanding fashions an eternal Son as the adequate image of himself. The Father and the Son affirm each other in mutual love, and each in affirming the other affirms himself. The reciprocal self-affirmation of the Father and Son which we call the Holy Spirit is like the Yes of God to himself and to his own life-as-dialogue. This divine interchange of life is neither capable of nor in need of enrichment or completion.

When God conceives of life other than his own and establishes through creation something other than himself, he conceives of and desires it only as a reflection of his own dialogical life. To recall a now familiar idea of Aquinas's, we can say: God the Father, as the originless, yet origin-giving, turning-of-God-to-himself, in this fruitful act of reflection on himself by which he produces his Son, informs him of his eternal plan and purpose for the world, freely decided upon. This plan and purpose is received and accepted by the ·Son. In the mutual Yes of the Father and the Son—that is, in the divine "We" which is the Holy Spirit—this plan and purpose is affirmed. Thus God's plan and purpose for the world has an inner trinitarian structure. God's creative planning and acting presuppose his trinitarian life. This does not mean that the Father, Son, and Holy Spirit act as a team in planning and producing the world. The early Church, reproached on the one hand for polytheism and on the other for godlessness, emphasized (Augustine stressed and elaborated this) that the trinitarian God in producing the world acts as a single principle of activity. This thesis may become more intelligible when we discuss the relation of the one divine nature to the three divine persons. It becomes especially clear in that type of theology which considers the nature of God in the first place, and understands the persons to a certain extent as "divisions" within the one divine essence. In this way God is seen as one single principle of activity. The three divine persons act by means of the one divine nature, which is their principle of activity. Even if one sees the unity of God as rooted not so much in his nature as in the first divine person—the Father—as is frequent in the theology of the Greek Church Fathers, the dogma is still intelligible. For in that case it is a single act which the three divine persons perform; but the inner structure of the act is more evident, insofar as the one single act is conveyed from the Father to the Son and from the Father and Son to the Holy Spirit.

This tenet of faith in no way prevents the acceptance of an internal trinitarian structure in the divine act of creation. *Vis-à-vis* the world, God reveals himself in his activity as a single principle. However, viewed as it were from the side of God, this one divine act has a structure which is trinitarian. Here, to be sure, we encounter the indissoluble tension between the unity and the threefold personality of God. We may not explain the oneness of God in creating in such way that the trinitarian aspect is overlooked, for that would be to imply that the trinitarian element could be eliminated from the doctrine of creation, from the root of the whole of Christian thought, without any loss to Christian faith. Such an abstraction would contradict Scripture not on a side-issue, but in regard to something which touches the foundation of the Christian faith. The idea of the oneness of the divine action in creating rightly lights up the doctrine of the one God, the monotheism attested to in Scripture. But this light should not become so dazzling that we lose sight of the dialogical structure of the divine life.

Although God made his decision to create the world freely, we cannot, as we have noted, speak of the decision as arbitrary. The God who is free is not arbitrary: he is bound in a certain sense to his own holy nature. We must ask, then, what motive God could have had for making the decision to create the world. This question can be answered only from the total picture which Scripture gives us of God; yet even in the light of this total picture, we can attempt only a tentative answer, for at the root of the world lies the mystery of the divine free will, the inner mystery of God himself, which is impenetrable to our eyes. If we nevertheless wish to attempt an answer, we may begin with the fact that in the New Testament God is called love. (Incidentally, it is not in accordance with Scripture but simply conjures up the ghosts of ancient Greece if we reverse the sentence and say: Love is God. Such a statement confers divinity on a powerful human experience and is mythical in character.)

An explication of this short sentence appears to lie in the biblical witness to the concern and compassion of God with regard to his creation. It corresponds to this total picture if we speak of love as the motive for the divine decision to create the world. This makes more sense still if we understand creation as the preface to the history of man's salvation. Here the question arises as to the kind of love to which God's decision to create the world can be ascribed. In the main we can distinguish between two types of love, Eros and Agape. "Eros" is the love which reaches out to the beloved thou in order to take him into the life of the lover for his (the lover's) own enrichment. "Agape" is the love which reaches out to the beloved thou in order to fill him with its own life. The first form of love is, so to speak, a child of our poverty; the second, a child of our wealth.

With regard to God we can speak in the strict sense only of this second form of love, Agape. Scripture does in fact indicate that love was the original motive for God's decision to create the world. The Book of Wisdom (11:24f., *J*) says: "Yes, you love all that exists, you hold nothing of what you have made in abhorrence, for had you hated anything, you would not have formed it. And how, had you not willed it, could a thing persist, how be conserved if not called forth by you?" Proverbs confirms (16:4): "The Lord has made everything for its purpose, even the wicked for the day of trouble" (cf. also Rom. 11:35f.; Rev. 1:8). At the first Vatican Council the Church professed her belief in the complete freedom of God's action in creating the world, and goodness as the inmost divine motive for creation.

The idea of love as the motive for the divine act of creation requires further analysis. Included in it is the idea that the lover has the power to reach out towards the thou; in other words, his capacity for dialogue. It implies further an awareness of himself, in virtue of which the lover is convinced that he can give himself to the beloved thou without encroaching on the latter's freedom, and that the beloved thou is able to receive and capable of understanding the gift of love. Here it becomes evident that the creative act of God is difficult or impossible to explain without the knowledge of his inner tri-personal life which we have through faith—that is, apart from the revelation concerning the interior divine dialogue. The dialogical life of God is lived in trinitarian form with infinite intensity. Now God's action in creating the world means his uttering himself, pouring himself into the non-divine. With this creative action he brings into being a new dialogical situation, because it is achieved by the power of the love expressed in the dialogue of his inner divine life; yet, in the dialogue with the non-divine, which is finite, he can express himself only in a finite way, in a way not adequate to himself. Only in the inner life of his Godhead, in his divine Word—the "Son"—can the Father express himself adequately and exhaustively. The uttering of himself, pouring out of himself, in non-divine reality, as the expression of himself, can only be an imperfect image, a reflection of the one adequate divine self-expression of the Father in the Son. Through and in Jesus of Nazareth God creates the perfect dialogical situation, which is at the same time the one he planned in the beginning. For Jesus, the Son, belongs to that relationship—that is, that dialogue—in which the eternal word lives with the Father. Hence Jesus on his side, from below as it were, is capable of dialogue with God in a twofold sense: he is addressed by God and he responds unconditionally. Since he is the representative of all men, all are drawn through him into dialogue with God, insofar as they receive through him God's saving word and in faith through him respond to it. (How the world of matter by its relationship to man belongs to the dialogue will be dealt with later.)

At the same time, through dialogue with God, men obtain the capacity for loving conversation with one another: in Scripture, Jesus is called the brother of all, around whom the rest gather as a family whose father is God (Heb. 2:11f.). Here we come to the inmost mystery of the love which must be considered as the motive for God's decision to create the world. In spite of his absolute perfection which, viewed metaphysically, is incapable of any enrichment or development, without past or future, it is obviously in keeping with God's nature that he can and wants to receive an affirmation of himself from the non-divine realm and not only from the "Yes" which he speaks to himself (through the Holy Spirit). In his self-giving love God desires to grant to the non-divine a share in the fulfilling dialogue of his own inner divine life.

There is a twofold aspect to everything creaturely. First, God affirms himself in an analogous manner in and through the finite. Secondly, this self-affirmation which fulfills itself in the finite is taken up into the inner divine self-affirmation which is the Holy Spirit and into the self-understanding of God which is the Son. This has incalculable significance for the proper self-fulfillment of the creature. We shall return to the subject presently.

We should not be doing full justice to the doctrine of the total freedom of God's decision to create the world if we viewed God in the Platonic or neo-Platonic sense as the *summum bonum,* the nature of which is to pour itself out. The concept of God as *bonum diffusivum sui* came into Franciscan thought in medieval theology by way of the theology of Marius Victorinus (c. 280–363). Though the phrase is susceptible of a pantheistic interpretation, he did not understand it in that sense. Later it was employed only in philosophical probings into the revealed truth that love is the motive for the creation of the world. The phrase *bonum diffusivum sui* was an attempt to express in neo-Platonic terms what Scripture says of God's freedom. Its chief inadequacy lies in the fact that it fails to convey the personal character of God: it can lead to the misunderstanding of God as not a "Thou" but an "It" reality. Hence its usefulness in theology depends upon its being rightly situated in the I-Thou metaphysics of Scripture.

Our reflections thus far have made it evident that God necessarily orders to himself the reality which he produces; he cannot create without relating the creature to himself. In this sense one must say that creation serves the glory of God; this is its primary purpose. Everything he creates is an inadequate reflection of what he himself is and therefore refers to him. This reference must be understood not only in an objective sense—as the will of God—but also in a subjective sense—as a task of the creature inherent in its character as creature. The creature's relation to God is willed by God himself, and creation cannot be itself without this relationship to God. In its very turning to itself, the creature essentially turns to God, even when it is unaware of it; for then its turning to God is unconscious or subconscious. But it is only when creatures consciously assimilate into their self-development the immanent meaning of their existence—namely, the turning to God—that they conform to the full sense of creation. Creation would not be intelligible if there were not present in it that possibility of the conscious, subjective relationship of the creature to God. Hence the concept of a purely material creation devoid of the spiritual principle would not do justice to the meaning of creation. Such a thesis in no way impugns God's freedom in creating: the idea that God is free implies that what he does is meaningful. The purpose of creation as it is often presented in Scripture, especially in the psalms and the prophets, is that the whole world shall be called to the praise of God, that the whole world be proclaimed as praise of God.

In this context the eschatological character of divine action becomes clearer. When God freely and lovingly pours himself into the non-divine, the reality which he produces has a beginning and a course to run; it does not reach its apex immediately. In the person of Jesus, in whom God's self-donation sums itself up and reaches its culmination, the divine intention has reached its goal. Strictly speaking, this may be said only of the risen Christ: all other creatures reach their goal by coming to share in the resurrection of Jesus. This participation has various stages; it begins with faith in Christ and terminates with the bodily glorification of each individual and of the entire physical cosmos. The creative activity of God has opened the way to an absolute future. It is the beginning of a road which leads through uncounted millions of years.

We see here again that theological statements are concerned primarily not with the nature of the world but with the course of the world from its beginning to its absolute future, to its final consummation. In theology, knowledge of the nature of things is requisite only insofar as it is important for our understanding of the course and purpose of the world.

When God through creation opened the way to an absolute

future, he assumed a great risk. The way into the future is not one along which men are to be drawn by force; it is to be travelled willingly. But this very freedom embraces the possibility that men will reject the way into that absolute future. It must be travelled in constant dialogue with God; and the form that this takes is the dialogue of men with one another. Dialogue with God is the meaning of the divine creative action. The person and event of Christ are a measure of the importance this dialogue has for God. We shall discuss more thoroughly elsewhere the greatness and the risk of the freedom inherent in it. A grasp of the basic Christocentric structure of the world will assist us in realizing, at the end of the treatment of Christology, that it is not in accordance with the biblical image of God if God and the world, the absolute and the relative, absolute being and the saving historical action of God, are viewed too much in distinction from each other.

THE REALITY OF THE CREATED WORLD

We turn now to another implication of the concept of creation, namely, the concept of man which it contains, and the idea implied in this about the reality which we experience. First of all, though the statement may seem odd, we must stress the reality-character of the world. The world has being in that it shares in the being of God. It cannot be confused with God. God is other than the world, yet the world stands in close connection with him. In creatures, belonging to God is indissolubly combined with separate, individual existence, dependence with independence. If we saw only the relation to God, we would undermine the reality of the creature: if we saw only the separate existence, the independence, we would lose sight of the creaturehood of things; we would be conceding divinity to creatures. Independence—that is, the individual being which is immanent in the creature itself—is an essential element of its creaturely character. When theology analyzes what is meant by being a creature, it must emphasize not only dependence on God but also independence of him, not as characteristics standing, so to speak, beside each other but as attributes of the creaturely being which intermesh and mutually penetrate and support one another. The creature is dependent in his independence and independent in his dependence. The creative activity of God means that God releases the creature into its own separate reality, into its independence, into its individual being, into freedom, and thereby relates it at the same time to himself. Because creatures stand in relation to God, theological statements can and must be made about them, statements which describe their connection with God. But because creatures are independent, non-theological statements also can and must be made about them. The analysis of the concept of creation leads to the thesis that non-theological statements *must* be made about creatures.

As the concept of creation evolves, theology itself legitimizes, even requires, non-theological statements concerning creatures. These non-theological statements have many dimensions—philosophy, science, culture in general. The statements which can and must be made on the basis of the theological analysis of creation are a prerequisite for our task of actively coping with and developing creation. As we shall see later, creation is entrusted to man in the form of a world and an environment which he is to shape, so that he himself becomes a created creator. The concept of creation justifies not only theoretical statements about the world but also our own creative treatment of it.

As a result of its relationship to God, the world points to him. This is the occasion for and beginning of the natural knowledge of God attributed to man by the First Vatican Council (DS 3001f.). This council does justice to the concept of creation when it rejects the view that the one true God, Creator and Lord, cannot be known with certainty by the natural light of reason through what is created (DS 3026). Because the creature continues to be dependent on God, one cannot limit or reduce God's creative activity to the construction of the world. The world, precisely because it is a creation, continues to be dependent on God by whom it is constantly preserved in existence; the powers immanent in the world itself are continually and transcendentally encompassed and supported by the universal divine creativity. The world is constantly directed towards God because it can never cease to be a creature; no development could render it independent of God, because independence of God is a contradiction of its inmost being. No evolution could result in the world's having a being, an existence of and and for itself, as does God.

If creatures have their own individual reality, then individual activity belongs intrinsically to them. Being essentially implies being active, in one way for men, in another for matter. For creatures, being active means self-realization. Whereas God's action cannot serve his own improvement, but is rather a pure expression of his perfection, man can achieve his own realization only by means of action, which is the expression of the degree of perfection he has achieved at any given time. In freedom he must reach out towards his true being, which lies in the future. He will attain this definitively only in that ultimate future in which the whole world and individual persons are transformed according to the model of the risen Christ and are admitted by God into eternal conversation with himself and with each other. But this activity also is subject to the law which governs everything that is created—namely, that it is an activity which really belongs to the creature and yet, at the same time, is dependent upon God, is produced by him.

The problem of simultaneous dependence and self-activity becomes acute with regard to the free actions of men. Here the question arises as to how the same action can be produced by God and at the same time by man in unrestricted responsibility. For several centuries theologians have tried to answer this question, albeit in quite different and contradictory ways, no one of which has been fully satisfactory. Above all, the Molinists and the Thomists have tried to solve this stubborn problem. Whatever solution one ventures to propose, we must not undervalue either of the two elements, the universal creative action of God or the individual activity —the freedom—of the creature. It would be mistaken to believe that the stress on the value of men's freedom which is the product of modern human self-understanding should be given greater weight in theology than the universal creativity of God. Scripture testifies both to the freedom of man and to the universal creativity of God, and even if it does not formally emphasize psychological-metaphysical freedom, but stresses rather freedom from the bonds of sin, nevertheless this psychological-metaphysical freedom is implicitly attested in everything that it says in general about freedom. Without psychological freedom, that responsibility concerning which Scripture makes far-reaching and momentous statements would not exist. On the decisions of men hangs the eternal fate not only of individuals but of the whole of creation; hence the attempt must be made to develop a synthesis of human freedom and God's universal creativity in which neither element is scanted. Most probably no solution can be reached by logic alone; insofar as one can be expected, it can be achieved only by the dialectical method. The dialectical thought process might take as its point of departure the revelation of human freedom and proceed to the demonstration of the dependence of the free man on God even in his free decisions; if this course is followed, God's universal creativity will ultimately remain in obscurity. Or God's universal creativity may be taken as the point of departure in a process leading to the demonstration of the individual free activity of the creature; in this case the freedom of man will be left in obscurity. In general one can say that the universal creativity of God, precisely because it is just that, has possibilities beyond our grasp because they are lacking in the realm of created reality. This would at least mean that God can deal with the creature in such a way that he remains entirely dependent on God without any risk to his freedom.

Theologians call the universal creativity of God in the individual activity of the creature the *concursus divinus naturalis,* and the general consensus in theology is that God effects every action of the creature. This thesis is a simple and necessary inference from the created nature of the world.

Bound up with the creature's independent being and action is its independent value. Every creature has an indissoluble and indestructible value of its own, simply because it exists, and this individual value is continually created by God. This does not mean that the creature can free himself from God or that he can exist and develop his own potentialities out of the resources of his own life. No creature, but only God, can exist completely of himself. Even in being-good the creature is in complete dependence on God, whose goodness his perfections image. Being-good gives man the possibility, as wonderful as it is perilous, of attempting to draw wholly on his own resources for the conduct of his life—that is to say, the ability to sin. In this sinful opposition to God he acts not only contrary to the will of God but contrary to his own nature: when he makes his being-good the occasion for enjoying himself and the world completely without reference to God, the real meaning of being-good is misapprehended and destroyed. In this being-good we see clearly once again the eschatological character of every creature and of the world as a whole. For the being-good of the creature within history is merely an incipient being-good: it has within itself the power and tendency towards perfection, towards that form in which the fullness of being-good is peculiar to him. But this form will be attained only when the creature relates himself definitely and unconditionally, vertically as well as horizontally, to God. That will not be possible until he participates ultimately in the glorified life of the risen Christ.

The universal creativity of God and the receptivity of the creature to it are the starting points for God's saving treatment of man, for his activity in revelation, for his saving efficacy. In fellowship with Christ man can experience God's universal creativity so vividly that, together with the apostle Paul, he is able to say: "It is no longer I who live, but Christ lives in me" (Gal. 2:20). Looking to the final consummation in the future, one is reminded of another passage in the Pauline epistles: ". . . let those who have wives live as though they had none, and those who mourn as though they were not mourning, and those who rejoice as though they were not rejoicing. . . . For the form of this world is passing away" (1 Cor. 7:29ff.).

That the world is derived from the love of God is decisively important for the relationship which earthly things have with one another. If one wants to describe the relation to God as vertical (be it the spatial image of height or depth), then he can picture the relationship which creatures have as horizontal. The things which go to make up the world differ greatly, yet they are closely associated with each other. They form a relational unity and an all-embracing one. Men in particular have such an intimate relationship that one may speak of a human family. The all-embracing unity of creation is and should become a brotherly unity in the human sphere. Men, for their part, stand in a special relation to the material world which is allotted to them as a gift and task of God, which we shall speak of later.

Notes

[1] Cf. Aquinas, *Summa contra Gentiles*, II, 22, II, 23; and F. Lortz.

‹ 7

Divine Providence

By means of a unique kind of causality God's creative love has produced the beginning of both the universe and human history and continues to produce them through constant creative activity. This means that God's creative concern accompanies the universe as it evolves towards the destiny which he has prepared for it. God's concern is directed, moreover, not only to creation as a whole but also to particular creatures, and especially to man: the divine plan of creation is a plan of salvation. God's eternal plan for the universe as a whole and for single individuals in the universe, and its temporal execution, are summed up by theology in the expression "divine providence." Scripture testifies not only to God's love as the underlying motive for his creative plan and activity but also to his continuing concern for the universe from the first moment of its creation to its final consummation. This assertion implies that neither the universe as a whole nor single individuals within the universe have as yet reached their final form. It implies further that God is continually and actively engaged in the universe. God's concern is not merely a loving gaze at things but constant activity on their behalf. The passages in Scripture which bear witness to this are so numerous that it is difficult to choose only a few.

God's active concern embraces not only the historical actions of men but also the events of nature. Everything which happens in

98

these two domains is brought about by God, even the free acts of men. To the thesis of the *concursus divinus* developed in the last chapter, the concept of divine providence adds the idea that the divine activity is ordered to the salvation of men; indeed, to the salvation of the entire universe. Hence nature and history do not run alongside each other as though they were two unrelated realities; rather, they constantly and mutually influence each other. Man is the destiny of nature; and by way of a reciprocal relation, nature in turn becomes the destiny of men. In his providence God acts as the Lord of nature and history, and at the same time as the solicitous Father of men. When the Old Testament recounts again and again the events which God has brought about in history, and is still bringing about in association with men, it does so both to render thanks to God and to evoke gratitude to him in the hearts of men. Thus, the final goal of world events reveals itself as the reign of God—that is, God as absolute love and power holding sway over history. Every individual event has a role to play within this comprehensive divine perspective, including even those events in which evil appears to gain the upper hand, for the apparent triumph of evil can be interpreted only in terms of the ultimate meaning of creation. In oppression and affliction man can learn that the world, to the extent that it is still apart from God, is always liable to ruin and failure.

The testimony of the prophets to the historical action of divine providence is particularly impressive. We may refer especially to Isaiah, Ezekiel and Daniel. At that period of world history in which the Assyrian conqueror demolished the ancient political structures of the Near East in order to build his own empire, Isaiah (or his disciples) was able to perceive in this frightful work of destruction a long-range plan of God; the coming of God's kingdom, a kingdom of peace and righteousness (Is. 2:2ff.), was revealed to him as the meaning of world events. He saw how God guides history towards the destiny he has willed for it; for even as he allows Cyrus to shine like a meteor by conferring on him an unheard-of triumph, he uses him to exhaust the resources of the age (Is. 45:1ff.). In a similar vein we read in Ezekiel (38ff.) that even the history-shaping powers hostile to God can do nothing other than serve his plan. Finally, Daniel praises God as the Lord of history (Dan. 2:20ff.):

Blessed be the name of God for ever and ever, to whom belong wisdom and might. He changes times and seasons; he removes kings and sets up kings; he gives wisdom to the wise and knowledge to those who have understanding; he reveals deep and mysterious things; he knows what is in the darkness, and the light dwells with him.

The goal of the whole of history is Jesus Christ. God reaches this goal in spite of infidelity, disbelief, apostasy, idolatry and the betrayal of the Revealer himself. Thus it is that even when men want to flee from God, they serve him and his designs. Even when men do evil, they bring God's plan of salvation to fulfillment though they neither know it nor will it. The clearest and at the same time the most dreadful example of this situation in the New Testament is Caiaphas. In the role of a prophet—namely, a herald of the divine message of salvation—he proclaims that it is better that one man should die than that the whole nation should perish (Jn. 11:50). Caiaphas is trying to justify the death sentence against Christ on political grounds; but the Holy Spirit, who employs Caiaphas as an instrument, draws an entirely different meaning from his words. Caiaphas is the spokesman for a monstrous crime, but by means of this very crime God achieves man's salvation (Jn. 11:49–52). Thus it is said that what God "wills" will happen (Jud. 9:5) and that what he does not "will" will not succeed (Is. 7:7). Ultimately, no decision from which God is excluded can prevail (Is. 8:10).

It would not do justice to the Old Testament to understand God's providence in a collective sense alone, passing over its meaning for the individual. The individual is not lost in the community as though he were a grain of sand; God is concerned about particular matters and individual men. Moreover, this is something of which the believer can always become aware, for God enters perceptibly into the life of a man, watches over that life and guides it, so that one can trust him and thank him. In the Christian view there is no room for an accident in the strict sense of the term, nor for an autonomous and arbitrary effect worked by a demonic power hostile to God. Such powers, to which even the gods were subject, played an important role in the religions of Israel's pagan neighbors. On the other hand, according to Jeremiah (1:5) the whole of one's life is encompassed by the concern of the Lord. He establishes the number of days and months of a man's life (Job 14:5), determines his very steps. Even the dark and enigmatic events in life come from him (Is. 45:5ff.). But the ways of the Lord are beyond man's understanding (Prov. 20:24).

Statements such as these are intended to represent living experience, not theoretical speculation. In the prayers of the Old Testament and in the psalms (cf. Ps. 23; 37:23f.; 39; 73:23f.; 54) it becomes especially clear that it is a question of the experience of God in the life of the individual. Here one particular factor must be emphasized. In the psalms the solicitude of God for "his own" and for all his creatures is seen not only in the fact that he provides them with the necessities of life but also in that he gives himself to men. A striking instance of this profound religious sentiment is to be found in the utterance of the psalmist: "The Lord is my chosen portion and my cup; thou holdest my lot . . . I keep the Lord always before me; because he is at my right hand, I shall not be moved" (Ps. 16:5,8).

The experience of suffering which befalls the just meant no small problem for the Old Testament faith in providence. As long as suffering could be viewed as a punishment for sin, it was accepted as such, but the more it became clear that the just also were stricken, the more was faith in providence placed in jeopardy. In the face of this difficult situation one tried to console oneself with the thought that there were hidden sins unknown to the evildoer himself, but known of course to God, for which punishment was being meted out. Such a solution could not satisfy for long. The experience of divine providence as love on the one hand and as justice on the other pushed in another direction. Man directed his gaze more and more to the future, first to the future within the world, but gradually to a future transcending the world. A hope in a providence characterized by such transcendence is much in evidence in those books of the Old Testament which originated in the Hellenistic period. We may well surmise that Hellenistic—in particular, Platonic—philosophy has contributed to this. To accept something of the sort would in no way contradict the inspired character of Sacred Scripture, for inspiration guarantees only the truth, not the "revelatory" or miraculous origin, of what is said. Furthermore, the understanding of such influences can be an aid to the interpretation of what is meant by the text of Scripture itself. In the New Testament the transcendent character of the kingdom of God has made a complete breakthrough. Hope now becomes hope in an absolute future. The apostles, of course, with their hope in the restoration of the earthly kingdom of David, still betray some of the Old Testament mentality. Jesus gradually leads them to transform such an expectation into hope in a future beyond history. The principal treatment of this subject in the New Testament is given to us by Matthew (6:25-34, *RSV*):

Therefore I tell you, do not be anxious about your life, what you shall eat or what you shall drink, nor about your body, what you shall put on. Is not life more than food, and the body more than clothing? Look at the birds of the air; they neither sow nor reap nor gather into barns, and yet your heavenly Father feeds them. Are you not of more value than they? And which of you by being anxious can add one cubit to his span of life? And why are you anxious about clothing? Consider the lilies of the field, how they grow; they neither toil nor spin; yet I tell you, even Solomon in all his glory was not arrayed like one of these. But if God so clothes the grass of the field, which today is alive and tomorrow is thrown into the oven, will he not much more clothe you, O men of little faith? Therefore do not be anxious, saying, "What shall we eat?" or "What shall we drink?" or "What shall we wear?" For the Gentiles seek all these things; and your heavenly Father knows that you need them all. But seek first his kingdom and his righteousness, and all these things shall be yours as well. Therefore do not be anxious about tomorrow, for tomorrow will be anxious for itself. Let the day's own trouble be sufficient for the day.

The key idea in these words of Jesus is contained in the proposition: Seek first the kingdom of God and his righteousness, and all the rest will be given to you. The kingdom of God, then, is the ultimate meaning or goal of providence. Jesus begins his preaching with the assurance that the kingdom of heaven is close at hand (Mt. 4:17). The kingdom of God has been established in his own person. From him it extends out over the whole of creation. All men, indeed the entire cosmos, are to be embraced by the reign of God established in the life, death and resurrection of Jesus Christ, until God is all in all, and thus the reign of God will have matured to its final form (1 Cor. 15:28).

God's reign over men is established when men submit to him in love. The obstacle to the kingdom of God is sin, that egoism which expresses itself in refusal to accept the word of God, in the weakness which gives in to persecution, in greed for worldly possessions, and in the selfishness which makes a man indifferent to the needs of his fellow men. The whole course of history is aimed at bringing God's reign to final victory over sin. This victory will make its appearance on the day of judgment. This does not mean, however, that the course of events leading up to that day constitutes a constant, progressive triumph of good over evil. On the contrary, the movement of history rises and falls. In the ultimate future which God's plan of creation envisages God's love, no longer concealed by the earthly veil, will be fully revealed. Looking towards this day, John prays in the name of the whole Church: "Come, Lord Jesus!" (Rev. 22:20, *NEB*).[1]

The providence of God is a divine activity ordered to the end of time, it has an eschatological character. Though it cannot be said that God does not trouble himself about the fate of men in this world, nonetheless the aim of divine providence is directed to the final consummation: everything on earth is preliminary to that consummation. God gives the man who makes every effort within his power to build up the kingdom of God everything he needs. Of course, man does not know what he needs: ultimately God alone knows that. When Scripture speaks of food and drink and clothing we should not think merely in terms of God's assistance for our natural life. The requirements for the final consummation of all things are what is at stake, and man of himself cannot determine precisely what these are: the values of all created things can only be estimated in retrospect, from the end of time. Thus providence may not bring prosperity and security; God may send failure and want. The working out of divine providence may not mean that our efforts will bear fruit or our human relations reach fulfillment. The most beautiful products of man's endeavors may be shattered, and it may seem as if the question Why? or For what purpose? really has no answer. So far as the ultimate answer to our questions is concerned, no judgment is possible, but we do know that what is really in progress is the growth of God's kingdom and the growth of men into that kingdom. Health, riches, success may hinder as well as help our development; what seems like adversity may be a blessing in disguise. To have faith in providence means to have faith in the mystery of God.

Thus providence does not mean for men, either collectively or individually, some kind of lasting temporal security within history; yet in his very insecurity man is protected by the solicitous power of God (Rom. 8:28-39). The ways of providence take their course in obscurity and we cannot test them; they are part of the mystery of salvation. We can only assent to providence in faith; we have no experiential knowledge of it. To be sure, now and then we may be granted a fleeting glimpse into its mystery. We experience its power when we see an unexpected pattern of meaning suddenly emerge from the entanglement of human encounters. Sometimes an unforeseen delay in our own plans in the end serves the purposes of a higher plan in which all our former hopes are fulfilled. Suddenly invisible hands lay themselves upon our hands and fill them with gifts which we could not have expected on the basis of human deliberations. These gifts provide us with new opportunities. Or these mysterious hands snatch away our favorite belongings, the possibilities and opportunities which were our whole life's content. And later we must acknowledge that had we kept these possibilities in our own hands, we would have developed them to our own disadvantage.[2] No passage of Scripture expresses so triumphantly, through a veil of tears, that confidence steadfast against despair and ruin, as the utterance of Job: "Even if he slays me, I will hope in him" (Job 13:15, according to the Vulgate; cf. 2 Cor. 4:16f; Lk. 12:4; Ps. 23:4).

Even though we do not know the ways of divine providence, still we do know that the goal which God has set himself will certainly be achieved. Human history moves towards the final goal determined for it by God in spite of all the attempts on the part of free men to frustrate it. God has determined this in a free decision. In his eternal plan for the universe he is subject to no immutable fate, to no law standing above him.

In the patristic period astrological superstition was sharply contested by Gregory of Nyssa, Diodorus of Tarsus, and Augustine, to mention only a few. The stars do not stand above God; rather God's light outshines them all. This view, of course, is not opposed to the opinion that between the movements of the heavenly bodies and the fate of men a certain loose correspondence prevails which does not abolish the freedom of man. Such a connection is probable in view of the close relation of man to the cosmos. In spite of its immutability, however, the divine plan of the universe is essentially distinct from the ineluctable laws of nature in their chain of cause and effect. It is also quite different from an inevitable fate which in its mysterious working assigns a man a definite role in the fabric of the whole universe and acts as his guardian in this role. One who trusts in providence is aware that he is in the hands of a loving and almighty Father, a Father who guides everyone, even when one's lot is difficult, towards salvation. God—Love—takes the cause of man into his strong and kind hands. There even death becomes the entrance into a great and rich life. Thus the admonition of the Apostle Peter: "Cast all your anxieties on the Lord" (1 Pet. 5:7), is realistic, not fanciful, advice.

Belief in divine providence should not paralyze human energy. Rather it challenges it. Because man knows that God himself is constantly at work in everything which a man produces, he can make every action an encounter with God. In this way the world is liberated from naked objectivity. It acquires a personal character, yet in the process its objective reality is neither endangered nor destroyed. As a result of the freedom granted to man by God himself, faith in divine providence does not deprive man of the capacity for initiative, of a readiness to take risks, of creative work. In fact, all these are set in motion by the divine activity. In this way new forms of political, social and cultural life will be developed from time to time. The Church itself cannot be bound to any one social or economic or political system if the freedom and dignity proper to man are to remain intact. Of course, one must take into account the fact that a social system functions best over a long period of time. Nonetheless, as a result of altered cultural or scientific or technological conditions, social systems become not only obsolete but even harmful. It is extremely difficult to determine precisely when one of these systems or structures must be replaced by a new one. Furthermore, one must face the fact that a social system which has been preserved up to now will not readily be given up by those who represent it, but will be vigorously defended, because it has proven itself for them. A new social system, on the other hand, is still untested and therefore appears to be full of uncertainty and risk. In spite of this difficulty, it must be emphasized that the various forms of human living-together—political, social, cultural—are constantly undergoing change. The further evolution of these forms is essential.

On the question of the relation of providence to human initiative, we quote Romano Guardini:

It becomes alive. But it does not become a magic world in which strange things happen and which ceases to exist the moment we come to grips with stern reality. To believe in Providence it is not necessary to abstract the harshness from the world. The world remains what it is. Providence implies that the world with its natural facts and necessities, is not enclosed in itself but lies in the hands of a Power and serves a Mind greater than itself. The laws of inert matter do not cease to apply once life takes hold of them any more than the laws of physical growth cease to apply when the human heart and mind are busy building up their world. They remain, but they serve a higher purpose. And once you discern this higher purpose you realize the service these forces and laws perform for it. Providence means that everything in the world retains its own nature and reality but serves a supreme purpose which transcends the world: the loving purpose of God.

But this love of God for His creatures whom He has made His children is alive like that of a human being for his dear ones. The love of a father for his child pursues him in all its developments, in all its fortunes, in all its ever-changing activities and decisions. So too the love of God for man is alive and ever new. And the whole world is drawn into the orbit of God's constant care for man. It embraces the whole world, past and present, in every passing moment of its existence and activity.

And so the world is renewed in every moment of time. Every moment has only one existence. It has not existed before and it will not come again. It springs from the eternity of God's love and takes all Being and all that is and all that happens into itself for the sake of God's children. Everything that happens comes to me from God, from His love. It calls me. It challenges me. It is His will that I should live and act and grow in it and become the person it is His will that I should be. And the world is to be perfected into that which it can become only through man—that is, through me.[3]

In this view divine providence is not only God's gift to man, but a task for him.

Prayer of petition deserves special attention in this context. It is in accordance with God's providential design that he grants us many things simply on the basis of our request, not as though we could exercise a determining influence on his decisions, but that by this means we acknowledge his sovereignty and manifest our trust in him. Prayer of petition does not mean that we must tell God what we need, or that we exert pressure on him to do what he would not do otherwise. Rather, in the prayer of petition, man opens himself to God's overflowing graciousness. When we petition God, we signify the way and the manner in which we dispose ourselves to him. In the prayer of petition, the living relation between God and man takes place as a relation of I to Thou. Man is capable of such an opening of himself to God only if he has the guarantee that God is turned towards him, that God does not look past him with indifference. Thus, it is faith in divine providence that makes human prayer of petition possible.

Even though faith in providence was always alive in the Church, at the beginning it was a long way from the formulations it received in later theology. The persuasion of the earliest theologians of the Church that God in one continuous act of creation produces everything, including the free actions of men, made a special treatment of divine providence superfluous. In spite of this, we do possess a series of treatises on providence from the ancient Church: Lactantius (d. after 317), Salvian of Massilia (d. 480), Gregory of Nyssa (d. about 408), Eusebius of Caesarea (d. about 430), Theodoret of Cyrus (d. 458), Chrysostom (d. 407). Augustine in his work on The City of God points out that the afflictions of the Jewish nation and the Roman Empire are subject to providence and serve its aim. In the above-mentioned works, the principal problem discussed is how the evil in the world, not only sin but also suffering, can be brought into agreement with faith in divine providence. Two ideas are stressed, the freedom of man and the eschatological consummation.

The Church has more than once, in opposition to dualist or fatalistic conceptions, expressed her faith in divine providence. She did so at the Synod of Prague in 561 (DS 459), in the confession of faith against the Waldensians (DS 790), against Wyclif (DS 1156, 1176f.) and most clearly at the First Vatican Council. Here it is stated: everything which God created, he protects and guides in his providence, reaching mightily from one end of the earth to the other and ordering all things with gentleness (Wis. 8:1). Indeed, all things lie open and naked before his eyes (Heb. 4:13), even that which happens through the free action of creatures (DS 3003).

We have already seen that the creation of man is the principal event in the creation account. When the creation of matter is mentioned, it is presented as taking place for the sake of man. In the creation account there is no mention of the creation of angels. However, Scripture does describe the influence of angels in salvation history; and these accounts are our only source of knowledge about them. In order to do justice to the importance which the creation of man possesses in Scripture, to the fact that man is the primary concern, in the following reflections man will be discussed first, then matter, and finally the significance of angels in the course of salvation history.

Notes

[1] *NEB:* From the *New English Bible, New Testament.* © The Delegates of the Oxford University Press and the Syndics of Cambridge University Press 1961. Reprinted by permission. Unless otherwise noted, New Testament quotations in the present work are from this translation.

[2] H. E. Hengstenberg, *Die Göttliche Vorsehung,* (Regensburg, 1940).

[3] *The Living God,* trans. Stanley Goodman (New York: Pantheon, 1957).

◄ 8

Man

At this point man will be discussed only insofar as he was created, and so inaugurated history. A complete theological anthropology will not be developed here. This will be presented when we come to consider the Church. Nonetheless, what is said in the following section about man lays the foundation for a theological anthropology. The first statement must be: man is a creature. This implies the tension in every creature between dependence and independence, its dependence on God and its own independent activity and value. As we have said, because of the independent value and activity that belong to man's nature non-theological statements can be made of him, as of every creature. In theological statements on man the point at issue is man's relation to God, and thus his salvation. Man's "nature" is discussed only insofar as the interpretation of his relation to God requires it. Since man stands in a different relation to God from the rest of creation, we must explain man's specific relation to God and account for its foundation.

Man is not created by God in the same sense as matter is created. Matter was created by God out of nothing. God produces it without any non-divine prerequisite. Man, on the other hand, according to the testimony of Scripture, was formed out of already existing matter; to that extent the thesis of creation out of nothing (*creatio ex nihilo*) does not apply in his case.

In virtue of his origin man exists in an indissoluble relationship with the rest of creation. Both the Fourth Lateran Council (1215) and the First Vatican Council have alluded to this fact. At the same time, however, there is between man and the rest of creation a fundamental and irreducible distance. Scripture sees the relationship in the fact that man comes from the earth, is allied to the earth and will return once again into the earth. It sees the distinction in the fact that man is the climax of creation. Scripture expresses this by calling man the image of God and by giving him a special commission from God to be master of the earth. We can clarify man's difference with respect to the rest of creation in the following manner. As we have seen, the innermost being of God is dialogical. The Father in conformity with his being carries on a dialogue with the Son. This dialogue comes to pass in that self-affirmation of God which we call the Holy Spirit. Now by means of an impenetrable and mysterious action which reaches its climax in the incarnation (cf. Phil.2:7, "he emptied himself"), God pours himself into the non-divine, with the result that a finite human reflection of the divine dialogue comes into being. This does not mean simply that there is a correspondence between the divine and the human, or that the structure of human dialogue corresponds to that of the divine dialogue. Rather, God continually and actively relates himself to our finite human world and draws it into his own interior divine dialogue. God is not seeking to enrich his own interior divine dialogue by the inclusion of finite reality. However, he does intend that his dialogue with finite reality shall represent, in an analogous way, the interior divine dialogue. This intention of God requires that finite reality shall be capable of dialogue with God, and with an unlimited intensity. Thus it is that God's pouring out of himself comes to its fullness in the incarnation of the divine Logos. If the interior divine conversation between the Father and the Son takes place in the Holy Spirit, then God's emptying of himself in the incarnation of the eternal Son means that now this conversation is extended, as it were, into our finite world. As a result the Father addresses our finite world through the Son, and our finite world in turn gives itself to the Father through the Son. Thus the man Jesus is the meaning and measure of everything human. To the degree in which a man falls short of Jesus, he falls short of the human. To the degree in which he enters into partnership with Jesus, he becomes the embodiment of the human itself. Man is that creature who in kinship with Jesus is sought by God as a conversation partner, and who has become and becomes capable of dialogue with God. The rest of creation enters into dialogue with God through man. Scripture repeatedly demonstrates its great desire to present the nobility of man, God's concern for man, the duty of man to devote himself to God, man's failure, and the never-failing mercy of God in which he continually calls man back to himself—God—and thus to man's own human being.

This is the purpose behind Scripture's description of the special way in which man comes from the hand of God. Scripture sees in this the proof of man's nobility and of God's everlasting concern for him. As we saw in the discussion of creation in general, the first book of Scripture, Genesis, presents two accounts of the origin of all reality from God, the Yahwistic and the Priestly. Both these accounts, though from different points of view, testify to the origin of man from God. Both accounts are interested in bringing out the distinct position of man in the whole of creation. The Priestly account, however, presents its testimony from a different point of view from that of the Yahwist. For this reason it is appropriate to discuss the two accounts separately.

The text of the Priestly Code reads (Gen. 1:26-27):

Then God said, "Let us make men in our image, after our likeness; they shall have dominion over the fish of the sea, and over the birds of the air, and over the cattle, and over all the earth, and over every creeping thing that creeps upon the earth." So God created man in his own image, in the image of God he created him; male and female he created them.[1]

First, it must be pointed out that this text is not the deposition of a primitive divine revelation. Rather, it is the result of a reflection made within faith. The experience which the people of Israel had with God and with themselves, in particular the experience both of God's loving concern and of his chastising justice, led the re-

flective believer to the insight that man is not God, and also that
he has never lived beyond the pale of God's concern. This means
that on the one hand man need never live outside the sphere of
God's loving gaze; on the other, he is incapable of fleeing from
God. The conclusion is that dialogue with God, whether a man
draws benefits or disaster from it, is an essential human characteristic. It is this experience of God's majesty and of his constant
activity that leads to the realization that man is created by God,
but that he is at the same time different from the rest of reality.
Looking back from the period of the covenant to the history that
preceded it, a dark and distant past illuminated by no documents,
it became clear to the sacred writer that from the beginning God
planned the salvation of man and that every calamity must have a
cause other than God. With his testimony to man's origin from
God, the author wished to depict the inauguration of that journey
at whose provisional term he himself stood, but which according
to God's promise would lead to a blessed future. The details of his
account were not meant simply to propose a theory concerning
man's origin or to display his own knowledge, but to summon his
contemporaries to remain faithful to the God who from the beginning had planned a partnership with the people of Israel. This partnership demands the gratitude of its human partner all the more
because in the beginning God was not allied exclusively to the
people of Israel. Rather, he is the sole and universal God of all
mankind. Nonetheless, he has guided the history of men to that
stage at which the people of Israel have become "his" people in
a unique way. If the creation of man is the inauguration of the
journey into the future, it would be a one-sided, indeed a false,
understanding of that creation to focus one's attention upon the
act of creation itself and not look beyond it into the future. The
creation of man, like that of the whole universe, is eschatologically
oriented. If we do not have an eye for the future, the account of
man's creation remains blind. The journey has been begun only
for the sake of the goal. The goal was not an accidental addition
but the very first thing willed. Mankind was created for the sake
of its future.

Whenever we set about interpreting the text quoted we are im-

mediately confronted by the Hebrew word "Adam." We usually
understand it as the proper name of the first man. But its primary
meaning is collective. The text means to say: as God created
plants and animals, so he also created man, or men. We learn in
a later chapter that in the view of Scripture the totality of mankind stems from a man named Adam. One may also say that the
sacred writer saw in Adam an individual who represents the totality of mankind.

The Priestly account reaches its climax in the assertion that man
is the image of God. It would appear that with this expression the
writer wanted on the one hand to deny that man himself is God—
something frequently claimed in the heathen milieu—but on the
other hand to emphasize that man is closely connected with God;
indeed, that God is really present in him. The one expression thus
testifies to both the immanence and the transcendence of God.
The plural in which God speaks of himself is striking. It may
simply be a grammatical formula, and in that case it would signify
nothing further. But it may also mean that God, in using "we,"
unites himself with the heavenly world, perhaps with the angels.
Should this interpretation prove correct, then man's status as the
image of God would be somewhat weakened, for the text would
now mean that man is similar to heavenly beings. The sacred writer
certainly seems to want to award man an extraordinary dignity; but
at the same time he appears to be concerned lest man should
understand himself to be God. In view of the deification of rulers
in the ancient orient such a concern is understandable, and the addition of the word "like" to the expression "image" appears to fit
in with it. In what does man's being the image of God consist?
To this question Genesis gives a clear answer: being the image of
God is to be understood functionally, not ontologically. Genesis
sees the image of God not in the being of man but in a definite
activity of man. It understands it as belonging to the order of action.
Man's being the image of God consists in ruling over the earth.
Man is appointed to rule. He is to reign over the beasts in the sea,
in the air and on the earth, and thus subject the earth to himself.
He is called to participate in the dominion of God himself. He is
crowned with majesty and honor (Ps. 8:5). We will see later that

this interpretation presented by Genesis of man as the image of God does not exhaust the human image of God. In the New Testament Jesus is called the image of God, and the rest of men are meant to participate in the image of God in Jesus Christ. There the functional nature of the image is supplemented by the ontological. Man and woman share in the divine majesty in the same way. Man was created by God in a double imprint, male and female. In this allusion of the text one can discern a protest against the oppression of women in those times. The sexual differentiation of man and his appointment to rule over the earth are closely related. Man is to increase on the earth. For this the domination of the earth is prerequisite. The earth is to support man. It is with this end in view that man as the master of the earth must cultivate it and care for it.

The designation of man as the master of the earth is a matter of great significance. It is aimed first at man's active mastery of the earth. Such activity, however, presupposes knowledge. Even though this is not in the text itself, it is in line with its general meaning. The text itself sets no limit to man's activity and his quest for knowledge, but one criterion is given: man's activity must further human life. It should not be overlooked that man belongs to God and has from him a commission to be master of the earth. Thus when man controls the earth he is fulfilling a divine command. On the other hand, man disobeys God when he allows himself to be mastered by the earth, by its grandeur and its wealth; and when, instead of being master of the earth, he sinks to being its slave. If we seek an expression for the relationship of man to the earth mentioned in Genesis, the term *homo faber* suggests itself. This must be complemented immediately by the expression *homo amans.* The two formulas combine in the expression *homo orans.* Man is supposed to form and shape the earth entrusted to him by God. He should assume a creative function. In doing this, however, he is not an absolute creator. He is a created creator, and his task is form-giving activity. In this activity he forms himself at the same time. Thus, while man directs the earth towards its perfect form, he serves his own self-formation. Man is a self-transcending being who goes out of himself—transcends himself—to the world, and in so doing he goes out of himself towards God. On the other hand, man cannot go beyond himself towards God without also going beyond himself towards the world. Were he to try to go out of himself towards God without also going out to the world, then his going beyond himself towards God would immediately imply disobedience to God. Conversely, were he to go out to the world without continuing on his way to God, he would be acting as though he were God, and not a creature commissioned by God. Thus the relationship mentioned above between the self-becoming of man and the becoming of the world appears in a clear light. Man does not exist in the world simply as a subject complete in himself, in opposition to an object to be known and shaped. Rather, even he achieves his true form, the unfolding of his being, only in and through the formation of the earth. In this sense man can be called the created creator of himself and the earth.

It is astonishing that man was spoken of in such sublime terms at a time when the Israelite people lived under severe oppression— namely, during the Babylonian captivity. Thus the text may also have been a comfort for the oppressed people. For it gives expression to the fact that an indestructible nobility has been conferred on man by God, a nobility which is not added on from the outside, but which resides in the very being of man, and which therefore cannot be lost through any external oppression.

The Yahwistic, the older text, reads as follows (Gen. 2:4b–7):

In the day that the Lord God made the earth and the heavens, when no plant of the field was yet in the earth and no herb of the field had yet sprung up—for the Lord God had not caused it to rain upon the earth, and there was no man to till the ground; but a mist went up from the earth and watered the whole face of the ground—then the Lord God formed man of the dust from the ground, and breathed into his nostrils the breath of life; and man became a living being.

According to this text the association of man with the earth is even more intimate than in the Priestly text. There were on the earth still no plants, because man did not yet exist to cultivate them. Men, then, are created in order to cultivate the earth. In the first (and later) text man is the goal of creation. In the second (and older) text, on the other hand, the cultivation of the earth is the goal. Man has of course a significance that goes far beyond that, for in being designated for the cultivation of the earth he is at the same time installed as the master of the earth. According to the Yahwist:

The world is not viewed as a cosmic system with the earth as the lower dwelling place of man and beasts, and heaven as the upper dwelling place of the celestial beings and God himself; with the heavenly bodies and the firmament, and the division of land and sea, as in Genesis 1. On the contrary, here the world is the immediate dwelling place of man. It is man's world in so far as it concretely determines the life of man as a being dwelling in and working on it . . . Only through man does the world become complete, without him it is only a landscape.[2]

Thus the Yahwist's account of the creation of the earth manifests an anthropological orientation. His presentation is directed towards man. Without man the earth is an unformed and barren steppe.

The picture of the formation of man out of the dust of the earth has a double significance. It indicates the stuff of which man is composed and proclaims at the same time his perishable character. A question may arise about the nature of the earth out of which God formed man. But the text says nothing about this. One need not, therefore, on the basis of this text, protest against the claim of natural science that man, insofar as his body is concerned, arose from organic nature or the animal kingdom. Though Scripture offers no support for this thesis, it raises no objection against it. What is of primary concern in this picture is the attestation of man's frailty. In Scripture dust is the symbol of perishableness (Ps. 22:15). Man is born from the dust (Wis. 9:15; 7:1). He should never forget his origin. His portion is weakness and death. Occasionally dust appears simply as an element of the underworld and as an expression of man's distance from God (Ps. 22:30). Man is so frail that he must pass away if God withdraws his breath (Job 34:14f.; 4:18–21). The projects of man vanish if God turns his face away from him (Prov. 19:3; Ps. 104:29; 146:4). As man comes from the earth, so he returns to it (Gen. 3:19). Man is appointed to cultivate and to care for the earth, and it will receive him once again into its womb. Man experiences the grandeur of God all the more intensely in view of his frailty (Job 4:19). The creature formed out of the earth becomes man through God's "breathing" into its nostrils the breath of life. God is the source of life (Ps. 104:29; Job 34:14; Eccles. 12:7). When God withdraws his breath, living beings fade away. Through this breathing into him of this breath of life, man is brought into proximity with God. The beasts also have life in them, but only into man has God breathed life. Perhaps one can say: If the Priestly author expresses the nearness of man to God through the concept of the image of God, the Yahwist expresses the same idea through God's breathing life into man. The content expressed is similar, the way of expressing it is different.[3]

It would be going beyond the text to see in the breathing of the breath of life into man the creation of the spiritual soul of man. The author of the Yahwistic text writes even more anthropologically than the author of the Priestly text. Nonetheless, one should not think that the Yahwist possesses a naive and childlike image of God. He conceives of God as noble and mighty. In the narrative of the Yahwist, God is depicted as the Lord to whom man owes unconditional obedience and who commands the fate of man and the world. However, for the Yahwist the main thing is to illustrate God's nearness to man. God is not like the great ruler of an oriental kingdom who dwells in inaccessibility. He is different from the gods of the heathens. He is graciously present. He is sympathetic towards men. The danger of humanizing God is clearly of lesser concern to the Yahwist than the danger of making God's friendship for man the occasion of liturgical solemnity.

The creation of woman is described in a special section. The text reads as follows (Gen. 2:18–25):

Then the Lord God said, "It is not good that the man should be alone; I will make him a helper fit for him." So out of the ground the Lord formed every beast of the field and every bird of the air, and brought them to the man to see what he would call them; and whatever the man called every living creature, that was its name. The man gave names to all the cattle, and to the birds of the air, and to every beast of the field; but for the man there was not found a helper fit for him.

So the Lord God caused a deep sleep to fall upon the man, and while he slept took one of his ribs and closed up its place with flesh; and the rib which the Lord God had taken from the man he made into a woman and brought her to the man. Then the man said, "This at last is bone of my bones and flesh of my flesh; she shall be called Woman, because she was taken out of Man." Therefore a man leaves his father and his mother and cleaves to his wife, and they become one flesh. And the man and his wife were both naked, and were not ashamed.

God wants to free man from his loneliness. Although according to the Priestly text God passes the judgment on the whole of creation that it is good, the Yahwist declares that Adam's loneliness is a state of real unhappiness. It is something from which Adam should be freed. The woman is to be his liberator. Apparently the tie with God alone does not suffice to free Adam from the natural feeling of loneliness. God himself confirms this. So he sets to work to remedy it. According to the scriptural presentation, God, in creating the beasts, is trying to provide man with necessary assistance. He makes, as it were, several attempts to remedy the loneliness of Adam. In each instance he brings what he has created to Adam, and Adam is supposed to decide whether it is that companion for whom he longs and who can release him from his loneliness. In each instance Adam manifests his decision by giving the beasts their names. The name is an expression of the creature's nature. If the creature is to be Adam's helper and companion, this must express itself in the kinship of its name. Adam gives to every creature brought to him the name proper to its nature. Yet the name which God wants to hear, the one which in Adam's judgment will express the fact that he finds in the creature brought to him a kindred being, does not come from the lips of the man. Does it not look like a failure on God's part when he must make several apparently unsuccessful attempts before he succeeds in the creation of the woman? Not at all. The origin of the animals from God is to be recounted. The creation of the animals is also intended by God. Therefore it is not an unsuccessful enterprise. However, it is recounted against the background of the story of man's creation. In the scene depicted by the inspired writer God condescends to the man. He submits his work to the judgment of the man in order to lead him to the insight that the companion he desires cannot stem from the animal kingdom. Rather, only a creature equal to man in dignity can be his companion and helper. The narrative of the creation of the beasts, then, serves as a framework for what is really the main point—namely, that woman does not stand beneath man but beside him.

Whatever the account of the creation of woman from the rib of man means we can say, in view of the mentality characteristic of the oriental, that to define the physical or biological origin of woman is not part of the narrator's intention. The text makes no pretense of presenting the event in detail: it has not the intention of teaching the way in which woman was created. It has, however, the intention of saying what she was created *as*. She is depicted as the being who complements man and seeks together with him an original unity. Why the rib is mentioned as material, or what idea the sacred writer associates with the rib, cannot be adequately explained to this day. The narrative has no counterpart within Scripture or outside it. Nonetheless, what the author wanted to say is certain: he wished to affirm the basic equality of man and woman and also to account for the drive of the sexes towards one another. According to his account, one of the fundamental institutions of human existence, the love between man and woman which achieves its fulfillment in marriage, is grounded in the origin of man. The notion of the original bisexuality of men frequently found in antiquity is not supported by the hagiographer. One may also see in the account of the creation of woman a protest on the part of the author against a view, current in his milieu, in which woman was considered an object of man and treated accordingly. Our text declares that a woman is a complete human being, equal in dignity to man, endowed with freedom, the power of decision and responsibility. She is not an object but a subject. When the biblical text says that the man and his wife were not ashamed although they were naked, this is a way of expressing the fact that the man and his wife were aware that they were joined to one another in a very special manner in complete trust, without mutual reserve and disdain. Furthermore, in the consciousness of this relationship they were able with remarkable freedom to give themselves to one another in the full possession of their own identities. In the New Testament Christ complements the account of Genesis by proclaiming a meaningful life of virginity.

Notes

[1] Text after Wolfgang Trilling, *Im Anfang Schuf Gott* (Leipzig: St. Benno Verlag, 1964; Freiburg: Herder, 1965), p. 62.
[2] Wolfgang Trilling, *Denn Staub Bist Du* (Freiburg, 1965), p. 22.
[3] *Ibid.*, p. 26.

‹9

Matter and Life: Evolution

From the point of view of Christian theology matter cannot, as in many dualistic philosophies and religions, be slighted out of a respect for spirit or be understood simply as an evil principle. For matter owes its existence to God, and over the whole of material creation stands God's judgment that it is good. Matter does not have its meaning in itself, but in man. It is an expression of God's concern for man. Matter represents living space for man. It also contributes to the formation of man's body. Through his body man is united to the earth and to matter; so much so, that according to Scripture man has come from the earth and will return to it again. As a result of its function as an expression of God's concern, matter cannot be understood simply in its naked materiality. Rather, the property of sign and symbol inherent in it must be recognized. For man matter is a sign pointing to God. For God it is an expression of concern for man. In the Logos matter's natural symbolic and significative power was raised to a new level. For the incarnate Logos and all his actions are signs of the presence of God in this world. In the resurrection of the dead matter comes to share in the glorification of the elect, and in this glorified state it acquires an eternal existence. Even if, as many Christians believe, matter had a beginning, it will have no end. Furthermore, matter will not simply go on existing forever in its present state, but in a transformed state, which for us is full of mystery, and which we cannot describe with the means now at our disposal.

In the life of the Church matter plays a special role insofar as it becomes under specific forms the bearer of divine salvation and grace.

According to the theory of evolution commonly held today, matter has evolved from very simple structures to ones of ever greater complexity. Growth is essential to it. The origin of life represents a special threshold in the process of the evolution of matter. Whether life is simply the way a particular structure of matter expresses itself is a scientific, not a theological question. Whereas previously, with an apologetic object in view, the intervention of God was considered necessary in order to explain the origin of life, it can be said today that theologians employ such an intervention of God only for the origin of the human soul—and even here only in a limited sense—but not for the origin of life. A more accurate account of evolution from the original state of matter to the abundance of forms today over the millions of years of the history of the cosmos is the task of natural science, not theology. Theology has only to establish that there is no contradiction between evolution and creation. Creation is the prerequisite of evolution. It cannot be replaced by evolution. Even the evolution of the original elements created by God does not eliminate God. For God remains continually immanent in his creation as the power active in everything. However, God does not thereby exclude secondary causes, the energies inserted in creation by him. Rather they are actualized by him in his universal operation.

On the basis of the biblical account of the origin of man, the Catholic Church and its theology long rejected the theory of evolution which holds that man developed from the animal kingdom. The question is, Does the biblical text exclude the idea of evolution in every form? In any case it excludes that radical, atheistic form of the theory which sees man as nothing more than the natural child of mother earth, her fertility and her creative power. Marxist scholars today support an extreme atheistic theory of evolution which is the foundation and real essence of dialectical materialism.

Labor plays a special role; it is considered the propelling force behind man. Labor has made man what he is. We can illustrate this by using the example of a hand: while it is the means of labor, it is also its product. Along with these propositions there is the conviction that modern man can be transformed into a new being by certain psychological and mechanical stratagems and that economically he can be managed like a pawn.

However, we may say with Ernest Benz:

Above all, these changes [in the sciences of anthropology and cosmology] have occurred since the evolution theory has come to prevail in the natural sciences.

In contrast to the theological concept that man as a fully developed being was placed into a fully developed world like a tenant who moved, with a duly signed lease, into a new completed, prefabricated apartment, anthropology and cosmology have come to the conclusion that not only is man himself, as a species, part of an immeasurably long chain in life's development, but also that contemporary man is still going through a constant development in consciousness. Furthermore, man is not only transforming his environment; he also exercises a direct influence on his own continuing evolution. It is this image of a changing man in a changing world, a world transformed by man, that can no longer be ignored by theology.

During a period when existentialist philosophers and theologians were increasingly writing off history in favor of a dialectics of the moment, anthropology has been opening new dimensions of history: It has explored thousands and hundreds of thousands of years of early history and prehistory; it has thrown light upon the development of man from prehuman and near-human animal to his appearance as *homo sapiens.*

During a period when theologians, concerned with the problem of existential decision in the present, had forgotten to inquire into the meaning of the future, the natural sciences, on their own behalf, have asked the question of man's future with an intensity that is astounding —because, indeed, our present knowledge of man's past development forces the question of man's future right into the foreground.

Hope was the original impulse of theology. But it abandoned it to secular movements like Marxism and communism. Instead, it became absorbed in contemplating the relationship between existence and death and became fascinated by the problems of evil and original sin. Anthropology, a natural science, is now restoring hope to its rightful place.[1]

In the opinion of most Catholic theologians of today a moderate doctrine of evolution is consistent with the scriptural account of the creation of man. The moderate doctrine of evolution can be distinguished from the radical one in three ways. It traces the process of evolution, with man as its climax, to the creative will of God. It contends that although the human body and psyche arise out of the continuous process of evolution, the human spirit does not; that the human spirit, resulting from a special divine creative will at a certain stage of development in organic life, originated as a new principle of being and activity which cannot be adequately derived from the previous level of development. According to this view, the scriptural account of the creation of man testifies to an actual event, the appearance of man on earth, and not merely to a certain relationship of man to God. However, it does not explain this physical, biological occurrence. It offers no information about the secondary cause (*causa secunda*) or about the processes within the world which God, as the primary cause (*causa prima*), employed. Its concern is not a scientific interpretation of the process but a witnessing to the creative will of God. Scripture witnesses to the latter in order to determine the relationship of men to God, God's action for man, and man's responsibility to God, which is founded upon his origin from God. According to this conception, Scripture reports the creation of man in order to determine his relationship to God from the point of view of the dialogue between man and God and of human salvation. The witness to human salvation includes the witness to the way of salvation from its beginning to its end because salvation takes place within history which has a beginning and an end in consummation.

It was only after long and serious debate that the encyclical *Humani generis* of Pope Pius XII (1950, DS 3895ff.) permitted theological discussion to accept, within limits, the theory of evolution without running into conflict with faith. Since then a "moderate" theory of evolution has not been considered contrary to faith, although now as before many theologians reject it as scientifically unproven and theologically untenable. The encyclical stresses that the theory of evolution is an hypothesis which has not been established with certainty.

That the theory of evolution, which until a few decades ago was considered contrary to faith or at least dangerous to it, is now regarded as a theological possibility does not mean that theology has simply yielded to the demands of science. In all these questions we must distinguish between what is of concern to theology and the method by which this concern is expressed. The interest of theology in this matter is centered on man's singular position in the world, and for a long time theologians feared that the hypothesis of man's descent from the animals would destroy or endanger his special status. Science cited arguments which necessitated a reconsideration of the position of theology and a more accurate determination of its scope. Only after much struggle did theology recognize that its concern could be distinguished from any method of expression without the abandonment of anything theology held with regard to man's unique position: this remains comprehensible and guaranteed even if we accept the idea of man's descent from the animals as an event willed by God. It is not to be wondered at that theology did not make this distinction earlier, for there seemed to be no reason to do so. However, when scientific progress faced theology with increasingly urgent new problems, it did not simply revert to now untenable positions but sought and won a deeper self-understanding. The crises which theology had to go through belong to those crises of growth which are an essential part of man's development even in his statement of the faith.

When modern science has applied its theory of evolution to man on the basis of fossils and the discovered remains of civilizations, it is still no simple matter to explain either theologically or philosophically how something developed can form itself out of something undeveloped, how a higher stage can be the product of a lower one, and how the different thresholds of being and existence can be crossed. One who maintains that evolution is a "fact" can nevertheless not dispute that this problem exists, even if it does not destroy the validity of the theory. From the theological point of view we can still say that God granted powers of development to non-divine reality and that he himself sets in motion, maintains, and supports creaturely causation in a transcendental fashion. Thus it is able, by means of divine activity, to transcend itself from within and rise to a higher level. Because God gives things the power to surpass and transcend themselves, from time to time they reach a new and higher stage of existence and being.

The theory of evolution clearly indicates the orientation of the nonhuman world towards man. Man's descent from the animal kingdom presupposes not merely a higher development of physical animal forms but also an unfolding of psychological patterns of behavior. As the precondition for man's activity, occasioned by the spirit, they aid him and are demonstrable in him as a motivating force. Ontologically the preliminary spiritual stages in the animal are connected with and yet different from the spirituality which is specifically human. The spirituality of man, which represents something new and independent, cannot be deduced as a continuum from the psyche of the animal, although it presupposes it. The only explanation for this spirituality is that man originated in a manner appropriate to him alone because of God's creative will.

This interpretation presupposes a particular idea of man which cannot be obtained from the theory of evolution. However, God's creation of the spirit was not an absolutely new intervention in his created work, in the sense of a revision. The spirit is not something foreign which has descended or fallen from heaven. It must be seen in the developmental context of subhuman and prehuman forms of life. It appears at the peak of the cosmic process of evolution as its product and yet as something new. Evolution focuses on man, the spirit, and the person. With Teilhard de Chardin, of whose views we shall have more to say later in this chapter, we can describe it as a process of concentration and personalization. As a result of man's vocation to share in the divine life, it presses beyond man to Jesus and beyond the historical Jesus to the new heaven and the new earth. God, standing at the beginning of time as the one whose reality lies in himself,[2] awaits the arrival of his creation in order to incorporate it into the movement of his own tri-personal life. Creation reaches its destination in a powerful upward thrust by fashioning more complex creations, more complex structures, and more highly organized forms of life with more perfect brains and nervous systems. The internal qualities which are the basis for the origin of the spirit willed by God are thus constantly in the process of development. Mankind hopes for the moment of arrival with God which will be the consummating culmination of a movement which was started with the first element. Spirit originates as a new principle at the moment of God's choosing and in the organism of his planning on the basis of his eternally divine creative will. The purpose of the entire evolution of the world is the origin of the human spirit in accordance with the eternal divine plan of creation. It is oriented towards man. When science asserts that on the basis of its resources it cannot be certain of this finality and that scientifically we must speak of coincidence, theology can point out that it is able to determine by theological reflection what science perhaps cannot. If there is a creator who plans and governs everything, then it is an obvious conclusion that evolution is directed towards a goal. From this standpoint, finality is a statement of faith and thus shares in the mysterious character of all such statements.

The claim that man and animal are materially and instrumentally connected is significantly modified by the doctrine that the creation of the spirit is a new principle in the evolution of the world. The spirit does not move into the physical organism the way a tenant moves into his house; it is present in the organism as an active principle, transforming it and making it subject to the spirit's own laws. How an organism which has been placed under the laws of the spirit can be transformed remains a deep mystery. Obviously a relation between body and spirit must be presupposed: spirit is capable of joining with matter, and matter is capable of joining with spirit. The spirit takes the related physical part of the animal organism and gives it its human character. The transformation of the animal organism into the human body begins naturally with the presence of the spirit as a new principle. With regard to the phenomenon of man it nevertheless represents a process which advances slowly.

Man is the climax of creation not only as a consequence of the divine creative will but also as a consequence of the meaningfulness inherent in creation. He grows, so to speak, out of the world which God continually upholds and sustains, and brings it to its immanent fullness. In a twofold sense man embodies everything that has come into being in the evolution of the world: psychologically, epistemologically and ontologically. With regard to the first, man with his reason can reach out to the totality of creation and incorporate it in himself: what is dispersed in the plurality of concrete visible reality he is able to unite in a spiritual field of vision. From the ontological viewpoint man unites all perfections of creation in himself; he is the most perfect of all earthly creatures. In a certain sense all other creatures are preliminary forms of man; even the most perfect animal does not embody all the possibilities realized in him. All other forms of organization of matter and life are present in the human constitution: the laws of physics and chemistry or physiology and psychology are valid within man as well as outside him.[3]

The claim that evolution is oriented towards man helps to answer a serious question concerning the origin of the spiritual soul. The question is, Can we speak of an evolution of man if the soul is not included? The fact that the ontological difference between man and animal is precisely here makes the question even more crucial. It really comes down to the question, How can God and man be at work together in the events of the world? How, on the one hand, can God's influence be so understood that the independence of the creature is not immersed in the divine universal activity; and how, on the other hand, can the creature be active without losing its dependence, its creaturehood? To say that the origin of the spiritual soul was exceptional is to reject that extreme monistic conception of evolution which sees the whole world as a homogeneous organism permeated by a single stream of life which rises through several stages to its highest form. The moderate theory of evolution does not regard the world as a complete, compact totality in which something not adequately deducible from the given could never arise. Rather, the world is so constituted from the beginning that it can form something new without alienating itself from its being or its autonomy. It is actually intended to produce something new. It reaches its ontological and meaningful fulfillment only in this newness. If this newness should fail to appear at the proper moment, the world would remain unfinished or be maimed. This correlation in creation must be understood as an element of the divine creative will. The fact that the spiritual soul originates by means of the divine creative will in the organism designed for it and forms it into the body is the supreme case of divine co-operation. The whole process of evolution which leads to the origin of the spiritual soul is sustained and even effected by God's activity without losing its relative independence. From the very beginning the goal of evolution is man.

Nonetheless, it could not reach this intended goal if God co-operated only in the ordinary sense; a special divine act is necessary. Divine assistance becomes especially intense when the soul is created; yet it does not occur separately from the process of evolution which is sustained by God and which is immanent in the world. This evolution cannot reach its goal without God's special activity; God completes the process of evolution itself. In this case God's activity has to a certain extent a categorical, but no transcendental, quality. Despite the proposition that the spiritual soul is not a natural product of evolution, we can in fact speak of an evolution of the whole man insofar as the whole of evolution aims at man, just as God's assistance and the evolution of the world which he sustains converge in the origin of man. In this process God and the world participate in different ways: the participation of the world, as the *causa secunda,* guarantees a continuity; God's participation, as the *causa prima,* guarantees a transition into a new, non-derivative form.

If we assert that God and the creation work together in the origin of man, we are not invalidating any claim of natural science but only adding something and making the partial explanation of science a complete one. The doctrine of co-operation also eliminates the Occasionalistic and Deistic interpretations of man's origin. According to Occasionalism, only God acts, and not the creature, who is simply the channel for God's activity; the creature is, so to speak, a pipe-line through which the divine stream of activity flows to a particular time. According to Deism, which was widespread among natural scientists of the seventeenth and eighteenth centuries, God created the world but is no longer active in it; every event is to be explained only by causes within the world. Insofar as Deism is presented as a total explanation, it denies the activity of God and the character of the creature as a creature. Occasionalism, on the other hand, fails to do justice to the independent activity of the creature. Occasionalism denies the *causa secunda*, deism the *causa prima*.[4]

Because spirit comes into being in creation with the origin of man, there is a completely new situation in the world: in man creation comes to itself. This involves several things. Creation can only come to itself when it understands itself as having been created, when it recognizes God as the creator. In man, creation becomes God's partner. The individual man can only become a person by limiting himself *vis-à-vis* what he is not, especially with regard to other personal beings, and by understanding his existence as at the same time individual and coexistent. This means that as subject he views the non-human beings presented by his environment as objects but his fellow men as other subjects. The subject-object relationship entered the world with the origin of man, as did inter-subjectivity.

Today we are indebted to Teilhard de Chardin for a special conception of the evolution of the universe. Even though he is not able to prove all his statements scientifically, but has only seen them as it were in a great vision, still they are well-founded and enlightening. The objections which present themselves against his unified theory of the course of evolution from the very beginning up to the consummation in the second coming of Christ certainly touch upon important elements of the Christian faith. However, they are not able to destroy the total picture which Teilhard presents. First of all, it is never an easy matter to understand Teilhard. Since he wished to live and die as a Catholic theologian, he speaks from the outset from a definite *a priori*. For this reason statements of his which are obscure and uncertain should be interpreted in terms of the Christian faith. As for the undeniable difficulties with his theory—for instance, the question of sin, freedom and related problems—we know that similar insoluble difficulties exist in the theological tendencies of schools of thought permitted by the Church. We need only consider the opposition between Molinism and Thomism. How, for example, Thomism can defend the freedom of man is an insoluble problem. Even theologians who recognize and accept Thomism are convinced that it cannot satisfactorily maintain the truth of human freedom. In spite of this, they see no reason to abandon the entire system. One may, therefore, proceed in a similar manner with respect to the total conception of Teilhard de Chardin. The intelligibility of his total view is discernible in the fact that he sees in both the process of evolution and the metaphysical relations of the whole of reality one vast unified system. In a certain sense it can be called a monistic interpretation of the universe, for Teilhard understands the theological principle as embracing, pervading and governing everything.

MONEGENISM

In the contemporary encounter between theology and natural science the question has arisen of whether mankind originated from one set of parents or from more. In the early centuries this question was not present on the theological scene, so though we may ask whether the Council of Trent wished to raise it, we must say that the council issued no formal statement concerning it, for it was not then an actual problem. In the encyclical *Humani generis* of Pius XII, on the other hand, we find the following passage:

There are other conjectures, about polygenism (as it is called), which leave the faithful no such freedom of choice [as in the assumption that man in regard to the physical realm descended from the animal world.] Christians cannot lend their support to a theory which involves the existence, after Adam's time, of some earthly race of men, truly so called, who were not descended ultimately from him, or else supposes that Adam was the name given to some group of our primordial ancestors. It does not appear how such views can be reconciled with the doctrine of original sin, as this is guaranteed to us by Scripture and tradition, and proposed to us by the Church. Original sin is the result of a sin committed, in actual historical fact, by an individual man named Adam, and it is a quality native to all of us, only because it has been handed down by descent from him. (DS 3897)

This text neither directly rejects polygenism nor supports monogenism. Nevertheless it states that it is not evident how Scripture —the encyclical refers to Rom. 5:12-19—and the doctrine of original sin as proclaimed at the Council of Trent can be reconciled with polygenism. In order to evaluate this proposition we must, as we have said, inquire whether the Council of Trent intended to teach formally that original sin was transmitted by descent from one single forefather or whether its purpose was to reject the Pelagian contention that the damage Adam did consisted only in setting a bad example. We might add that the text leaves open the question of whether polygenism may be advocated if it can be shown that it is compatible with the true doctrine of the Church on original sin. If it can, the text presents no basis for its rejection. Perhaps we might take the parallel which Paul establishes between Adam and Christ into account here.

Paul calls Christ the second ancestor of the human race in a spiritual sense. He can fulfill this function even though there is no biological or hereditary connection between him and all other men: God designates him as the salvific representative for all other men because of his position in the total creation. Similarly, we could perhaps argue that an individual man could have acted as God's appointed representative for all other men, so that a community of joy and despair would exist between him and all the rest of mankind. As attractive as such an argument appears at first sight, we must bear in mind the basic structural, historical difference between Adam and Jesus. The whole of creation—its process of coming into existence and the human history which takes place within that cosmic process—is Christocentric from the beginning. We cannot ascribe such a position to Adam, and therefore we must assume some other connection between Adam and all other men if his action is to have saving or pernicious consequences for them. That connection, then, would be descent. This does not mean, of course, that Adam's sin is inherited like some sort of biological element or like a material possession; rather, his descendants share in his sin on the basis of their biological connection with him. Romans 5:12-19, which the Church sees as giving evidence for original sin, seems to come close to monogenism unless we assume that it is

simply using the Old Testament text with no intention of addressing itself didactically to our question. As far as the first two chapters of Genesis are concerned, we cannot find any real trace of
monogenism. However, we do seem to find it in Genesis 3, for here
the sacred writer sets out to explain the religious state of men,
their sinfulness and their lost condition. He does this by referring
to man's origin and starting point. In accordance with ancient
oriental social and religious modes of thought, the author sees all
of humanity gathered together in the first man. He depicts concretely in the first man the characteristics of all of mankind. Adam
has a corporate meaning for him. H. Renpens is fundamentally
correct when he says:

Certainly an ancient text has something to do with an ancient teaching whose essential core is then made doctrine after much vacillation
and deliberation. But it is an entirely different question whether we
claim that this text is the true point of departure for an intellectual
process of growth which ends in a dogmatic formulation or whether
we want to see the completed dogmatic formulation in the ancient text.
In the latter case we are reading too much into the text. But coupled
with this is the other extreme: we can see too little in a text if we
believe that nothing is present as long as there is no clear formula.
Precisely where Scripture is concerned, which is the first human written expression of God's mighty acts, we must give our attention not
only to what is expressed in completely thought-out formulas but also
to the considerable effort and attempt to reach a formula. Very often
a thought is still being shaped, is evolving, is struggling with the great
reality which is supposed to be comprehended and which is experienced
and known more than thought of in concepts.[5]

We can express science's answer to our question by using the
image of a field of origin. To be sure, this field of origin from which
man comes was small according to contemporary scientific opinion.
God chose out of the small population of the biological realm
from which man descended one single organism among several and
permitted the spirit to arise in it. The remaining specimens of the
population either developed in a different fashion or died out.

God did not have to allow the spirit to originate in every protohominid simply because it had reached a certain level of organization and material structure. It is not meaningless to think that although several types of beings had developed to that stage in which the creation of the spirit would be logical, God did not, in fact, create the spirit in them. To explain this occurrence we may draw upon the idea that nature makes experiments. Those specimens which failed to achieve their goal represent nature's slips. Science can prove that from the time the presence of man is scientifically ascertainable, he appears in a definite, even if perhaps small, group. But science cannot explain with its own resources how this initial population began. Even if it could establish an unbroken morphological sequence, it still could not determine where in the sequence the first human being appears who is no longer an animal. Natural science will presumably not be able to determine this even in the future. It can show when man can be observed for the first time but not when he first appeared in fact. When theology upholds the traditional proposition that God created spirit in only one of a species out of a biological realm which had reached a certain level of organization, it is motivated to do so not by philosophical reflections, or by scientific observation, or by direct revelation, but by the analogy of faith.

THE ESSENTIAL ELEMENTS OF MAN

When we speak of body and soul as the essential components of man in connection with the doctrine of creation, we are only indirectly concerned with the problem of man's origin. The question, although a metaphysical one, has existential consequences: the structure which God gave men is the basis for his superiority over other creatures. To understand more fully the correlation of body and soul we must refer to the idea of evolution. Man is not a creature composed of two elements but is a single being in whom matter and spirit are essentially united. Out of these two principles arises a third thing which cannot be identified with either of them. In the process of evolution each succeeding stage represents something more than the preceding one. Out of the lesser comes a greater. If we speak of evolution, we must assume that each new development really has more life, power and vitality than the previous one. As we have already noted, the difficult yet decisive question then arises as to how a thing that is less developed can produce something more advanced. While this is first of all a philosophical question, it has fundamental implications for theology. For such a process to be possible there must be a reality distinct from creation which is behind the events in creation constantly providing the world with new energy. This reality which acts in the world and yet is distinct from it can supply this energy only if it is absolute being. We call this absolute being the living God. He constantly grants new powers of life to the world, so that in its natural impulse to go forward it is able to achieve greater fullness of being. God's bestowal of new powers of life results not merely in quantitative enrichment but in matter's more intensive possession of itself. Matter becomes richer and at the same time more complex. In this complexity matter constantly finds more power to possess itself. If we accept this explanation, we must decide whether we can still speak of evolution in the usual sense, or if we must not speak of a continuously new creation.

We can retain the word "evolution" only if we use it to mean a synthesis of creaturely and divine activity. We must assume that the activity of the absolute is intensified in creaturely activity and that therefore the latter increases in depth. It is conceivable that matter, in its forward thrust, reaches a certain point, under the influence of new powers of life and energies granted by the absolute, at which it endeavors to go beyond its previous form of existence. By itself matter cannot reach a new form, but this is granted it by absolute being. At one point Thomas Aquinas says that the soul arises from the potentialities of matter (*educitur ex potentia materiae*). We call the bestowal of such newness—which stems from matter but yet is not created by it—God's creative bringing-forth of the spiritual soul. When absolute being grants new life and new energies in this case we have the creation of the spiritual human soul. Thus without obliterating the essential difference between spirit and matter, we can see that the soul is the highest realization of evolution that matter aspires to, but can reach only by the transcendental activity of God. Matter must have a certain structure for the spiritual soul to exist; there can be no soul without a body. The soul is not spirit in a non-material form but is spirit in a form which matter exacts and puts its stamp upon. Conversely, the soul acts upon matter; the body is the soul's expression of itself outwardly. These reflections represent a synthesis of the ideas of Thomas Aquinas with those of Hermann Schell and Teilhard de Chardin on the subject of evolution. Here it becomes evident that on the one hand, with the origin of man, evolution has reached its apex, but that, on the other hand, from this point on, a new impellent principle is at work. The idea of evolution offers us insight into the metaphysical structure of the universe, and at the same time into that process of becoming, founded in anthropological ontology, which is essential to and characteristic of man. It also indicates man's increasing desire for an ever new future.

When we emphasize that man consists of body and soul, we must explain this commonplace statement because the distinction is not sufficient in itself. The body is certainly matter fashioned by spirit and the soul is spirit limited by matter. Because of its relationship to matter, spirit is the soul of man, and because of its relationship to spirit, matter is the body of man. Body and soul unite to form the reality which we call man. As we have seen, Scripture refers to these two elements of man without distinguishing sharply between them or presenting any formal doctrine concerning them. The distinction first becomes apparent in the literature of the Hellenistic period. To a certain extent Scripture speaks of this distinction, though only incidentally, when it mentions man's involvement in the material world as well as his conditioned fate, or when it relates conversations between God and man. Man is a result of the fact that God created a body and breathed the breath of life into it.

When Christ says that the whole human self is subject to God, he means the body and soul which together compose the totality of man. God is responsible for both elements (Mt. 10:28). Because man has a body, he is involved in history and nature and is at their mercy. Although his body can perish outwardly, man does not lose his hold on his self. God can plunge the entire human self, body and soul, into perdition. When Scripture now and then speaks of body, soul, and spirit, seeming to assume a tripartite structure of man (1 Thess. 5:23; Heb. 4:12), it does not mean three distinct elements of human nature but is suggesting with various expressions the different tasks of the one spiritual soul. Because Scripture is principally interested in salvation history, its use of the words "flesh" or "soul" or "body" does not always correspond to our use of them when we speak about man in metaphysical terms. For example, the word "flesh" in the Pauline texts does not mean the material body but the entire person in his alienation from God and in his bondage to sin. "Moral" and "religious" modes of behavior—such as idolatry, incontinence, wrangling, and anger—belong to the works of the flesh. The word "soul" must also be seen in relation to salvation history: it refers to the entire man in relation to redemption. If we look for reference to the dichotomy of body and soul in Scripture, we must not merely examine words but take into consideration their context. As we have said, we cannot see in the second chapter of Genesis any reference to a spiritual soul in the account of God's breathing life into man. But we can say that our subsequent perception of the spiritual soul of man is an amplification of the Genesis account of creation. Scripture says that the spiritual human soul gives life and is the conveyor of thought and understanding, of will and aspiration, of feeling and perception (Deut. 34:9). Joy and peace (Pss. 86:4; 94:19; Jer. 6:16; Lam. 3:17), longing and love (Ps. 63:2; Song of Solomon 1:7; 3:1), sorrow and pain (Job 27:2; Ps. 42:6f., 11; 43:5), hate and contempt (Is. 1:14; Ps. 11:5; Jer. 15:1; Ez. 25:15; 36:5), aversion and disgust (Job 10:1; Jer. 6:8; Ez. 23:17) are experienced by the soul. The longing for God dwells in the soul. It can lift itself up to God (Pss. 25:1; 86:4; 143:8). It can wait and hope for him (Pss. 33:20; 130:5f.); indeed, it thirsts and longs for him (Pss. 42:1f.; 63:1; 84:2; 119:81; 143:6). Comforted by him, it rejoices and rests in him (Pss. 34:2; 35:9; 22:20; 63:8; 103:1f., 22; 104:1, 35; Is. 61:10). But we must not forget that in the Old Testament until the Hellenistic period man was regarded as a unity, not consisting of distinct structural elements, but with different aspects and functions of one and the same object. Before the Hellenistic period we find no texts which mention a principle independent of the body and distinct from it. We must ask, then, whether Greek ideas, particularly Platonic, did not have an influence on such an interpretation of man. This assumption would not be at variance with the idea that Scripture is divinely inspired; in that case, we would have to view Greek philosophy as playing the role of a midwife. The various functions in the light of Greek philosophy are relatively distinct, though closely connected, principles. The New Testament affirms that man has a spiritual soul endowed with reason when it compares the spirit of man with the spirit of God, as in 1 Corinthians (2:11). Just as only the human spirit knows what occurs within man, so only the spirit of God penetrates into the hidden life of God. God exists in himself because of the divine Spirit; the Spirit is the divine "within." In the Spirit God says "yes" to himself. Similarly, the human spirit is the "within" of man. In and by means of his spirit he is present to himself and possesses himself because he is constantly going out from and returning to himself. To know his own spirit means that a man enters into his own within, comes to the recognition of himself.

We shall not speak of the characteristics of man's spiritual soul, even its immortality, in this context. The difficulty implicit in the question of the immortality of the human soul is that the New Testament promise points to the transfiguration of the entire person and the awakening of the dead in conjunction with the resurrection of Jesus Christ rather than to the immortality of the soul. We shall analyze this problem when we discuss theological anthropology in connection with the doctrine of the Church. For the moment we shall confine ourselves to pointing out that the spiritual soul of man is distinguishable from the soul of the animal, which behavioral animal psychology has investigated with increasing thoroughness, by the fact that the human spirit reflects upon itself and can stand over against itself, so to speak. It is also capable of comprehending and assimilating by means of ideas the whole reality, the entire universe. The animal cannot reflect and its perception is limited at any given moment to its immediate environment, in the sense of its biological-psychological existence.[6]

Man is himself in that he exists in a body molded by his spirit.

At the same time, in his bodily existence he transcends himself towards nature, the human thou, and the human community. Hence the body is the medium by which man's individuality and self-being expresses itself; and it is also the medium for the expression of man's bond with the universe and of his involvement in history. We can see that man is a creature and not God because he tires, becomes ill, and undergoes physical death. Conversely, man's return to God, to the fullness of life, and his salvation, are revealed in the overcoming of death and of the illness which is its anticipation. The mysteries of sin and salvation are accordingly mysteries of physical man. They take place in the body and have their effect on the body. The Son of God himself appeared in bodily form to give human history a new beginning (Jn. 1:14). The believer is incorporated into Christ in the physical event of baptism. He must prove and carry out his love for Christ in his body. The central celebration of the Christian, the Eucharist, is a physical event in which the participant experiences belonging to the body of Christ and growing more deeply into it.

In his physical being man experiences to a certain degree that he is a product of history as well as its creator. In his physical existence he is called upon to accept and appropriate historical events without estranging himself from his own being. At the same time he is summoned to promote human history in its efforts to create patterns and dimensions of life which are worthy of man.

We can clarify the relationship between the soul and the body somewhat further. Because of the soul, matter is formed into the human body. The soul determines the form of the matter, with the result that it is not lifeless or merely vegetable or animal matter but is the human body. Matter which is no longer connected with soul ceases to be a part of the human body even if its physical form continues to exist for a time, as with the removal of a hand or a leg. The soul is the fundamental explanation of the fact that a man is a man rather than something else even if it is not to be identified with the man himself. It is responsible for the fact that the acts of man are human, that even his eating and drinking and his bodily functions are somewhat different from the same functions in animals.

According to Scripture the body is not an object we possess which exists outside our actual being. Not only is it the natural basis of our existence and the tool upon which we depend, it is the living form of our being and the necessary expression of our individual existence. The meaning of our life finds its realization in the body. For this reason we are not to despise the body as if it were a prison of the soul, or fear it as the enemy of the spirit. But it cannot be regarded in a materialistic sense as identical with man himself, as if man were able to find his life's goal and meaning in material events. The body is to be understood as the bearer of a spiritual, personal life which is subject to the call of God and receives its nobility from the fact that it is the image of God.

At the Fourth Lateran Council (1215, DS 800) the official Church incidentally asserted its belief that man is constituted of body and spirit when it pointed to God as the creator of every reality, including man. At the Council of Vienna it taught that there is a unity of body and soul in man in which the rational soul is the essential form of the human body (DS 900–901).

The unity of being which body and soul form has the result that both physical and spiritual events have a unity of effect on man, and also that body and soul mutually influence each other. Scripture calls the unity of body and soul the "heart" of man. It also uses this word in the sense of personality. Man first learns about his personhood as man from Scripture, not from philosophy. According to Scripture the heart is the living center in which the human self possesses itself, the innermost region where man comes to awareness of himself and from which all his decisions originate. Courage and bravery reside in the heart; man withstands danger with his heart; concern, parental feelings, and joy stir in the heart; sorrow and pain dwell within the walls of the heart. Feelings and passions, desires and longings and—above all—love live in the heart. Our good and evil thoughts, our self-contrived visions, our judgments and condemnations come out of the heart. All our plans and decisions originate in the heart. The heart is the organ with which the human self reaches out towards God and grasps him and also that with which man betrays God in unbelief; it is the place where God enters man. God transforms mankind by the men to whom he gives a new heart. This biblical conception of the heart as the immanent ground of the totality of body and soul has been alive in theology from Ignatius of Antioch through Augustine, Bonaventure, Elizabeth of Thuringia, Gertrude the Great, Francis of Sales, Blaise Pascal, to John Henry Newman. It would be a denial of the wholeness of the one nature of man if either spirit or body were considered or treated as a separate and independent entity. This would be the case, for example, if the body were used only as a means to pleasure, and not also as an implement of self-dedication. The physical side of man would be destructively separated from the spiritual if capacity for labor were simply treated according to supply and demand, like that of an animal or machine, and not seen as a part of a personal self which has dignity, rights, feelings, and purpose.

ADDENDUM

In connection with the problem of the origin of man we call attention again to the fact that Scripture does not attest directly and formally to God's creation of the spiritual soul. Nevertheless, it is possible to infer such a divine creative activity from an analysis of the idea of man which Scripture gives us. The idea of man given to us in Scripture is, therefore, the precondition for the statement of faith that God brought forth the spiritual soul of the first man at the appropriate hour; i.e., that because of his eternal will to create he allowed it to originate in suitable structures of matter without its being simply an expression, an epi-phenomenon, of those structures, and so derived from them.

We must probably assume that what is true of the first human soul is also true for every spiritual soul, although there is no official doctrine on this point. By and large theologians until now have believed that God creates the spiritual soul in the moment when the parental cells unite and fulfill the conditions necessary to produce a new human being. This concept, called creationism, follows from the essential difference between physical and spiritual being. Generationism represents another thesis which is coming into increasing favor. According to this view, at the time of procreation the parents give the new child, together with the living germ cells, spiritual potentialities, the fusion of which creates the soul of the new child. Augustine himself vacillated all his life between generationism and creationism (and admitted that he knew nothing about the subject). The danger in generationism is that it may minimize the essential difference between the physical and spiritual life of man. Although the Church itself has no formal doctrine, it has indicated in a series of statements an inclination towards creationism (DS 360–361, 381, 1007, 1440–1441, 2015, 2017, 3220f.). With reference to creationism we must say that even if God directly creates the spiritual soul in each child, the parents are the true procreators. In the act of procreation parents are concerned not only with the formation of a physical body but with the whole man, with the child. Because they are creatures parents cannot reach their goal without divine assistance: in this case, because the goal is of a unique type, they need a special act of divine co-operation. However, it must be said that God never refuses this assistance. Even though God and parents work together, we must nevertheless say that each child owes its existence completely to its parents and also completely to God, to each in a different way. Since it must be presumed that God creates a suitable soul for each particular body, the fact that the child originates from its parents means that they are responsible not only for its physical character but also for its spiritual one (the meaning of heredity). We can take offense at the idea of God's assistance only if we believe that the relationship between God and the world is Deistic, and therefore deny the idea of a *creatio continua*. If this concept of the evolution of world events includes the idea that creation is going on at all times and that something new is always coming into existence, then it is only a special case when the new thing that arises in the creation which is constantly occurring is the spiritual soul of man.

Notes

[1] From *Evolution and Christian Hope* by Ernst Benz, translated by Heinz G. Frank. Copyright © 1965 by Nymphenburger Verlagshandlung

GmbH., Munich. English tranlation © 1966 by Doubleday & Company, Inc. Reprinted by permission of Doubleday & Company, Inc.

[2] The view of Hermann Schell, who at the beginning of the twentieth century advocated an evolutionary theology which exhibits important affinities with that of Teilhard de Chardin. Cf. H. Mynarek, "Grundlegung einer naturtheologischen Anthropologie," in *Theologie und Glaube*, 56 (1966), pp. 225–243.

[3] H. Dolch, "Der Mensch in der werdenden Welt," in *Lebendiges Zeugnis* (Paderborn, 1961), pp. 7ff.

[4] *Ibid.*, pp. 17f.

[5] *Urgeschicte und Heilsgeschichte* (Mainz, 1959), p. 221.

[6] See H. Autrum, *Tier und Mensch in der Masse* (Munich, 1966).

Readings for Part II

Mouroux, J. *The Mystery of Time*. New York, Desclée, 1964. Part I, ch. 2; see also Macquarrie, J. *Principles of Christian Theology*. New York, Scribner's. Ch. 10.

Rahner, Karl. "The Order of Redemption within the Order of Creation" in *Mission and Grace*, I. New York, Sheed and Ward, 1964.

———— "Monogenism" in *Theological Investigations*, I. Baltimore. Helicon, 1961.

Renckens, H. *The Religion of Israel*. New York, Sheed and Ward, 1966.

———— *Israel's Concept of the Beginning*. New York, Herder.

Schoonenberg, P. *Covenant and Creation*. London, Sheed and Ward, 1968.

Teilhard de Chardin, P. *The Phenomenon of Man*. New York, Harper Torchbook, 1961.

III

The First Sin and Original Sin

‹ 10

The First Sin

THE SIN ITSELF

We turn our attention now to a very controversial and much discussed problem of today. We will begin with the primeval sin of man and its consequences. Scripture speaks of the first sin in the narrative of the garden of Eden, the so-called paradise narrative. The word "paradise," of course, does not occur in the Hebrew text. It was introduced through the translation of the Hebrew text into Greek.

The Lord God took the man and put him in the garden of Eden to till it and keep it. And the Lord God commanded the man saying, "You may freely eat of every tree of the garden; but of the tree of knowledge of good and evil you shall not eat, for in the day that you eat of it you shall die." (Gen. 2: 15–17)
Now the serpent was more subtle than any other wild creature that the Lord God had made. He said to the woman, "Did God say, 'You shall not eat of any tree of the garden?' " And the woman said to the serpent, "We may eat of the fruit of the trees of the garden; But God said, 'You shall not eat of the fruit of the tree which is in the midst of the garden, neither shall you touch it, lest you die.' " But the serpent said to the woman, "You will not die. For God knows that when you eat of it your eyes will be opened, and you will be like God, knowing good and evil." So when the woman saw that the tree was good for food, and that it was a delight to the eyes, and

147

that the tree was to be desired to make one wise, she took of its fruit and ate; and she also gave some to her husband, and he ate. Then the eyes of both were opened, and they knew that they were naked; and they sewed fig leaves together and made themselves aprons.

And they heard the sound of the Lord God walking in the garden in the cool of the day, and the man and his wife hid themselves from the presence of the Lord God among the trees of the garden. But the Lord God called to the man, and said to him, "Where are you?" And he said, "I heard the sound of thee in the garden, and I was afraid, because I was naked; and I hid myself." He said, "Who told you that you were naked? Have you eaten of the tree of which I commanded you not to eat?" The man said, "The woman whom thou gavest to be with me, she gave me fruit of the tree, and I ate." Then the Lord God said to the woman, "What is this that you have done?" The woman said, "The serpent beguiled me, and I ate."

The Lord God said to the serpent, "Because you have done this, cursed are you above all cattle, and above all wild animals; upon your belly you shall go, and dust you shall eat all the days of your life. I will put enmity between you and the woman, and between your seed and her seed; he shall bruise your head, and you shall bruise his heel."

To the woman he said, "I will greatly multiply your pain in childbearing; in pain you shall bring forth children, yet your desire shall be for your husband, and he shall rule over you."

And to Adam he said, "Because you have listened to the voice of your wife, and have eaten of the tree of which I commanded you, 'You shall not eat of it,' cursed is the ground because of you; in toil you shall eat of it all the days of your life; thorns and thistles it shall bring forth to you; and you shall eat the plants of the field. In the sweat of your face you shall eat bread till you return to the ground, for out of it you were taken; you are dust, and to dust you shall return.

The man called his wife's name Eve, because she was the mother of all the living. And the Lord God made for Adam and his wife garments of skins, and clothed them.

Then the Lord God said, "Behold, the man has become like one of us, knowing good and evil; and now, lest he put forth his hand and take also of the tree of life, and eat, and live forever"—therefore the Lord God sent him forth from the garden of Eden, to till the ground from which he was taken. He drove out the man; and at the east of the garden of Eden he placed the cherubim, and a flaming sword which turned every way, to guard the way to the tree of life." (Gen. 3:1-24)

To begin with, something should be said about the literary form and the sense of the narrative as a whole. The author doubtless wants to relate how the history of man, and in particular the history of God with man, began. He feels all the more compelled to do this because between the people of Israel, to whom he belongs, and God an intimate bond has existed for centuries, ever since the events on Mt. Sinai: God was experienced in an unforgettable manner then as the saving and healing God. Yet in spite of this, sin and catastrophe now rule over Israel. How can this be possible? Where does evil come from? This is the fundamental question which interests the author. His answer reads: not from God, but from human actions. Thus his narrative becomes at once a defense of God and an appeal to men to resist sin and renew their confidence in God. The author is undoubtedly convinced that he is relating an actual event. For this, ancient traditions stood at his disposal. Of course, one may not assume that they reached back into that dim past age of which he speaks; there were no records of that period! The question arises whether he really could relate anything actual, or whether what he reports originates in his free imagination and is therefore no more worthy of acceptance than the myths of his heathen environment. The narrative which he offers us has no counterpart in extra-biblical sources, but many of the individual motifs can be found there. They have been taken over by the author for the presentation of his own narrative. He has likewise shaped in a free and independent composition the Israelite traditions which he found, so that one must treat his narrative as his own work. He is not merely a compiler but a real author.

He has arrived at his narrative through plunging himself into devout meditation on the idea of God which was alive in his people. What he has presented, he has discerned as a member of the Israelite community of faith. That in essence at least there is question of an actual event in the narrative is attested by the inspired character of Scripture. The New Testament provides us with the ultimate guarantee: only in the light of Christ, or in the light of the apostle

Paul's preaching of Christ, can we be certain that there is an actual event at the root of the garden of Eden narrative. The event at stake is the sin. It is the key idea in the narrative presented by the Yahwist. For him the main thing is to declare that an offense stands at the beginning of human history, that this offense has brought ruin upon men and that it i 'he fertile source of innumerable sins. One should not overlook tue fact that the stories of the tower of Babel, of Cain and Abel, and of the deluge also lie within the Yahwist's view of history. In order to specify its type more accurately, it has been called a wisdom narrative. The special relation of the author's narrative to the older wisdom of Israel, which flourished in the rich cultural period of Solomon, has been cited as the basis for this classification.[1]

When we turn to the interpretation of the narrative, naturally only the more important aspects can be stressed. The author begins with the affirmation that from the very beginning God has been concerned about man. He represents this concern by recounting how in the midst of a barren landscape God formed a garden, a cultivated tract of land with plentiful water and luxuriant vegetation. This is described as a gift to men from a solicitous God. But it is not a fantastic garden of wonders. The people who were placed in the garden by God were not supposed to lead an idle and frivolous life. They had to care for the garden and till it. Here the Yahwist employs a theme similar to that of the Priestly text. As the garden is assigned to man as God's gift, so man is assigned to the garden, the earth, as its cultivator. The tree of life standing in the middle of the garden is of special significance. It is clearly conceived of as a symbol of the immortality for which men long. This longing is mentioned in numerous oriental myths. Next the tree of the knowledge of good and evil is mentioned. This tree plays a special role in the course of events. Nevertheless it is questionable whether it is actually a symbol, and not merely a didactic construction. Perhaps the tree of life and the tree of the knowledge of good and evil are identical.

The fateful event begins with a command of God. In this command God reveals himself as man's Lord as well as his guardian. It serves at the same time as an admonition and as a means of directing man's attention to God. It is an expression of that watchful and anxious love which desires to protect man against the dangers of his own greatness. Man stands in an intimate relationship with God: this is brought out in the process by which God breathes life into man. But this nearness to God, the greatness and dignity of man, was also his peril. The image of God, he could forget that he was only an image and attempt to set himself up as God. In any case, it was not the intention of the command to set up a taboo. Man is appointed to cultivate and administer the whole world; there is no region which is excluded. Man is not to be denied access to any particular part of creation.

That the two human beings were subject to temptation is a profound mystery. In that moment—after an evolutionary process of millions of years—in which creation, owing to a special act of God, could open the eye of mind and reflect upon itself, it recognized itself in and through man as created and as an image of God. The level of consciousness of that period must not be interpreted in an unrealistic manner, yet the instinctive presentiment—indeed, the instinctive realization—of the created character of its own being and the creator character of God is to some extent implied. However, precisely this consciousness of intimacy with God contained in self-reflection became a temptation for man.

In the light of the New Testament we can say that even the first men, in spite of their nearness to God, lived the life of faith. The longing to see is bound up with faith: the life of the believer is not static but full of movement and restlessness, straining towards an approaching reality. There is in him an irresistible drive towards the remote, towards the future. This reaching out and striving for God cannot be considered nonexistent in the lives of the first men. There was in them an insatiable longing for something still unfulfilled. That the self-consciousness inherent in man, his ability to reflect upon himself, could realize itself in a manner contrary to God's will is due to the freedom intrinsic to him. Freedom was the noblest and at the same time the most dangerous of the divine gifts. God dared, as it were, to grant man a share in his noblest attribute, in his own sovereignty; for though God cannot delegate his omnipotence, he can nevertheless grant a participation in it. But in the event the gift proved too great for the recipient's weakness.

As for the unfolding of the account of the sin, the fine psychological style with which the author narrates how this first sin took place has often been pointed out. It is with the sin in view that he introduces the serpent. He probably conceived of the serpent as real. For in those days it was not thought so extraordinary that a beast should speak. The serpent awakened in the woman a threefold desire: sexual desire, aesthetic desire, and intellectual desire for the knowledge of good and evil, or the desire to be like God. If the author added the serpent to the narrative, there may have been a variety of motives. Perhaps he was interested in accounting for man's fear and hostility when confronted by a menacing serpent in the underbrush: this would be shown to have its foundation in the behavior of the serpent towards man at the beginning of history. This hypothesis is called an etiological explanation. Such an interpretation attributes to the author an attempt to explain the behavior of men towards serpents and of serpents towards men by searching for the cause, and indeed a cause which lies far back in history. Nevertheless, an interpretation of this kind still remains on the surface. One must take into consideration the fact that in the Canaanite religion the serpent was a type of divine animal, venerated for its wisdom and its power of healing. The secret of a sublime divine knowledge was attributed to it. In opposition to this myth the author explains that the serpent is not an animal which cures but one which harms; that it does not bring life but death. The serpent motif is a negative formulation of the law of faith ruling the entire Old Testament: You shall have no strange gods beside me. Here then the author is promoting a demythologizing theology.

Though in the narrative the serpent turns to the woman first, a greater susceptibility to temptation on the part of woman is not the issue here. The tragedy in this whole situation is that the woman was supposed to assist man in the fulfillment of his life; this is why God presented her to man. But the gift became for him an occasion of disaster. God overwhelmed man with his blessing, but man turned the blessing into his own misfortune. Here we see an apologetic tendency at work to defend God against the reproach that he was responsible for the evil in the world.

As for the type of sin, one must distinguish between the internal and the external event. In the internal order human beings were induced by the serpent to distrust God. The serpent wants to nullify God's plan and destroy men; to prevent men from continuing to take God's word seriously. It sows in their hearts the desire to act like God. God, on the other hand, is portrayed as a jealous being who, in his egoism, wants to withhold from men that greatness which is proper to himself but to which men have a real right. Thus disobedience, pride, and disbelief are the causes of man's sin. It is disbelief especially which plunges men into disaster: throughout the Old Testament we encounter its fatal role (e.g., Sir. 2:9–13; 3:26–28; 11:14f.). Sirach 10:12–18 says:

The beginning of man's pride is to depart from the Lord; his heart has forsaken his Maker. For the beginning of pride is sin, and the man who clings to it pours out abominations. Therefore the Lord brought upon them extraordinary afflictions, and destroyed them utterly. The Lord has cast down the thrones of rulers, and has seated the lowly in their place. The Lord has plucked up the roots of the nations, and has planted the humble in their place. The Lord has overthrown the lands of the nations, and has destroyed them to the foundations of the earth. He has removed some of them and destroyed them, and he has extinguished the memory of them from the earth. Pride was not created for men, nor fierce anger for those born of women.

(Cf. Sir. 23:27 and also in the New Testament Mt. 19:23–26; Lk. 15:18,21; Jn. 4:27; 1 Jn. 3:8; Jn. 8:34.)

We know nothing about the form which the sin took in the external order. There is no reason to believe that it was a sexual sin. God himself brought the woman to the man with the explicit instruction: Be fruitful and multiply. He presented woman to man that they might become one flesh. The total impression the narrative gives does not admit of a sexual interpretation: one cannot use the serpent for it. It is true that the serpent was frequently a male sexual symbol, but as we have already seen, in the Canaanite religion it was in addition understood as symbol of wisdom and of the gods and goddesses who bestowed life. The desire awakened by the serpent to know good and evil plays a special role in the sin. The expression "the knowledge of good and evil" certainly implies a distinction between the two, but it has a wider significance. In Hebrew thought, to know does not, as in Greek thought, signify theoretical knowledge. It means practical knowledge, and practical in the sense of productive. It means much the same as to acquire mastery over the thing known, to have command over the known. Thus the further knowledge extends, the greater becomes man's capacity for disposing things. In the drive for knowledge lies the struggle for the authority to control things, for autonomy and unlimited power. Even though the object of this knowledge is called "good and evil," these terms must be understood in a wider sense. In the language of the Old Testament the formula "good and evil" can mean much the same as the whole of reality, everything that is found in the realm of man. Here it is probably best understood as meaning the administration of human life. That does not mean that the moral order is excluded. Morality, however, is only one element in the total human economy. Since the total human economy, the administration of human life, has been determined by God's creative act, man, when he attempts to know good and evil, undertakes to determine the administration of his own life and exclude the influence of God. He wants to set the standards for all his activity. He claims complete autonomy. Man alone wills to be the measure of all things, refusing to acknowledge God as the norm for his life. Thus the desire for the knowledge of good and evil is an anti-theistic attitude of which the eating or not eating of the fruit of the tree is a symbol. It is a profound mystery how man, since he is but a creature, can arrive at the desire to live in a fully autonomous manner separated from God. The beginning of an explanation is suggested by the Yahwist when he attributes a godlike quality to man. In the similarity of man to God, in the godlike being of man, lies the reason that man can succumb even to the temptation to be God, to live and to arrange matters like God. On the other hand, however, he is only a poor creature. If he attempts to overcome his creaturehood and expand the divine element in himself, if he seeks to increase the divine life in himself beyond his created limits, then the divine spark in him becomes his doom in a mysterious reversal. Stier brings out this meaning of the Yahwistic text as follows:

It is certainly to the credit of the Yahwist that he saw man thus (Gen. 11:1–9; the building of the tower): able, or driven, to reach beyond himself and in an usurped but genuine godliness to rule despotically in the world, only to founder on God in his self-violation and be thrown back to the earth as a criminal. This should not be misunderstood in such a way that Adam, the first man, is dissolved into a type, becomes everyman. Adam is not merely a symbol of the *adam*. Still it is permissible to say that in the traditional picture of the nature, activity and fate of the first man, Adam (1 Cor. 15:45), the Yahwist found those features sketched which he saw redrawn in the nature, activity and condition of historical man—the two of them gazing at one another. If one sees in the Yahwist a child of the late period of Solomon or the period immediately following, one may assume that he has drawn in the picture of the primeval man a type of the contemporary man of his own era. It was an era in which the sacral ordering of life underwent secularization, power became despotic and wisdom became rationalism. In a polemic stance he held up to the optimism of that emancipated age the primeval sentence of doom under which the whole of presumptuous human nature stands.[2]

THE CONSEQUENCES OF THE SIN

Sin brought disaster upon man. Let us analyze this disaster briefly. The eyes of the two sinners were indeed opened; they acquired knowledge. But it was not a knowledge which enriched them but one which inhibited and shackled them. The understanding which they had acquired conferred on them no power over the world, its properties and energies; rather this knowledge is synonymous with their feeling of nakedness. The word "naked" has a deeper meaning than the expression "unclothed." It does not mean simply bodily nakedness, it means much the same as miserable, poor, helpless. "Nakedness" is a symbol of shame and privation, impotence and want (cf. Ez. 16:8–13,39; Hos. 2:3). Instead of becoming like God and having power over nature, the two human beings are plunged into helplessness and misery; just the opposite of what they had hoped for. This is why they feel shame in God's presence. In his plan they were to be masters who subdued creation. Now they must acknowledge their guilt before him. Thus there is now something uncanny in his nearness, they cannot endure his gaze and the sound of his words. They try to hide from him from whom no one can escape, and their fear increases when the rustling of the trees tells them that he is present in the garden. The spite which rebelled against God crumbles into fear in the presence of holiness. A close look at the text reinforces the impression of human helplessness. Of the serpent it is said that he is *arum* (wise). According to the promise of the serpent, man could expect to become wise too, but instead he becomes *erom* (naked) and dishonorable. The two human beings experienced in each other's presence that they were naked. An isolation of the one from the other has emerged out of their community in sinning, and the new experience of shame makes them repellent to each other.

This feeling of shame refers to sex and sexual desire only secondarily. In the first place the reciprocal feeling of shame is awakened and fed by the experience of helplessness. Sin has forced its way like an alien power into the life of the sinners; now they are ruled by the power of sin and no longer have mastery over themselves. Man, who should be the master of the world, is no longer even master of himself. As a result of their moral impotence Adam and Eve discover that they are no longer able to cope with the sexual attractiveness of evil. In sexual desire the superior strength of evil takes a frightening form. This does not mean that sexual desire was first awakened by sin or that in itself it is perversion, but that through sin sexual desire was released from its integration in the whole person and became autonomous. Adam and Eve learned that they faced a serious temptation no longer to regard and love one another as persons but to use each other as things. The sexual appetite at work in them drove each of them to seek his own gratification. They were ashamed in one another's presence because they felt impelled not to esteem and love each other as persons but, on the contrary, to use each other

as things affording mutual gratification. The gratification of lust
evolved out of a loving encounter. The relationship uniting them
was no longer determined by personality but by objectivity. In a
profound sense they were exposed to one another. They could, of
course, cover their bodies and restrain their inordinate desire, but
they could not conceal and overcome their helplessness in face of
the desire for one another, now situated in the rule of sin. Before
the sin they wished to conceal nothing in one another's presence
because the relationship between them in its every dimension, even
the sexual, was taken up into the love of God. This expressed itself in mutual trust and esteem and was thus fulfilled in a genuine
dialogue of love. Their innocence in the presence of one another
rested on their innocence before God. But now this security and
openness is something that belongs to the past.

THE JUDGMENT

It is in tune with all this that Adam and Eve, standing before a
demanding and judging God, push the blame off onto one another.
It sounds as though Adam is reproaching God himself when he
says: "The woman whom you gave to be with me, she gave me
fruit of the tree, and I ate." The woman in turn puts the blame
on the serpent. Both seek to cast off responsibility for the sin, but
they do not succeed. Adam and Eve as well as the serpent are
affected by God's sentence of judgment. Moreover, each is pun-
ished by the one whom he has led astray. If one stops at the
literal sense of God's sentence as it is related by the Yahwist, it
can appear that the author intends to proclaim a change in nature;
in the nature of the serpent, in the nature of the woman and in
the nature of the soil. On this the view of Aquinas is instructive:

Some say that animals which are now savage and kill other animals
would have been tame in that state, and not only towards man but
towards other animals too. But this is altogether unreasonable. For
man's sin did not so change the nature of animals that those whose
nature it is now to eat other animals, like lions and hawks, would
then have lived on a vegetable diet.[3]

The Genesis text does not testify to a structural change in the serpent. As we mentioned above, the author is quite probably thinking in terms of an actual serpent, but the narrative has a deeper level: man's relation to God is at stake. According to the author, it is clear that there is a power hostile to God in the world. As we have already noted, he most likely saw evidence of this in the heathen cults in which the serpent is a symbol. Whether these idolatrous rites on their part were in turn contrived by a power in the background hostile to God is yet another question. The Book of Wisdom explains that death has come into the world through the serpent (Wis. 2:24). It seems to see in the serpent a symbol of the devil. Nevertheless the Yahwist himself did not reach such a conclusion and one may not fairly read it into his text.

Accompanying God's curse on the serpent a promise is given. The question is whether one can infer the conquest of the serpent's race from the fact that, as it says in the text, the serpent can only wound the heel of man while his own head is being crushed. At first glance this distinction creates the impression that, whereas the serpent would be destroyed, the race of man would only be wounded. But if one looks more closely, quite another meaning is seen. For even if the serpent only wounds the man's heel, it will inject poison into the wound, and the wound will be fatal. Thus the chief stress must be placed not on the disparity of bodily members but on the type of attack. The serpent can and will snap at the heel of man, but man will crush its head. When man collectively is called the antagonist of the race of the serpent—the demonic powers—this is also an allusion to the weakness of the human race. It is a sinful race. Nevertheless it is at the hands of this weak race that the conquest of the serpent will come. In the text of Genesis a future figure stands out who will have no share in the weakness of the human race. Who this figure is, of course, will only become clear in the New Testament. Since the coming salvation is alluded to in it, God's word of promise has been called a pre-Gospel (*proto-Evangelium*).

As for the sentence on the woman, it must be acknowledged that her nature was not altered by sin either. Even without sin

pregnancy and childbirth would have imposed a strain sufficient
in itself to cause pain in the human organism. What have changed
are the dispositions and resourcefulness of woman. As a result of
the psychic weakness introduced into humanity by sin, she is incapable of perfecting in love what objectively occurs in her and
integrating it into the whole of her personal being. Furthermore,
her relation to her husband has changed in its ethical, not its biological, dimension. As a result of her own desire she is exposed
without the power of resistance to the carnal appetite of her husband. Accordingly, the sexual distinction of man and woman
created by God leads to the oppression of the woman by the man.
Sent by God as man's equal to liberate him from his existential
loneliness, she is degraded to a slave of her husband and his lust.
In this thesis of Genesis one cannot but see a protest against the
oppression of women.

In the sentence on Adam it should also be remarked that the
earth has undergone no change in its laws because of sin; work
is not primarily the result of sin. Even before the sin man had to
till the earth and care for it, and this implies a certain amount of
toil and hardship. But the relation of man to the earth is affected
by sin in a twofold way. First of all, the earth in a mysterious
manner shares in the diminution of human existence introduced by
sin. This mysterious relationship cannot, of course, be represented
conceptually. Its disastrous effect is that man, owing to his selfishness, his lust for power, his arrogance and his greed for wealth,
misuses the earth. Contrary to its original ordination, the earth is
robbed of the ability to offer man all he needs in unimpaired fruit-
fulness. As a result of the corruption of nature through man's guilt,
he must wrest what he can from her, instead of receiving all that
an unalloyed stewardship of nature would have given him. The
fact that man in his exploitation of the earth employs the laws of
nature laid down by God does not justify his violent methods. His
knowledge of nature's laws is precisely what enables him to make
incursions into nature capable of disrupting her entire economy
(e.g., the devastation of vast regions). In conjunction with this it
should also be noted that as a result of the weakening of human
intellectual and moral powers, those energies in man which would
enable everyone to fulfill with creative joy the world-shaping task

incumbent on him are not effectively employed. Man must repeatedly provide himself with an incentive for his task. This becomes apparent when success is denied him and he would prefer to give up. The sentence of death which God imposes, without executing it immediately, hits man the hardest: he must live under sentence of death. His life consumes itself until it expires. God's warning to men, reported by the Yahwist, that as soon as they eat of the tree of the knowledge of good and evil they must die, implies the promise that had they abstained from eating it—namely, in the event that they did not choose to try to regulate their lives autonomously but were ready to acknowledge God as the norm of their lives—they need not have died. Thus, according to the Yahwist the subjection of men to death must be understood as a consequence and an expression of their disobedience. The first men seem to have had the prospect of a biological life continuing without end. Of course, if one examines the matters more closely this idyllic notion becomes somewhat vague. Freedom from death was not to involve an everlasting existence in the manner of life with which we are familiar; but the transition to another existence was not supposed to be fraught with the pain, torment, absurdity and untimeliness which are bound up with death in our experience. In this passage the longing common to the oriental mind for inexhaustible and endless life expresses itself, a longing depicted in numberless literary documents, biblical and non-biblical (cf. the Gilgamesh Epic).

Such a longing is nonetheless unfulfillable. No human effort, however great, can produce eternal life. Man must be aware, and remain aware, of his limits. If he goes beyond them he achieves nothing, but on the contrary destroys himself. The biblical text admits the following variations: if it is difficult for us to remain within the limits of life set down for us, this has its foundations in moral weakness. Death belongs to human nature; the one born of dust is subject to corruption. The human ego, the person, must on the basis of his created being experience death; the forces of life exhaust themselves, yet it is a challenge to us to undergo death obediently and lovingly in dedication to God. The less a man is shackled by sin, pride and egoism, the more he is able to devote himself to God and thus make God's will his own. Had he not sinned, man would, according to the Yahwist, be able to accept without reserve—lovingly and obediently—the event in which the earthly form of his existence is to be transformed. Even so, he would certainly not have been spared the transformation. There is no need to suppose that he would have led an endless life in his earthly form, nor even that he would have been allowed to do so, but he need not have been anxious about his death, nor could he have fallen into death unawares. In particular, he need not have feared being called into God's presence: man engaged in a dialogue of friendship with God would have had no reason to fear him. It is not death itself but the experience of dying in which the difference lies: if man had remained innocent he would have experienced death quite differently. Hence, what would have been spared man if he had not sinned can scarcely be described by the word "death" in the usual sense. The objective transitoriness of human life and of life in general has not been altered by sin, what has changed is the way in which man meets the question of his finitude and transitoriness, ethically and religiously. Nevertheless it must be acknowledged that man could, were he free from sin, accept without reserve in his personal fulfillment whatever his nature demanded of him.

For a better understanding of this interpretation of the consequences of sin, it will be helpful if we pursue briefly the question of what is meant by the world in which man lives. This question cannot be answered simply. We know from long endeavor to grasp the correct meaning of human understanding that the world in which we live consists of two components; that which is objectively given and our encounter with it, the extant on the one hand and our own consciousness on the other. We cannot know or conceive the world as it is in itself. What we encounter is always only the world known by us and at the same time determined by our knowing. For all their profound differences, Kant and Aquinas agree that only the known world is our world. These reflections show us that the world cannot simply be understood objectively as that which exists in itself; rather it must be understood as that which comes to pass on the basis of our own effort. The world is the product of that which is given to us and our own construction. In a simple everyday experience we see this thesis confirmed. Friendship or love confers on man a perspective in which he sees this world in a new way; in such cases he is experiencing the world in its relation to another person. Thus the world of his experience becomes something different for him. The lover uncovers new meanings and new depths in the world.

From this view of the world we gain access to an understanding of the Yahwist. He does not teach that the world of the first man is to be distinguished structurally from his own. It was the same world as ours; if there is a difference, it lies in human experience and practical knowledge. Scripture throws light on one such difference in experience and life. Men could have and should have made the things of the world their own with a different authority and power, with a deeper and more intense capacity for experience, than they actually have. The difference in the world meant by our narrative is a difference in relation to the state of human consciousness. According to the Bible the condition of human consciousness has been altered through sin. It is determined by guilt, and this is fundamental. Through guilt it has, in the conviction of the biblical writer, lost its full power. The sin, since it represents a break between God and man, has introduced into man a break in himself; having become guilty, he can only exist as a broken man. And thus the healing power of love has become weakened.

THE TEACHING OF THE CHURCH

On the basis of the biblical account of the first sin the Church, in the course of the historical development of dogma, has made fundamental declarations of its faith. These have been interpreted by theology in a variety of ways. The declarations of faith made by the Church on the original condition of man and the consequences of the first sin are important for a complete understanding of Christianity, for from these follow the Church's pronouncements on original sin. The subject of original sin, along with those of the first sin and personal sin, forms the dark background for understanding the saving person and activity of Jesus Christ. One should

not, of course, overlook the fact that the statements of the magisterium, like those of the Old and New Testaments, are very sober
and economical. The councils of Carthage (418), Orange II
(529), and especially Trent (1545-1563), and the decree of the
Biblical Commission of 1909 name as special gifts of the original
state freedom from sin (innocence and immortality), integrity,
complete freedom of the will, justice, grace and holiness (DS 222,
239, 242, 370; 371, 383, 389, 621, 1511f., 1521, 3525). Against
Michael de Bay (DS 1901-1980) and the Synod of Pistoia (DS
2616) it was stressed that these gifts do not belong to man's created nature but are free gifts from God.

NATURAL AND SUPERNATURAL

To understand the teaching of the Church in this matter it is first
of all necessary to discuss a concept which has played an important
role in theology and about which there has been considerable historical and systematic inquiry, but which even to this day is not
completely clear: the concept of the "supernatural." Formally the
supernatural is that which is superior to the natural. The supernatural, then, is not the transcendent or mysterious or occult, and
the natural the normal or ordinary. The difficulty in understanding
the natural and supernatural lies in the fact that we cannot with
certainty obtain an adequate concept of the basis of comparison:
the natural. If we try on the basis of experience to describe nature,
this procedure viewed theologically suffers from the fact that we
cannot say with complete certainty how far the "natural" world we
encounter in our experience is already under the influence of the
supernatural. There has never been a state of pure nature *(natura
pura)* in reality, for from the beginning God invited creation into
the movement towards a supernatural destiny. Thus it is quite
understandable that the problem of natural order or natural law has
at different times met with different answers. With this qualification
in mind we can say that theology is accustomed to designate with
the term "natural" what pertains to the essence of a thing or a man,
what evolves out of that essence and what contributes to the perfection of that essence. In this definition the Aristotelian concept of

essence in distinction to the biblical concept of existence—the Aristotelian metaphysics of being in distinction to the biblical metaphysics of the person—plays a positive role. For Greek philosophy the important thing was to account for the essence. Hence in the history of theology the concept of the "supernatural" in distinction to the "natural" was developed with a special thoroughness in that age in which Aristotle played a large role in theology. In this sense everything is supernatural which surpasses the natural essence and its possibilities. Employing the usual theological terms, the supernatural, then, is that which is benevolently added to nature by God as a free gift to which nature has no title. Such a definition of the supernatural seems at first glance to be satisfactory. In truth, however, it suffers from a conceptual fuzziness, for we can never adequately define the natural essence of things and the world. We can arrive at the essence only by reasoning *a posteriori* from experiential functions to their essential foundation according to the principle: *agere sequitur esse*. But in the sciences our knowledge (experiential) is continually increasing.

In any case this formal distinction exists only between the concepts nature and supernature: what must be conceptually distinguished never was, nor is actually, separated. For from the beginning God intended an order of supernatural happiness. To confirm this we need only reflect upon the Christocentric character of the divine project of the universe.

This remark already takes us beyond the mere formal-conceptual distinction to a determination of the content of the supernatural. The supernatural in its final form consists in the dialogue made possible by Christ, a dialogue of the creature—man—with God, who will then appear unveiled. Everything which leads up to this belongs to the dimension of the supernatural. The material world itself is taken up into this dimension. From the standpoint of content one can proceed to an understanding of the supernatural and the natural by starting with the supernatural; that is, with the biblical teaching of man's saved existence, or the existence of man in Christ. In analyzing this existence one can eliminate everything that is essential for salvation or existence in Jesus Christ. What remains after eliminating all the factors pertaining to salvation is nature. The supernatural, then, is the criterion for the definition of nature. Once again this does not, of course, yield an absolutely certain result. Only one thing may be said with certainty: even the man not united to Christ, even the "ungraced" man, is a man. He does not lose his human nature by forfeiting the element of grace, which belongs to "being in Christ."

The question of the relation of the supernatural to the natural is a source of much controversy today. In no case can the supernatural be understood as alien to the natural. The natural is planned and willed by God as the bearer of the supernatural, the grace of salvation. Grace does not destroy nature, but presupposes it, elevates it and perfects it. This is easy to understand. The natural, as a result of its origin in God, is open to God. God can influence his creatures without destroying them because of the complete and substantial dependence of every individual creature on him. It is precisely the influence of God, *creatio continua,* which preserves the creature in its created existence. His supernatural influence is an invitation to the creature to enter into his personal triune life. Moreover, the creature is called and prepared for this precisely as a creature so that he can hear and accept the call. This is, of course, always a call away from human autonomy and pride into love, and therefore a call to sacrifice and self-surrender. The highest form of this sacrifice and self-surrender was the death on the cross of Jesus Christ, which reached its fulfillment in his glorified life (cf. Christology).

Theology asks whether nature, which is open to God, has a merely passive receptivity for the supernatural, or whether it positively reaches out to this call. If it has only the first, then the supernatural appears to a certain degree to be a foreign invasion of the natural. If only the second holds true, then the supernatural no longer appears to be a pure gift. In answering this question one should not proceed with an abstract conceptual method, but in a concrete and realistic manner. The second alternative would mean that man in his relation to God is so formed that he is positively adapted to the vision of God—to dialogue with God. He cannot, of course, realize this goal with his own resources. Thus the supernatural in the strict sense would consist in the fact that God calls man to something which corresponds to man's essence but which he could never reach through the unfolding of his merely natural powers. This is possibly also the opinion of Thomas Aquinas, though he has been interpreted differently.

A distinction has been made between the strictly (substantial) supernatural and the accidental supernatural (preternatural). This distinction arose out of the disputes with Protestantism, Baianism and Jansenism. By the strictly supernatural one means the supernatural order, participation in the triune personal life of God, which is in no way attainable by natural powers; by the preternatural, that which occurs in a "supernatural" manner, the restoration of natural order by miraculous means is meant; e.g., a miraculous cure of a sick man.

THE ORIGINAL STATE AND ITS LOSS

As the Church's doctrinal declarations show, it is a Catholic article of faith that God intended holiness and righteousness for the first human beings but that they incurred God's judgment and displeasure through sin. The holiness and righteousness contemplated by God was a pure gift. One may find an allusion to the graciousness of God's behavior in the assertion of the Yahwist that God lived in familiar intercourse with men. What is more important, looking forward from the Old Testament to the New, we can say that Jesus Christ has re-established what the first men gave up, and indeed has far surpassed it. Thus, from the new order and the new creation that have come through Christ one can infer that which should have belonged to the first men but which they lost through sin.

It has been traditional in Catholic theology to suppose that the first human beings possessed, besides righteousness and holiness in a genuine partnership with God, the so-called preternatural gifts *(justitia originalis* in the narrower sense), gifts of integrity, freedom from suffering and death, from inordinate appetites and ignorance. In the past these gifts have been described extravagantly in theology, but the gradual triumph of the concept of evolution has now forced us to come to grips with the question of whether Adam actually was a superior man intellectually or culturally. It must be conceded that no special cultural or intellectual elevation was required for the favor bestowed on the first man. Moreover the favor surpasses, because it is supernatural, the level of consciousness of even the most highly developed man. It corresponds with the Old Testament description of the formation and origin of the first man, and it is not incompatible with the New Testament, to see the so-called preternatural gifts as rooted in the original holiness and righteousness which God had conceived and intended for man and in the activity which would have flowed from it. If man had not rejected God, the holiness and righteousness in him would have taken effect in his life in such a way that his relation to himself, his fellow men and his whole material environment would have been without discord. But this is not the reality of the matter. As a result of sin the grace granted to man by God can take effect only in a fragmented way. It will have its full effect only in the resurrection of the dead at the second coming of Jesus Christ. The risen Christ is the model of how union with God can exhibit itself in a man who belongs entirely to God.

The individual gifts need to be discussed in more detail. Concerning death the essential things have already been said. Death belongs to the nature of man. But as a result of sin it has the added character of punishment; that is to say, what belongs to the nature of man, his transitoriness, is now bound up with anxiety, pain and glaring absurdity. As for the freedom from suffering and pain which in the past theology ascribed to the first men, we know that suffering and pain imply a modification in our biological and intellectual life, and that they inhibit further development. In a certain sense of course pain is indispensable for organic life, because it gives warning of dangerous disorders which would otherwise remain hidden and pursue their destructive work unhindered. But it is an obstructive modification of the organism which leads to the sensation of pain, and the degree of pain depends on the strength of the sensation. According to the Yahwist, man has to experience pain in a new way as a result of his guilt: its intensity is influenced by the degree of his love of God. Scripture declares that if a man is filled with love of God—if he lives, so to speak, instinctively in that love—then pain cannot pierce him to such a degree that he is overcome by it. The experience of love in everyday life may serve as an example. A lover may experience pain, may be in mental and bodily torment, but if with his whole being he is captivated by a human thou, he carries in himself a joy which is not touched by his suffering. He is, as it were, absorbed by his love to the exclusion of everything else. The paradisal world may not be represented as a state of such enchantment that it spared man all pain. According to Thomas Aquinas the garden of Eden even had thorns and thistles.[4] Significantly, however, Thomas adds that these were not intended for men. Man, having incurred guilt, selfishly misuses and exploits the material world put at his disposal by God. This, of course, has repercussions on the condition of the world, which in turn has an effect on human life. Thus a change takes place in men which leads indirectly to disorders in the material realm, and these again have repercussions on men.

These reflections show that the various theories of natural science regarding prehistory are not touched by the doctrine of the original state of man. Scripture is not a textbook of the cultural history of mankind, but deals with the relation of man to God for salvation or disaster. To represent this, of course, the writer draws his means of expression from the reservoir of his own knowledge of cultural history.

Another point is the question whether primeval man was equipped with extraordinary knowledge. Scripture says nothing about this; it only assures us that man was able to move with instinctive certainty, even though by no means without danger, amid the forces of nature and the animal world. Genesis is not opposed to the view that the first man lived in an intellectual twilight. He did, of course—indeed one can probably say that had he been suddenly transported into a scientific and technical world like our own he would have become frantic. He knew little, he understood almost nothing. However, what he did know, he knew by its ultimate principle. Aristotle describes man as a rational animal; that is, a being who seeks the ground of things and strives to live according to it. This is realized in primeval man. His relation to God enabled him to strive for and to discover, even if only obscurely, the transcendent ground of being. It is this power which, according to Scripture, was weakened by sin.

A word remains to be said about the problem of freedom from concupiscence—or rather, from disordered concupiscence (inordinate appetite). Appetite can be understood in two stages. The first signifies the faculty of sentient desire which arises spontaneously and automatically, preceding deliberation and the free decision of the will. Even after this it can persevere in a direction contrary to the decision of the will and thus is able to hinder freedom and deliberation. Such a tendency is automatically given with the corporeal-spiritual nature of man as created by God and therefore is not evil in itself. But insofar as the desire tends to a good whose affirmation would be disorderly and therefore sinful, concupiscence presents a temptation to evil. This is the second stage, from which the first men were supposed to be free.

What follows is introduced to provide a more accurate explanation of concupiscence. Under the influence of Greek philosophy concupiscence was understood simply as the opposition of sentient desire to the judgment of reason, an interpretation based on the opposition of body and mind, sensuality and reason. This tension is characteristic of ancient Greek thought. But for biblical revelation the idea that evil has its roots in the sphere of the senses is not entirely correct. According to Scripture the sinfulness of man is rooted not in a metaphysical dualism but in a dualism of salvation history. The inclination to sin, according to Paul, comes from the whole human ego. Inordinate appetite consists in the fact that man has an inclination to reject God and to make himself independent. It lies in a religious ethical dualism between self-exaltation and dedication to God. Accordingly, freedom from inordinate appetite means, with respect to its structure, the integration of all human powers into a life devoted to God. With respect to its material content it means freedom from manifold perversion; namely, from the temptation to rebel against God and shut oneself up in egoism against one's fellow man, from the inclination to violate the world in which man necessarily lives, and finally from the opposition in man of the sentient and intellectual spheres. It should be acknowledged that this last element—repeatedly and too exclusively emphasized—has been recognized as belonging to freedom from concupiscence through the assistance which Greek philosophy provided for the interpretation of revelation. Also, it must be admitted that this gift is only hinted at in Genesis; in the statement that the two human beings were naked and were not ashamed. How this statement is to be understood was explained earlier. We find another scriptural reference to it in the epistles of Paul. According to Paul inordinate appetite is closely related to sin. Before sin and without sin it does not exist. In reference to these texts the Council of Trent declared that disordered appetite arises from sin and leads to sin. This does not mean that one may represent the freedom from disordered stirrings which has been attributed to the first man by dogmatic theology as a life of weak and crippled natural powers. The first men had a human capacity for enjoyment, understanding and love, but they lived in the totality of their personal being.

THE DURATION OF THE ORIGINAL STATE

An important question remains. There has been considerable reflection in theology upon whether the first human beings were called immediately by God to a life in grace, or whether this was only to be theirs after a trial; indeed, whether the life of familiar intercourse with God actually took place or only lay in God's intention. The acceptance of a trial is not irreconcilable with the fact that God planned and carried out the creation of the entire universe for the sake of the absolute happiness to come. Probably the best answer one can give to this last question is that Scripture has given us no information on the subject. However, it is reasonable to assume that the first men turned towards God at that moment in which they could reflect on themselves and God. Thus, at that moment at which in a suitably developed organism consciousness emerged, and man recognized himself as a creature and as the representative of the whole of creation, he turned towards God. At that moment men experienced themselves as the measure of things. And indeed they were not completely deceived in this. For there is a sense in which man is the measure of all things, as God intended him to be. Nonetheless, at that same moment men probably rejected the idea that they themselves have a measure—that God is their measure. If this thesis is correct, then the grace of the original state was never objectively realized; or, better, the integrity of the original state was never objectively realized. The statement of the Council of Trent on the "loss" of the grace of the original state cannot be cited as an objection. For this question did not lie before the council. Moreover, even the term "loss" still makes sense if the first men did not accept the gift of happiness destined for them by God.

The observation that men did not incur a radical loss of salvation is important. God did not omit from his saving concern the men who had become sinful. To be sure, God does not grant a return to what had been forfeited, for history cannot be reversed, but he does grant a new beginning. God gave with his judgment the promise of a future salvation. Thus, even after they had become sinners, men were never obliged to live without grace. God's promise remained with them constantly.

The question of the age of the human race is excluded from our discussion. Scripture gives no information about it, and hence theology is not qualified to treat the subject. If today an extremely great age is frequently estimated by natural science, there is no reason for theology to object. Statements on man lying within its domain are not endangered.

Notes

[1] Trilling, *Den Staub Bist Du,* pp. 95f.
[2] *Adam,* p. 18.
[3] *ST,* I, q. 96, a. 1, ad 2.
[4] *ST,* I, q. 69, a. 2, ad 2; II, q. 64, a. 2.

‹ 11

Original Sin

We now turn to a problem of considerable importance for the understanding of Christianity, the question of original sin. The first men were to receive the grace which God had destined for them as representatives of their descendants, the whole of mankind: they were also to lose it as the representatives of the whole of mankind. This is what we mean when we say that the grace was to be inherited grace, the sin inherited sin. Thus the question arises of the fact and the essence of inherited—that is, original—sin.

THE MEANING OF THE EXPRESSION

The doctrine of original sin, as Pius XII said, belongs to the indispensable content of the Christian faith; even if it is not, as Schopenhauer thought, the heart and center of Christianity, it is one of the foundation stones. The fact that even today there is no theological consensus with regard to the essence of original sin presents a considerable problem for the discussion of questions connected with it. The understanding of original sin has developed gradually in the Church. In theology today the problem is discussed with renewed liveliness and vigor in connection with the concept of evolution. Above all, the question of the essence of original sin and its association with the first human being has become a controversial issue.

172

Before dealing with the sin itself the meaning of the word "sin" in the compound "original sin" must be clarified. The word sin in this expression is to be understood in an analogous sense. In the ordinary use of language one understands by sin a freely willed transgression of a command of God for which the transgressor himself is responsible, and in this sense what we mean by the expression original sin is not a sin: one could therefore, in the everyday way of speaking, deny original sin if this did not provoke the misunderstanding that it is not a sin in any sense. Original sin is to be understood as a condition placed before every personal decision. If we call original sin a sin, and indeed in an analogous sense, we mean that original sin is at once similar and dissimilar to sin in ordinary linguistic usage. Here, as in the rest of theology, a stronger accent should be placed on the factor of dissimilarity than on that of similarity. The similarity is qualified by an even greater dissimilarity. This means that original sin is a mystery; it evades our full comprehension. The problem lies in the chiaroscuro of faith. Hence it is understandable that, like the self-disclosure of God which took place in Christ, it is also a source of scandal.

THE FACT OF THE ORIGINAL SIN

Scripture

We shall deal first of all with the scriptural foundation for the Church's doctrine of original sin and its development in theology. This will be followed by a presentation of the Church's doctrine itself. In the Old Testament the wisdom narrative of the Yahwist was never interpreted in the sense we have given it: that the human condition is grounded in the sin of the first man. In particular, an inner connection between the general state of sinfulness and the first sin was never stressed. The general state of sinfulness was presented simply as a fact of experience (Gen. 6:5; 8:21; Job 4:17; 14:4; 25:4; 1 Kgs. 8:46; Is. 64:5; Sir. 8:5; 17:20; Prov. 20:9; Pss. 130:3; 143:2). That death is a result of the sin in paradise is expressed for the first time in Sirach 25:23 and Wisdom 2:8f.—that is, in the Hellenistic literature. In the Old Testament no doctrine of original sin is found. Nevertheless the Old Testament does offer a few starting points for the later development: the beginning of sin with Adam, the influence of bad example, the universality of sin, the solidarity of men with one another.

In the New Testament we encounter a similar situation. We find for the first time in Paul's Epistle to the Romans a text which can serve as the foundation for the idea of original sin developed later. The text reads (Rom. 5:8-21):

But Christ died for us while we were yet sinners, and that is God's own proof of his love towards us. And so, since we have now been justified by Christ's sacrificial death, we shall all the more certainly be saved through him from final retribution. For if, when we were God's enemies, we were reconciled to him through the death of his Son, much more, now that we are reconciled, shall we be saved by his life. But that is not all: we also exult in God through our Lord Jesus, through whom we have now been granted reconciliation. Mark what follows. It was through one man that sin entered the world, and through sin death, and thus death pervaded the whole human race, in as much as all men have sinned. For sin was already in the world before there was law, though in the absence of law no reckoning is kept of sin. But death held sway from Adam to Moses, even over those who had not sinned as Adam did, by disobeying a direct command—and Adam foreshadows the Man who was to come. But God's act of grace is out of all proportion to Adam's wrongdoing. For if the wrongdoing of that one man brought death upon so many, its effect is vastly exceeded by the grace of God and the gift that came to so many by the grace of the one man, Jesus Christ. And again, the gift of God is not to be compared in its effect with that one man's sin; for the judicial act, following upon the one offence, issued in a verdict of condemnation, but the act of grace, following upon so many misdeeds, issued in a verdict of acquittal. For if by the wrongdoing of that one man death established its reign, through a single sinner, much more shall those who receive in far greater measure God's grace, and his gift of righteousness, live and reign through the one man, Jesus Christ. It follows, then, that as the issue of one misdeed was condemnation for all men, so the issue of one just act is acquittal and life for all men. For as through the disobedience of the one man the many were made sinners, so through the obedience of the one man the many will be made righteous. Law intruded into this process to multiply law-breaking. But where sin was thus multiplied, grace immeasurably exceeded it, in order that, as sin established its reign by way of death, so God's grace might establish its reign in righteousness, and issue in eternal life through Jesus Christ our Lord.

This text shows that at the center of Pauline thought there stands not sin, but salvation through Jesus Christ. The reference to sin is so to speak embedded in gratitude for salvation. Paul speaks of sin as a dark background for the glory of God's radiance. His mention of sin is inspired by the exultation and gratitude of one whom God has snatched from the abyss of sin, and who now looks back at the horror from which he has escaped. Here perhaps one should recall the etiological method which must be taken into consideration when interpreting primeval history in the Bible (Gen. 1–11). Set free to preserve freedom, living in Christ, saved from the forces of destruction, filled with the depth and height of divine things and impelled by the Holy Spirit, Paul asks in retrospect how in spite of God's goodness the disastrous situation before Christ could have come about. Romans 5 is an explanation undertaken in the spirit of his faith in Christ. The more luminous the epoch introduced by Christ seems to the apostle, all the darker must the preceding period appear to him in the light of salvation history. How completely he is filled with the experience of faith in the saving action of Christ is probably best expressed in chapter 8 of Romans (verses 34f.). Thus, the point of departure of the apostle is his experience of Christ. What he says about the sin of Adam and its enduring effect is an attempt to define the condition of man without Christ.

Permit us to quote the comprehensive interpretation of the passage in Romans which Otto Kuss gives on the basis of a very detailed exegesis:

As soon as man reflects on his existence, he sees himself confronted with the realities of sin and death. He will try to understand these over and above all the other disturbing facts of life. And the believer is extremely interested in learning what the gospel has to say to him, immediately or mediately, precisely on this subject. Paul integrates the realities of sin and death into his theological view of life, which is determined by the all-embracing polarity: "the disaster-domain (*Unheilsbereich*) of Adam—the salvation-domain (*Heilsbereich*) of Christ." He must of necessity—in conjunction with the Old Testament and contemporary reflections—place death and sin within the disaster-domain of Adam. Indeed, sin and death correctly and properly characterize the domain of Adam as disastrous. The text of Romans 5:12 traces the death of all men back to Adam in order to be able to derive life—the real, eternal life destined for all men—much more manifestly from Christ. The text of Romans 5:19—at least according to the formulation going beyond that of v.12—speaks not only of the fact that all men have been subject to the regime of the power of death through Adam, but also that they all "became sinful." If an isolated consideration of v.19a, perhaps, still leaves a "way out," a look at v.19b (according to which Christ is clearly designated as the absolute and sole cause of the "righteousness" of the many) shows that the fundamental sinfulness of the many meant here goes back to Adam alone. In a third text, 1 Cor. 15:21,22, which comes into consideration here, it is clear that there is discussion only of inherited death, not inherited sin: "For since it was a man who brought death into the world, a man also brought resurrection of the dead. For as in Adam all men die, so in Christ all will be brought to life." According to v.21 the physical death of man is to be traced back to Adam as the cause. In v.22 the comprehension of death intended here appears to broaden. It might possibly mean the total disaster striking all men in Adam without exception. This "death" is on the same comprehensive scale as the salvation coming through Christ which signifies resurrection and life. . . .

If looking back one surveys the whole once more, a number of important reasons appear to urge the thesis that Paul in a decisive place has gone beyond the view prevailing at his time of the origin and nature of man's radically doomed situation. Paul speaks of "original sin," and he offers an adequate and solid foundation for the doctrine of original sin of a later age. An examination of the pertinent texts of the Old Testament, Jewish apocrypha—especially apocalyptic—rabbinical teaching and Philonic religious philosophy shows that here, in general, one can probably speak of more or less clear premises for a doctrine of "original sin," but that the decisive conclusion was nowhere clearly and unmistakably drawn. The hopelessness of an isolated preaching of original sin would have been too hard to bear for an age which possessed no means to free itself from the burden. Only intimations of the desperate situation emerge here and there. Paul is the first to be able look more closely into the darkness, because Paul believes and knows that the light has already conquered. He sees God, man and the world in the perspective of salvation become a fact in Jesus. He is able to treat the great religious question of his time unreservedly and effectively, because he approaches the needs of his time and of every time from above, not from below. When he attained faith in Jesus Christ, he perceived at the same time the true countenance of the world abandoned by God. From the brightness of this knowledge he looked back and discovered only more darkness where up to now it had seemed to him to be so bright. From here on it becomes quite clear: grace is the central concept of the Pauline theology of sin, and the whole problematic of sin of the major Pauline epistle merely represents the background for the doctrine of salvation. Where God stakes everything in order to save man the corruption must be colossal. Only the comprehensive knowledge of what has taken place through Jesus Christ gives the apostle the ability and the courage to fix his gaze on the pre-Christian condition of man: faith in salvation become a reality through Jesus Christ is the fountainhead of the Pauline "doctrine" of "original sin." The apostle is not interested in speculation on the difficult questions which appear if one reflects further on details, nor in the great effort and subtlety employed by later theology. This was reserved for the development of the doctrine. In the doctrine of original sin developed by Augustine from his special situation in the history of dogma—supported, of course, by his erroneous understanding of Romans 5:12d (*in quo*—in Adam)— the guilt-character of the sin transmitted to all men by Adam is quite unmistakably brought into the forefront for the first time . . . By this means the way is opened in the future for the momentous fixing of an exegesis possible for Romans 5:12d (even after the rejection of the Augustinian interpretation) but for Romans 5:19 quite obvious.[1]

This interpretation presupposes Christ's saving work as its foundation. Even one who sees no formal evidence for original sin in verse 19 must admit that the text points in the direction of the Church's later doctrine, and for this it offers an adequate starting point. Even if verse 19 considered purely philologically is open to the hypothesis that the topic of discussion is personal sin intro-

duced and occasioned by the sin of Adam, still the official interpretation of the Church guarantees the truth of the other possible
interpretation: namely, that every man through his entrance into
human society becomes subject to the power of sin and is sinful.
The apostle Paul also had in mind the sinfulness belonging to all
men by nature owing to Adam's fall when he said: "In our natural
condition we, like the rest, lay under the dreadful judgment of
God" (Eph. 2:3). In the Pauline epistles the way in which the sinfulness of individual men is linked to the sin of Adam is an open
question. Thus we reach the conclusion that while the Epistle to the
Romans, like the rest of the Pauline writings, presents no formally
developed doctrine of original sin such as was stated by the Council of Trent, the doctrine of original sin could evolve over the
course of the centuries from the Pauline theology to the formulation of Trent without any violence to the scriptural text. The doctrine of St. Paul is the product of meditation on the situation of
men before Jesus Christ. Jesus himself did not teach that because
of Adam's sin all men were in a condition of sinfulness.

The Development of the Scriptural Teaching
in Post-Apostolic Teaching

At first the Pauline theology of original sin was not developed
further in post-apostolic theology. However, in the Apologists we
encounter the notion of an hereditary corruption and the bad example of Adam. Irenaeus understands the corruption afflicting
mankind since the first sin as guilt: in Adam the whole of mankind
rebelled against God. Tertullian speaks of a *primordiale delictum*.
Augustine was by far the most influential in the development of the
doctrine of original sin in the direction of the Church's later teaching. In his struggle against the Pelagians he declared that as a result
of the first sin all men are a *massa damnata* on which the wrath of
God rests. Augustine placed a strong accent on concupiscence,
without completely identifying it with original sin. As evidence for
his thesis of original sin he points to the baptism of infants, which
he noted had been practised since apostolic times. He employs in
addition the Epistle to the Romans, especially 5:12, which (follow-

ing the sense of the Latin text with the expression *in quo),* he considers direct and immediate proof of original sin. Nevertheless Augustine placed substantially greater weight on the reflection that there must be an original sin because Christ has come to save all men without exception. That is, the whole of mankind is in need of salvation. For this we have the clear testimony of Scripture. Starting with the universal testimony of Scripture, Augustine asks why men are in need of salvation, from what must they be saved: obviously from sin.[2] Men, and indeed each man individually, are separated from God so long as they are not reconciled to God through Christ. In this view the point of departure for the theology of sin is no longer reflection on the condition of "Adam" before sin and the consequences of sin for Adam. Here the foundation of the thesis of original sin is simply the fact of the universal need for salvation. Thus Augustine advocates the doctrine of original sin not for its own sake, but rather because he sees in it the explanation of a more profound and universal truth of Scripture, namely, the necessity of salvation. Even little children can come to God only through Jesus Christ; so long as they are not united to Jesus Christ, an obstacle stands in the way of their union with God. What should this obstacle be if not original sin, since there can be no question of personal sin? Augustine, then, does not begin with original sin and then go on to prove the sinfulness of all men. Rather, he begins with the universal necessity of salvation. That Adam's sin could have such a far-reaching effect he sees in both the position of Adam as the representative of mankind and in the solidarity of the human race.

In the theology of the Greek Fathers the accent falls on the freedom and responsibility of the individual. In the sin of Adam, nonetheless, they saw the reason for the calamitous state of the world and the wretched condition of men. Anselm should be mentioned in connection with the Augustinian-Latin way of thinking, insofar as he proposed a thesis which is important for the whole of later theology: that the essence of original sin is to be seen in the lack of the righteousness which man should have and the corruption of human nature which that lack or privation occasions. Abelard denied the transmission of Adam's guilt to all men and like Chrysostom only acknowledged an inherited punishment. On the other hand, Anselm's thought was further developed by the scholastic theology, Franciscan as well as Dominican, of the thirteenth century. Bonaventure, like Thomas Aquinas, distinguished between the formal and the material element of original sin. He sees the first in the loss of *justitia originalis,* the second in our disordered concupiscence. However, he sees these elements primarily as a unity. Thomas Aquinas goes beyond this when he states that the first sin involves each man in its guilt because the one who committed the first sin is the protofather of all men. John Duns Scotus sees the formal element of original sin in a simple lack, the absence of original justice, whereas the material element consists in the obligation to possess original justice. According to Scotus there can be no question of a corruption of nature. In the Nominalist theology of the fourteenth and fifteenth centuries original sin was understood simply as the imputation of the first sin to all men by a positive act of God.

Luther returned to Augustine but went beyond his view by completely identifying original sin and concupiscence. Calvin agreed basically with Luther. On the whole, Reformation theology placed the greatest emphasis on the thesis of the total corruption of man. In the Protestant theology of the Enlightenment (e.g., Theodore Lessing) the doctrine of original sin was seen simply as a reference to the original barbaric state of mankind and the enduring power of the sensual even now. Alongside Lutheran orthodoxy, there is in contemporary Protestant theology a widespread abandonment of the traditional doctrine of original sin based on the difficulty of explaining the character of guilt in it. Karl Barth, for example, characterizes the traditional doctrine of original sin as a contradiction in itself. By "original sin" he understands the sinful act of each individual man for which the individual is most responsible.

The Development of the Church's Doctrine:
The Council of Trent

The Catholic doctrine of original sin is a particularly instructive example of the development of scriptural beginnings into a dogma of the Catholic Church. An official Church declaration on original sin was made for the first time by the Council of Carthage in the year 418. This was the first council to deal with the expression *vitium originale,* although it did not invent it. The term had a precursor in the vocabulary of Tertullian, and the expression *peccatum originale* in particular had been used by Augustine for a long period before the council—that is, since the year 397. Augustine, like all the theologians after him and the Church in its teaching, never understood the sin of Adam by the expression *vitium originale;* it always meant the sin contracted by Adam's descendants.

The declaration of the Council of Carthage was directed against the British monk Pelagius and his disciple Caelestius. At the beginning of the fifth century, Pelagius tried to check the moral laxity which had made inroads in the Church owing to the extensive secularization since Constantine by stressing the capacity for good residing in the human will. His disciple Caelestius systematized the ideas of his teacher, first in Rome and then in North Africa. According to Pelagius sin is simply a personal decision of the individual; a sin inherited on the basis of a familial relationship with Adam cannot be admitted. Adam's sin exercises a corrupting effect on man only as a bad example: man, with his concupiscence and his mortality, nevertheless stands on the same level as Adam before his sin. Even if he had not sinned, Adam would have died. Children at birth are therefore in the same state as Adam before his sin. Owing to his freedom, man is able and obliged to do good.

Against this thesis the Council of Carthage, attended by two hundred North African bishops (DS 222f.), defended the thesis of original sin as a real offense by citing the Church's practice of infant baptism—to the considerable embarrassment of the Pelagians. Appeal was also made at the council to Romans 5:12 and chapters 2 and 3 of Genesis. Since the Latin text of the Epistle to the Romans was the one used, the discussion turned on the Latin translation *in quo*—that is, the relative not the causal sense. As for the baptism of infants, it is undeniable that it goes back to an earlier period, but here the Church was in advance of theological interpretation, for up to that time there had been no adequate theological foundation for the Church's practice. The principal text of the Council of Carthage is located in Canon 2 (DS 223). Since the text of this canon, essentially unaltered, was taken over almost literally by Canon 4 of the Council of Trent, we need not quote it separately at this point.

It is significant that the Council of Carthage stated that there is in man an original sin, a sin which comes from Adam. But the method of transmission and the essence of original sin were not more precisely defined by the council. Pope Zosimus confirmed Canons 3, 4 and 5 of the council's decisions and they were later admitted into what is called the Indiculus. In citing the ancient practice of infant baptism, the council appealed to the words in the baptismal formula: *in remissionen peccatorum*. Since infants cannot commit personal sins, the sin which is washed away in baptism can only be original sin. In citing Romans 5:12 the council appealed once again to the traditional interpretation of this text— a real tradition even if the Latin translation does not correspond to the wording of the Greek text.

The next council which concerned itself with the question of original sin was the Second Council of Orange in the year 529 (DS 371–392; especially 371f.,378,383). The Second Canon (DS 372) of this council, in which the decisive statement on original sin is located, has with unimportant omissions been taken over by the Second Canon of the Council of Trent, so that it is also unnecessary to quote it separately here. The literal wording of the First Canon (DS 371), however, should be quoted.

If anyone says that it was not the whole man, that is, both body and soul, that was "changed for the worse" through the offense of Adam's sin, but believes that the freedom of the soul remained untouched and that only the body was made subject to corruption, he is deceived by the error of Pelagius and contradicts the words of Scripture: "The soul that sinneth, the same shall die" (Ezechiel 18:20); and: "Do you not know that to whom you offer yourselves as slaves for obedience, to him whom you obey you are the slaves?" (Rom. 6:16): and: "By whatever a man is overcome, of that he also becomes the slave" (see 2 Pet. 2:19).

This text contains no inconsiderable problematic. The question is what is meant by the expression that the whole man, body and soul, has been changed for the worse, and that the freedom of man, the freedom of the soul, has not remained uninjured. To what extent has freedom been impaired? To answer this question one must study carefully Canon 8 (DS 378) and Canon 13 (DS 383) of this same council. According to both these canons the will, wounded by original sin, has suffered a diminution of its freedom. It has been weakened and is inclined towards evil. Thus, though the wound is grave, freedom is not destroyed. For that time this was a definite innovation. It contradicted the tradition dating from Augustine and spread by Prosper of Aquitaine according to which the will has been rendered impotent as the consequence of sin: it has become a slave of sin, so that one can only speak of a *servum arbitrium*. Neither Augustine nor Prosper of Aquitaine, who was a faithful echo of Augustine, meant to imply, by the thesis of the loss of free will, that metaphysical-psychological freedom was destroyed: this, as Augustine expressly emphasized, remains intact. However, man could no longer employ his free will in a meaningful way—that is, for the realization of good. What, then, is it useful for? What kind of freedom is it in which the will no longer has the power to do what is right? It must in fact be admitted that so far as a meaningful or, more accurately, a salvific use of freedom is concerned, free will has vanished. This thesis seems to be completely in harmony with Scripture, and especially with Paul's line of thought. In Paul's view freedom is a good belonging to salvation. It is re-established only through Jesus Christ, by whom men were restored to true freedom. Such a formulation implies, of course, that men had some freedom before Christ's saving action. However, it was not the freedom to do what is right but only a freedom to sin, a destructive liberty. Considered in this way, the will was enslaved by sin.

The decrees of the Second Council of Orange were unknown to the Middle Ages: they were first discovered and used by the theology of the post-Reformation period.

The Council of Trent furnishes the normative text for the Catholic doctrine of original sin. Owing to the importance of the subject, it is necessary to give the text itself DS 1510–1515):

Our Catholic faith, without which it is impossible to please God (see Heb. 11,6), must remain in its purity, sound, unshaken, and free from errors. The Christian people must not be carried about with every wind of doctrine (see Eph. 4,14). But that serpent of old, the perpetual enemy of the human race, in addition to the many other evils with which he troubles the Church of God in our day, has revived old controversies and started new ones about original sin and its remedy. Therefore, the holy, ecumenical, and general Council of Trent has assembled lawfully in the Holy Spirit. . . . She wishes at this time to turn her attention to recall those who have strayed and to strengthen those who have remained in agreement; and having followed the testimony of Holy Scripture, of the Holy Fathers, and of the approved councils, and the judgment and consent of the Church, she determines, professes, and declares the following doctrine on original sin.

1. If anyone does not profess that the first man Adam immediately lost the justice and holiness in which he was constituted when he disobeyed the command of God in the Garden of Paradise; and that, through the offense of this sin, he incurred the wrath and the indignation of God, and consequently incurred the death with which God had previously threatened him and, together with death, bondage in the power of him who from that time had the empire of death (see Heb. 2,14), that is, of the devil; "and that it was the whole Adam, both body and soul, who was changed for the worse through the offense of this sin" (see 174:371); let him be anathema.

2. "If anyone asserts that Adam's sin was injurious only to Adam and not to his descendants," and that it was for himself alone that he lost the holiness and justice which he had received from God and not for us also; or that after his defilement by the sin of disobedience, he "transmitted to the whole human race only death" and punishment "of the body but not sin itself which is the death of the soul": let him be anathema. "For he contradicts the words of the Apostle: As through one man sin entered into the world and through sin death, and thus death has passed into all men because all have sinned" (see Rom. 5,12; (175:372).

3. If anyone says that this sin of Adam, which is one by origin, and which is communicated to all men by propagation not by imita-

tion, and which is in all men and proper to each, is taken away either through the powers of human nature or through a remedy other than the merit of the one mediator, our Lord Jesus Christ who reconciled us to God in his blood, having become for us justice, and sanctification, and redemption (see 1 Cor. 1,30); or, if anyone says that, through the sacrament of baptism rightly conferred in the form of the Church, this merit of Christ Jesus is not applied to adults and to infants alike: let him be anathema. Because "there is no other name under heaven given to men by which we must be saved" (Acts 4,12). Hence the words: "Behold the lamb of God, behold him who takes away the sin of the world" (see John 1,29). And: "All you who have been baptized into Christ, have put on Christ" (Gal. 3,27).

4. "If anyone denies that newly born infants are to be baptized," even though they may have been born of baptized parents, "or says that they are indeed baptized for the remission of sins but that they do not contract from Adam any original sin that must be expiated in the bath of regeneration" to obtain eternal life; "and, consequently, that for them the form of baptism—for the remission of sin—is to be understood, not in a true, but in a false sense: let him be anathema. Because the words of the Apostle: 'As through one man sin entered into the world and through sin death, and thus death has passed into all men because all have sinned' (see Rom. 5,12), cannot be understood in any other way than as the Catholic Church everywhere has always understood them. Because of this rule of faith, in accordance with apostolic tradition even infants, who have not yet been able to commit any personal sins, are baptized for the remission of sin in a very true sense, that they may be cleansed by regeneration of what they have contracted by generation." For "unless a man be born again of water and the Holy Spirit, he cannot enter into the kingdom of God" (John 3,5).

5. If anyone says that through the grace of our Lord Jesus Christ conferred in baptism the guilt of original sin is not remitted, or even says that not everything having the true and proper nature of sin is taken away but is only brushed over or not imputed: let him be anathema. For God hates nothing in the regenerated because there is no condemnation for those truly buried with Christ by means of baptism into death (see Rom. 6,4), who do not walk according to the flesh (see Rom. 8,1), but putting off the old man and putting on the new man which was created according to God (see Eph. 4,22ff.; Col.

3,9f.), are made innocent, without stain, pure, no longer hateful, but beloved sons of God, heirs, indeed, of God and joint heirs with Christ (see Rom. 8,17) so that absolutely nothing delays their entrance into heaven. It is the mind of this council and it professes that concupiscence or the tendency to sin remains in the baptized; but since it is left to provide a trial, it has no power to injure those who do not consent and who, by the grace of Christ Jesus, manfully resist. Moreover, those who compete according to the rules will be crowned (see 2 Tim. 2,5). As for this concupiscence, which the Apostle sometimes calls sin (see Rom. 6,12ff.), this holy council declares that the Catholic Church has never understood that it is called sin because there is, in the regenerated, sin in the true sense but only because it is from sin and inclines to sin. If anyone thinks the contrary: let him be anathema.

Soon after the Council of Trent the magisterium of the Church once again dealt with the question of original sin in opposition to some theses of Michael de Bay. De Bay held that original sin was not so much a condition of fallen nature as a perversion of the human will. In his opinion the sinful tendency of the will proper to each man from birth is corrected only by a conscious turning to God in pure love. According to the Catholic view the factor of voluntariness is situated not in each individual man, but in the voluntary act of Adam as the protofather of men. Pope Pius V in the year 1567 condemned the following theses:

Voluntariness does not pertain to the essence and definition of sin; nor is the question whether every sin must be voluntary one of definition, but of cause and origin (DS 1946). Hence, original sin truly has the essence of sin without any relation or reference to the will from which it took its origin (DS 1947). Original sin is voluntary by reason of the habitual will of an infant, and it holds sway habitually in infants because there is no contrary exercise of choice in the will (DS 1948). And under the sway of this habitual will it happens that an infant who dies without the sacrament of regeneration, when he does obtain the use of reason, actually has hatred for God, blasphemes God, and rejects the law of God (DS 1949).

Unlike the early Church in its controversies with the Pelagians, the Council of Trent did not address itself to the question of the actuality of original sin; rather, it was concerned with how the significance of original sin is to be understood. Precisely this question raised special difficulties, for by carrying Augustine's thesis to an extreme Luther had exaggerated the effects of original sin. Some of the council Fathers were nonetheless of the opinion that no material differences existed between the conception of the Reformers, Luther in particular, and that of Catholic theology; that such differences as did exist belonged more to the formulation than to the reality itself. Luther, sharing the view of the late scholastic theology (Gabriel Beil) in which he was formed as a student, thought that the whole of Catholic theology had fallen into the abyss of Pelagianism and that it was therefore essential for the teaching of Scripture and of St. Augustine to be recovered.

The council (June 17, 1546; DS 1510–1516) wanted to dispose of the doctrine of original sin as quickly as possible. This was probably why it simply used the texts of the Council of Carthage (418) and the Second Council of Orange (529) for the repeated condemnation of the theses of Pelagius, condemned long since. When interpreting Trent it is important to note that the presentation of the doctrine of original sin begins with the theology of man's original state and his fall. In this way the medieval doctrine of the sin as the loss of holiness and justice is united with the Augustinian thesis that all men descended from Adam are deserving of damnation. Trent rejects the idea that only human misery is derived from Adam and not the sin adhering to each man. In a subordinate clause of the third section (DS 1513) the council takes a position on the question (discussed in the Middle Ages and also at the council) of the unity or multiplicity of original sin and the means of its transmission. The council says that the sin of Adam is one in origin, that it is transmitted by generation, not imitation, and that it is in each individual man as a sin proper to him (*inest unicuique proprium*). By this last thesis an opinion advocated by A. Pighius (d. 1542) and others was clearly rejected. According to this (rejected) view, Adam's sin as an act is past, and it was sin only as an act; nevertheless it continues to exert a moral effect as guilt, and indeed as a unique guilt which is imputed to all men. Pighius believed that by distinguishing between the *actus peccati* and the *reatus peccati* he could answer the difficult question of how a man can be a sinner without even being able to commit a sinful act. With the formula mentioned above, the council placed the unity of the sin in its root, its source, but at the same time emphasized its multiplicity by holding that the sin adheres to each individual. In this third section, however, the council does not place the emphasis on the sinfulness of each individual owing to the transmission of Adam's sin, but on the need for salvation through Jesus Christ. At the Council of Trent, as in the case of Paul, the doctrine of original sin is only the background. One can even say that the doctrine of original sin at the council, as in Augustine, serves as the basis for explaining the universal necessity of salvation. In Section 4 (DS 1515) infant baptism is defended, apparently in opposition to the Anabaptists. But, in addition, infant baptism makes sense only if something is present in the infant which must be washed away by baptism; in other words, if sin is present in the infant. In the background here is a reflection similar to that which we found in Augustine. Actually section 4 contains nothing different from Canon 2 of the Council of Carthage, which was so strongly influenced by Augustine.

In modern theology it is primarily those elements in the Tridentine texts which support discussion in connection with the thesis of evolution that are singled out. Above all there is the question of whether Adam is an actual historical figure—even if of the most remote and shadowy past—and is to be understood as an individual man, or whether he represents only a literary construction. Connected with this question there is the problem of whether the human race originated with a single pair (monogenism) or a multiplicity (polygenism) of first parents. It is rightly emphasized that the fact of original sin can be preached to modern man as worthy of belief only if what one must understand by original sin is expressed in a manner which he finds worthy of belief. It may justly be maintained that the Council of Trent, in the passage on the transmission of Adam's sin to all men, did not answer—indeed, it did not even treat—the question with which we are here concerned. This view is supported by the fact that, as we remarked earlier on, Trent could hardly have taken a formal position on a question which did not belong to the problematic of that time but has emerged only lately, in connection with the idea of evolution. But granted this view of what the council settled, it nevertheless must be acknowledged that the opinion occasionally proposed by Catholic theologians today that original sin consists in the persistent and efficacious bad example of the first man does not reproduce the teaching of the council. If this conception were to prevail in the Church, it would mean not merely a reformulation of Trent's teaching but a profound change in its declaration of the faith. Such a transformation is not possible without giving rise to a contradiction in the self-understanding of the Church, and it cannot, therefore, be proposed either by the Church itself or by theology without the abandonment of dogma—that is, without giving up what has been the mind of the Church up to now. A "rethinking" of this sort would represent such a decisive attack on the hitherto existing world of faith that the consequences would be incalculable. One could, of course, suggest that the necessary distinction made in theology between the manner in which the faith is formulated and the content of the faith furnishes legitimate reason for a change in the Church's thinking on original sin. For the interpretation of an ecclesial declaration of the faith, the underlying intention of the declaration must be distinguished from the linguistic formulation: the latter is, and must be, clothed in the culture and language of its own time. Language, as an element in the self-development of man and human society, is in constant flux. Hence one must view, for example, the thesis that original sin is transmitted by generation as not being fixed by Trent despite the literal sense of the Tridentine text. Nonetheless such an interpretation as is now being proposed would read too much between the lines of the council text. For what the council intended to express is precisely the fact that the sin of Adam inheres in each individual man, and not that it only influences him as an example; and hence the distinction between the content of a statement and the form of a statement leads in our case directly to the conclusion that the doctrine of the sinful state of Adam's descendants was what the council intended to state. The council's declaration would therefore lose its meaning if one were to deny the

sinful state of man. It is hardly necessary to emphasize that theological considerations, and not emotional reactions, are alone pertinent to our problem.

THE NATURE OF ORIGINAL SIN

As for the nature of original sin, there is no detailed, official and
binding teaching of the Church on this question. Thus we are
faced with the not inconsiderable difficulty that while the *fact* of
man's sinful state is established by the Church's teaching, the
essence of what is declared a fact—and hence whose actuality cannot be contested without contradicting the Church—is not adequately and officially explained. The consequence is that whereas
we know that there is an original sin we do not know for certain
what it is: there is, therefore, in the Church's teaching on original
sin an inevitable element of uncertainty. One can probably say of
the Tridentine teaching what is likewise true of the teaching of the
apostle Paul: the council's declarations on original sin are an attempt, based on Scripture, to determine the state of man *vis-à-vis*
salvation without Christ.

With respect to the essence of original sin, which is the core
of the problematic, perhaps the following can be said: as Scripture,
Augustine, the theologians of the Middle Ages and the Council of
Trent unanimously declare, each individual man is directed to
Christ. Without Christ he remains in a condition of misery. The
state of original sin is the state of being without Christ, however
one may describe it. It is a state devoid of that living and saving
relation to Christ which is established through faith and sacrament.
(The possibility of salvation for children who die without baptism
before they have reached the age of reason will be discussed later.)
When the medieval and modern scholastic theologians explain that
original sin consists in the lack of that holiness and justice—
sanctifying grace—which according to God's will man should
possess, only the objective, not the personal, element in grace is
taken into consideration. However, we know that grace involves
both a relation to God (*gratia increata,* Uncreated Grace) and its
objective counterpart, sanctifying grace (*gratia creata,* created

grace). It is not a contradiction of Catholic teaching, but rather an essential element of it, to say that the graced man exists in a living relationship to Christ and to God, the Father. This relationship reaches its fullness in the *visio beata,* the life of glory. Grace, then, includes a personal and an objective element, but the personal element is the higher, and in the definition of the essence of original sin a stronger accent must therefore be placed on it. This does not lead to a denial of the traditional (since Anselm) theological conception of the essence of original sin, it only places it in the correct context. The objective element is dependent on the personal element: when the personal element is missing, there is an actual absence of the objective element.

Original sin means that man is enclosed in himself and cannot, owing to his weakness and his incapacity for love and commitment, break through the walls of his self-imprisonment. As long as man's spiritual immaturity makes him incapable of a real decision, he remains unaware of his condition; but as soon as a conscious decision becomes possible for him, the man in original sin experiences his incapacity for transcendence. Only if God in the initiative of his creative love breaks into this self-enclosure and thus opens the way to true freedom can a change take place. As the result of original sin, God must make his breakthrough anew in each man: he makes it at any given moment through the Christ-event. Christ has brought a new epoch into being: yet it must be actualized for each individual personally if it is to exert its saving effects in him.

The condition of man in original sin, then, can be described as an "incapacity for dialogue." With respect to its personal element, original sin consists in the lack of desire and capacity for dialogue with God, and consequently for loving and altruistic (and not simply aimless) dialogue with one's fellow men. It is the incapacity for being a genuine partner. Because he is without the bond with Jesus, the Man for others, man is content in his inability to make contact with others, in his arrogant and self-seeking isolation. He is dominated by the power of sin.

The tendency to sin (concupiscence) must likewise be situated within the complex essence of original sin. Medieval theology did not overlook this point: it called concupiscence the material element in the essence of original sin.

The bad example of Adam also plays an important role in the definition of the essence of original sin. Bad example provides an external impulse to sin: it is not simply an interesting picture presented to man's view but a dynamic reality. Pelagius's doctrine was rejected by the magisterium of the Church only insofar as it was proposed in isolation; separated, in the manner of heresy, from the whole and made independent of it. But there is no contradiction of the Church's teaching if the power of bad example is incorporated in the definition of original sin.

Seen from an evolutionist viewpoint, the result of original sin is that man in the process of evolution—which according to God's free decree aims at Christ—does not move towards the future with a salvific directedness to Christ. He is so constituted that he advances in a certain sense apart from the ultimate and innermost intention of evolution, although he need not be aware of this inner deficiency. In spite of his biological, intellectual and cultural progress he is shut off from the innermost goal of evolution, which transcends its natural processes.

THE POSSIBILITY OF ORIGINAL SIN

The question still remains of how this condition constituted by the lack of a personal saving relation to Christ, and through him to God the Father, can be called guilt. Around this question the mystery of original sin deepens: nevertheless an attempt can be made at an answer. It can be said that God views man as a unity, one great family, with the result that there is in mankind a solidarity of one for all and all for one. This idea is fundamental to the whole biblical order, and from it is derived the law of representation according to which, in certain circumstances, one person can take the place of another. There are numberless instances of representation within the biblical history of salvation, occurring for both good and evil. The decisive act of representation was performed, and is performed, by Jesus Christ. He makes God, the Absolute, clearly manifest to us in this world, so that we can reach God through him. Through Jesus we can hear God's call to us: Jesus himself receives this call and mediates it to us. It is through him, therefore, that we too are able to come to God. But whoever does not come to God through Jesus Christ remains far from God, imprisoned in the merely created, in his own self. He is unable to reach beyond himself. And yet this is what must be accomplished if he is to attain to his own selfhood. He must leave himself behind in order to reach out to what lies before him, to God. Since this can take place only through Jesus Christ, and cannot take place apart from him, for men the world without Christ is closed to God.

That this is the case has its foundation in the fact that there was, and still is, another act of representation, the negative one: Adam, the sinful ancestral lord of men, has blocked the vista to God. In the beginning the world was to attain God through him, but since in Adam man has shut himself off from God and is no longer open —pervious—to God, men remain at a distance unless they attain to God through Christ. They remain imprisoned in the world and in their own egos, in their self-exaltation and self-assertion, because they have no way to God so long as they do not travel the way who is Christ. That Adam in his representative function had such immense significance that he was able to obstruct the view to God not only for himself but also for all mankind is wrapped in the mystery of God's plan for man's salvation—on which we cannot pass judgment.

In addition to the solidarity of men, the historicity of man is also expressed in his relation to Adam. The historicity of man means that he is always a product of history. He is, of course, also the lord of history in that he creates and shapes the history lying before him. But his lordship is a very limited one. At any given moment he finds himself in a determinate social role within an already determined form of society. Indeed, he encounters himself in the process of being molded by his social role. Thus man is at once a creature of history and a creator of history. He can be characterized as the created creator of history. That the sin of Adam has blocked man's way to God is expressed in the fact that man is substantially shaped by his history, and not merely in an intra-historical sense but in a sense transcending history.

Reflections of this kind place the personal element of original sin in the foreground: that is, man in the state of original sin does not have a living relation to God because he does not have a living relation to Christ. The objective element is not, however, neglected; it is simply moved to second place. Because man is created for God and claimed by God as his own, the directionlessness of man—his lack of the right relation to God—is a real defect.

When the Council of Trent says that original sin is transmitted not through imitation but through generation, it in no way means to designate the reproductive process as the instrument for the transmission of original sin. It is entrance into the human community which is the condition for participation in the corruption that has entered history through Adam's sin and the lack of the right relationship to God. This lack of the right relationship to God is universal—Paul speaks bluntly of the power of sin—but it affects each individual in his own personal fate and in his personal existence.

Without assuming a divine decree constituting Adam the representative of all men it would be equally possible to explain the involvement of all men in the fall by showing that Adam's act at the beginning of human history took root in history as a disastrous *a priori* (Karl Rahner) and therefore continues to be unceasingly effective in history. For the adequate understanding of such a proposition, however, it would be necessary to develop much further our theology of the beginning with its full implications.

As we noted above in the section on evolution, the Church has made no formal decision concerning the problem of monogenism versus polygenism. No doubt it is quite significant that *Humani generis* states that the Catholic does not have the same freedom with regard to this problem as he has concerning the idea that man evolved physically from prehuman organisms. Recalling that the encyclical sees no possible way to view *(nequaquam apparet)* polygenism as consistent with the Tridentine doctrine on original sin, we may ask whether this text is contradicted if we accept the statement that although when the encyclical was promulgated there seemed no possibility of agreement, time may alter the situation, and even now the theory of polygenism can no longer be rejected with complete certainty.

The questions remain open as to whether the doctrine of original sin as participation in the primal sin in point of fact requires monogenism as opposed to polygenism; whether there is only the one alternative, either acceptance of the doctrine of original sin and rejection of polygenism or acceptance of polygenism and rejection of the doctrine of original sin. We have no reason to think that we are faced with any such dilemma. The majority of contemporary scientists support the proposition that man had more than one ancestor. They agree that the present human species derives from a number of original forefathers, from a group of people (even if a small number). If this proposition should prove to be correct, then, we may claim, original sin as a universal phenomenon can be maintained no matter whether one or many or all of the members of the original population sinned. According to traditional theology, we could regard the first sinner as God's representative of mankind to come, or we could say, with contemporary explanations, that the primal sin remains implanted in history as a fatal *a priori*.

THE CONSEQUENCES OF ORIGINAL SIN

In theology a complex of evil consequences have been distinguished from the essence of original sin. This distinction, in spite of its fundamental correctness, cannot be adequately carried out, for concupiscence is considered both as a "material" element and a consequence of original sin. Even the absence of "justice" is considered both as essence and as consequence (the judgment of God) of original sin. If both the Second Council of Orange and the Council of Trent say primarily of Adam that his whole human nature has undergone a transformation into a worse condition and that his will has not escaped unscathed, the statement is extended to apply to the whole human race. Above all it is the wrath of God—that is, the

chastising judgment of God—which strikes the sinner. Original
sin also has its effects in the natural sphere. They are called mortality, passibility, ignorance and concupiscence.

It can be said that man's natural powers have not been weakened
in themselves by original sin in the sense that his understanding or
memory or biological energy has diminished. Quite the contrary:
since the emergence of the first man both biological and intellectual
forces have steadily increased, for evolution goes on unceasingly,
even if at an extremely slow pace. It pushes on to ever higher peaks.

It should be said once again that for Paul the word "death" has
a meaning deeper than that of mere biological death. It means the
end of earthly life of course, but it also means eternal death—
rejection by God—the two events forming a unity: total death. This
is the death which threatens man in the state of original sin, and it
can be conquered only through Christ. The "corruption" of human
nature, therefore, consists in the fact that with the loss of the
saving relation to God, that dynamism in man which helps him to
live in genuine fellowship, to use his freedom in a meaningful way,
to integrate all his experiences and adventures into a unity within
himself, ceases to operate—that same dynamism which enables
him to accept death and suffering, knowledge and desire, in a personal way, so that all these things become part of a genuine self-
realization and not simply the possession of objects and the experience of events. Even the man freed from original sin for dedication to Christ—the "new creature"—no longer has within him
the power to achieve such an integration without a struggle.

In medieval theology *ignorantia* and *concupiscentia* were held to
be the special consequences of orignal sin.[3] *Ignorantia* is not to be
identified with lack of education: ignorance is a burden which
weighs upon all men and seems to increase with the progress of
knowledge. For the greater the increase in knowledge the less a
man is able to assimilate its whole range. Indeed it is now generally
acknowledged that experts are no longer capable even in their own
specialties of keeping up with the ceaselessly advancing growth of
knowledge, much less of mastering all the learning in their own
fields. But the *ignorantia* which theology has in mind has no connection with this kind of incomplete comprehension: it could exist

even in one who carried the whole of modern scientific scholarship in his head. It is what both the Old and the New Testaments describe by the term "foolishness," what Erasmus meant by "folly." This foolishness consists in the fact that a man neither relates to God nor judges in the light of God, himself, the creation, the events of history and the world in its detailed arrangement. Such a man lacks the wisdom which, in face of the whole of material progress, discerns and recognizes both the connection of the world with its first cause—the Absolute—and the true future, and therefore the ultimate meaning, of the world. His foolishness is also based on a decision: it is to a certain extent identical with the refusal to love. Concretely, this presents itself today in the form of materialism, skepticism, atheism and even gnosticism. One should not, of course, overlook the fact that this foolishness is not, as a rule, recognized for what it is by the one who has fallen prey to it. At the opposite pole is the phenomenon which looks like foolishness but is not— the foolishness of God which revealed itself on the cross. The cross of Christ is foolishness for the human spirit which remains imprisoned within the world, but this very cross is the wisdom of God, for it opens the way to the Absolute.

As for concupiscence, let us refer to what was said earlier with regard to that subject. Here it may be emphasized that concupiscence takes effect as a rupture within man himself, as estrangement and the hostility of one man against another within the human community; it manifests itself in cruelty, bloodthirstiness, lust for power, arbitrariness, tyranny, sloth and cowardice. Through Jesus Christ the way has of course been opened for man to overcome this enemy of a truly human, truly fraternal, life. But it is to be feared that he succeeds only to a limited degree; for, owing to the fires of concupiscence which still smolder within him—the sinful appetite which still holds sway—fallen man has incomplete control of himself even after the bond with Christ is restored. He is unable to integrate into his true self that which rises from the depths of his own nature or flows into his consciousness from his environment. It is the task of a lifetime to achieve his personal integration progressively in dedication to God through Christ, in love of neighbor, in fraternal formation of the world, and thus to fulfill himself spiritually. Later on, in the presentation of a theological anthropology based on the Christ-event, we shall return to certain details of this which cannot be discussed here.

Because the problem of original sin is being discussed today from so many different angles and such contradictory solutions are being proposed our presentation will not be complete without a brief survey of the most important and most characteristic views insofar as they differ from the traditional explanation. We cannot go into all the minor differentiations: the crucial questions are those of monogenism versus polygenism, the historicity of Adam, and the fact and the nature of an original sin.

The Jesuits Alszeghy and Flick,[4] professors at the Gregorian University, start with the presupposition that in the evolutionary process characteristic of all reality man has developed from lower organisms, has even emerged, perhaps, at a number of different points, and that mankind as a genus had gone through a development similar to that of an individual as he grows from child to adult. Men, therefore, could have existed for a long time without the *use* of reason and freedom. At a particular stage of their hominization men had the capacity to choose between good and evil. By freely choosing good they would have furthered their own evolution and that of the whole creation, but they disobeyed God. In this way sin entered the world and became its master. Nevertheless God did not give up his plan of allowing men to share in his life; he achieved it in another way, by the mystery of Easter.

The authors seek to do justice to the biblical and Church doctrine by the assumption that man, in the stream of evolution, was destined for supernatural communion with God but failed to reach this state owing to his recalcitrance: hence paradise existed only virtually and not really. The first sin has led to all other sins and has placed all mankind in a situation contrary to the will of God which derives from man's failure to seize freely an opportunity of advancing towards a higher human existence within evolution. The transmission of original sin is explained by the use of the biblical concept of "corporate personality." In this view the first sinner represented the whole of mankind, for even if not all men were descended from him, they are still one in their derivation from the same primal matter before becoming human and in their destination to participate in the life of God. The problem of monogenism versus polygenism hereby disappears.

Our main reservation with regard to this interpretation is that it does not seem to do full justice to the reality of the "original state of man" defined by the Council of Trent.

P. Smulders [5] begins with the idea that all mankind is called to the fullness of the body of Christ. Every action of the individual or the community is meant to serve this goal, and the real nature of sin lies in man's failure to live up to this vocation. The consequence is that he is shut up within himself. Original sin consists in that human condition in which every man has an orientation towards self-realization outside communion with God. The foundation of original sin is that now irrevocable step, taken at the beginning of mankind's path, which was hostile to God and evolution.

Whereas Alszeghy and Flick's theory explains original sin by the concept of a "corporate personality," Smulders explains it by showing the significance of the beginning which determines all that follows but is not itself determined by anything prior to it. In both cases the transmission of original sin is rightly removed from the realm of biology.

Smulders proposes further that the causality of the first sin does not exclude later sins from collaborating in this causality. The children of Adam would not only inherit the sins of their fathers but would perpetrate them on a higher cultural level with a maturer self-confidence and a greater control over themselves and the world. Sinfulness grows and develops with the evolution of mankind. This interpretation of original sin does not require the theory of monogenism.

P. Schoonenberg, S.J.,[6] emphasizes the social and cosmic nature of sin. He rejects the idea that sin is only a by-product of the evolutionary process which therefore gradually vanishes with the advance of evolution. Sin has world-wide significance; it is the "sin of the world" (see John 1:29). This is one result of the solidarity of mankind. The sin of the world consists in the deeds of individuals and the sinful situation which they evoke. Every free action is an appeal to others to act freely. Every sinful action places others in a situation which is less free and more conducive to sin. Schoonen-berg thus differentiates between a sinful situation and the condition of existing in a situation conducive to sin *(sündiges Situiertsein)*. The latter he terms a human existential. He identifies this condition (with a certain degree of discretion) with original sin. He under-stands it at times as inability to love, as inclination to evil, as isola-tion and fear, as the division and hopelessness of the world, and at other times as the lack of a life of grace, as death to supernatural life. It does not become sufficiently clear, however, whether he regards these elements as the result or the content of a situation conducive to sin, or whether one is the result and the other the content. It is difficult to understand how the graceless situation of the world can elicit a condition conducive to sin as an existential of the individual, or how the doctrine of the Council of Trent that a condition of sin exists in each individual can be explained by the proposition that the inner condition of man is determined from without.

Schoonenberg's most important proposition implies that "Adam's" influence is to be equated with the influence of the world. In contrast to the classical doctrine of original sin in earlier theol-ogy, he maintains, Scripture does not mention any doctrine of sin outside personal sins. Augustine, in his struggle against Pelagius, was the first to do this. Sin has a history. We must understand its dynamics within the process of evolution. It is always aggression against God; against the world, which God has graced through salvation history; and, in all this, against Christ. It began with Adam and reached its culmination in the execution of Christ. The condition of original sin has gradually become universal. This proposition is correct: that original sin never occurs in isolation from the general human situation (as a matter of fact, Augustine emphasized this) and that it reached its most intensive actualization in the killing of Jesus. In our opinion, however, this viewpoint does not give sufficient attention to the primal sin in its relation to original sin and does not duly recognize the universality of original sin—that is, the universal need of salvation.

H. Haag [7] claims that Scripture witnesses only to the incursion of sin, its considerable expansion, and men's inability to free themselves from it. If the Council of Trent says anything further about original sin, then it must be interpreted in the light of the new exegesis. Here the fact is overlooked that this view contradicts the idea and possibility of a real doctrinal development in the Church, and therefore it stands in opposition to the idea of a teaching magisterium in the Church. In any interpretation of a decision of the Church regarding a matter of faith, we must inquire into the intention of the decision, and distinguish the form of the statement from its central core. But according to the Council of Trent an inner condition of sin which precedes each personal decision is the minimum of Church doctrine to which we must hold in this question. The proposition that original sin is the sinister power which the first sin exercises over men falls short of the doctrinal concern of Trent, however strong the impulses stemming from that primal sin actually are.

In view of its wide acceptance we shall mention the concept of original sin set forth in the Dutch Catechism under the heading "The Power of Sin." This approach has many points in common with Schoonenberg's. The text starts by saying that every man who comes into the world is a fellow man of the incarnate Son of God. Men are aware of a deep guilt which is prior to their own responsible decision. The inescapability of wars, which are malignant eruptions desired by almost no one, the unconsidered arrogance of colonialism and racism, the egoistic inability of men to love one another—all show the truth of the text: "The whole world may be exposed to the judgment of God" (Rom. 3:19). Chapters 1–11 of Genesis, which are not historical but symbolic narratives, containing the core of the whole history of mankind including its future, describe the phenomenon of sin. Adam, Cain, Noah and those who built the tower of Babel represent mankind as such. The fifth chapter of Romans proclaims how complete is the reign of sin and death over mankind and how grace and restoration have come abundantly with eternal life through Jesus. Everything else is literary form and not message. Although the significance of the primal sin may not be overlooked, the point in question is not principally that man sinned and is now corrupt but that he sins and becomes corrupt: it becomes a question of sin and not of stages of evolution or degeneration. The sin in the environment influences men by example and often by coercion. It destroys sensitivity to value, especially the ability to love: thus sin comes to power. The result is that everyone who belongs to the human race is affiliated with a deep-seated opposition to God which, lying at the root of his personal decisions, takes effect in all his actions: he is held back by reluctance in the face of real love. As Scripture does not trace the true unity of the human race to descent from Adam, it likewise does not attribute human solidarity in evil to descent from one man. Rather it comes from all sides, in all the ways in which men have entered into relations with one another. Sin, which infects all men, was not committed by one Adam at the beginning but by Adam, man, by every man. At the time of Augustine (about 400) this universal sinfulness which man had learned about both from Scripture and from experience came to be called "original sin." Whereas "original sin" was previously spoken of more in connection with children, this recent trend places the accent on adults. Original sin is the sin of mankind as a whole. It is heard as the keynote in every personal sin, and only in personal sin does it first receive its form. Baptism is a dedication to life struggle against personal sin.

This explanation accommodates sin to the evolutionary process without naturalistically divesting it of its religious significance. Furthermore, it is understood as a reality which operates in man. The social character of sin, the solidarity of men which Augustine already so emphatically stressed, is underscored.[8] Sin is portrayed as the dark background for the salvific act of Jesus Christ and is thus properly placed in the course of salvation history. On the other hand, the beginning of sin seems to be undervalued. There is also the question whether a merely symbolic interpretation of the first eleven chapters of Genesis does not go against the sense of the Council of Trent.[9]

Of the Protestant theologians we shall mention only Karl Barth and Paul Tillich. Barth rejects all idea of a burden resting on men as a result of Adam's sin. Each individual is responsible for his own actions. Since Adam each man sins again and again. Barth even spoke of a transcendental disposition to sin which stems from the finite character of human life.

Tillich understands the biblical account of the fall as a symbol for the transition of every man from essence into existence. He understands essence as a pre-historic condition of pure potentiality. The fall lies in the actualization of this potentiality. In this unavoidable transition man estranges himself from his essence. Accordingly, original sin is to be understood as the tragic guilt of existential self-estrangement. Jesus Christ is the only man who, in free self-realization, overcame self-estrangement in exemplary fashion. Tillich seems to come close to Manicheism, although he expressly rejects it.

Notes

[1] *Der Römerbrief, Übersetzt und Erklärt* (Regensburg: Pustet, 1957), pp. 272–274.

[2] *Sermo* 293, 11; *PL*, 38, 1334.

[3] A. Kraus, *Vom Wesen und Ursprung der Dummheit* (Cologne, 1961).

[4] "Die Erbsunde in evolutiver Sicht," in *Theologie der Gegenwart, 9* (1966), pp. 151–159, and *Il Creatore: L'inizio della salvezza*, 3d ed. (Florence, 1964).

[5] *Theorie und Evolution* (Essen, 1963).

[6] *Theologie der Sünde* (Einsiedeln, 1966).

[7] *Biblische Schöpfungslehre und kirchliche Erbsündenlehre* (Stuttgart, 1966).

[8] See M. Seybold, *Sozialtheologische Aspekte der Sünde bei Augustinus* (Regensburg, 1963).

[9] P. Lengsfeld, *Adam und Christus* (Essen, 1965).

Readings for Part III

Burke, P. "Man without Christ" in *Theological Studies,* March 1968.

Davis, C. *Theology for Today.* New York, Sheed and Ward, 1963.

de Rosa, P. *Christ and Original Sin.* Milwaukee, Bruce, 1967.

Dubarle, A. M. *The Biblical Doctrine of Original Sin.* New York, Herder, 1965.

Rahner, Karl. "Concupiscentia" in *Theological Investigations,* I. Baltimore, Helicon, 1961.

Schoonenberg, P. *Man and Sin.* Notre Dame: University of Notre Dame Press, 1965.

‹IV
The Angels

›12

The Work of Salvation of the Good Angels

THE EXISTENCE OF THE ANGELS ACCORDING TO SCRIPTURE

Before we begin our analysis of the Christ-event itself a group of creatures important in salvation history remain to be discussed: the angels. Their creation is not explicitly attested in Scripture, but they appear in salvation history as creatures of God, his messengers and the executors of his will. When they first appear in history God's dialogue with men has already begun. Unlike numberless spirits who appear in extra-biblical sources, they do not have an independent sphere of activity alongside that of God: like all other creatures, the angels are created for Christ; he is their Lord and Head (Col. 1:16). For one who does not understand this the angels can become a source of danger: he may give to them that place in his faith which belongs of right to Christ alone (Rom. 8:38; cf. Col. 2:18f.). However exalted the angels may be, Christ stands above them (Heb. 1:4f.).

As with the rest of creation, we shall only discuss angels in their relation to salvation history. The ontological problems associated with them will only be treated insofar as this is necessary to an understanding of salvation history. Scripture itself speaks of angels not to complement our knowledge of creation, but simply as they relate to mankind. Otherwise it is extremely reserved on the ontology of angels. This salvation-history outlook has never been lost sight of in the course of Church history. Nevertheless it must be noted that in medieval theology the section on creation which dealt with angels was utilized chiefly to solve problems in metaphysics and epistemology. According to Aquinas the angels also belong to that body whose head is Christ. Even their holiness is, according to him, stamped by Christ. John of the Cross holds that the Son of God became man in order to gather saved mankind together with the angels into the Church. Nicholas of Cusa sees a Church constituted by God out of the angels and the men united with God through Christ.

The use of the word "angel" right into the Middle Ages to describe a mission, not to explain the essence of a type of being, is in accord with the viewpoint of salvation history. It is only since the Middle Ages that the expression "angel" has been employed as descriptive of a type of being.

The existence of angels is attested by Holy Scripture, but we may also ask whether their existence is knowable through natural reason. On this point it is to be noted that in extra-biblical material we come upon numerous "angelic" beings, who frequently appear in half-divine, half-human forms: these are elements of the usual mythical and polytheistic picture of the world and God. In Greek philosophy incorporeal intelligences which regulated the heavenly bodies were accepted. Such beings, then, are elements of the ancient view of the universe and are so intimately bound up with it that with the passing of that world view the reason for belief in their existence has also been lost. This extra-biblical belief in angelic beings is not the residue of a primitive revelation—as we have frequently emphasized, there is no foundation for the acceptance of a primitive revelation. These "angelic" beings, then, have to be recognized as the projection of human mental images and wishes onto a mythical picture of the world; yet one can see in Aristotle's acceptance of incorporeal intelligence the results of metaphysical reflections. In the hierarchy of being Greek philosophy acknowledged and affirmed the superiority of mind over matter, resulting in a clear ascending scale: matter, intellect in matter, pure intellect. The difference between pagan angelic forms and the biblical angels is so profound that one cannot claim that it is possible to know from nature that angels exist. Unlike such conceptions, the biblical angels belong completely to the monotheistic world picture seen in the Bible and must be understood as elements in the divine plan of salvation. One is forced, therefore, to admit that it is only within this divine plan of salvation that their peculiar being can be known —that is, on the basis of divine revelation alone. Augustine is right: we know of the existence of the biblical angels only by faith. The theory of evolution raises no slight difficulty for modern minds, for if in the total event of evolution man, and above all, Jesus Christ, is the summit towards which all is directed, then it is difficult to find a place for the angels in this process. Natural reason cannot prove their existence, it must simply be accepted as a mystery. Evolution is apparently limited to the intellectual-material world, though it might be possible to see an evolutionary element in the participation of angels in salvation history: in any case they are associated with the final consummation of creation.

Scripture texts attesting the activity of angels increase with extraordinary frequency from the time of the Babylonian exile—obviously contact with the religious world of the Babylonians is responsible for this. Babylonian influence traceable in Scripture brings us again to the often discussed question of how the content of a statement in Scripture is to be distinguished from its form. This problem, taken up officially in the Church for the first time by Pius XII in his encyclical *Divino afflante Spiritu,* acquires a special importance for the interpretation of the biblical texts in which mention of angels occurs. It would be going too far to see in the angelic forms of Scripture merely mythical figures, to demythologize them to the extent that by angels one understood nothing more than symbols for God's operation. In many texts it is true that the angel is to be understood as such a symbol, but not all the angel passages can be understood in this sense, though those statements in Scripture in which there is talk of "the angel of the Lord," do appear to be simply testifying to the mighty operations and government of God in history. In some passages in which according to the

Hebrew text God himself is at work, an angel is named in the Septuagint translation (e.g., Ex. 4:24; Job 20:15; cf. Ps. 8:5; Job 1:6; Pss. 97:7; 138:1). There are other passages in which it must be admitted that by "angel of the Lord" God himself, insofar as he acts in human history and shapes it, is meant (cf. Gen. 32:22–32; 22:11f.; Ex. 3:2; 14:19; 23:20–23; Zech. 1:8–14; 2:2f.; 4:1–6, etc.). Possibly awe in the presence of God—a man did not dare to come into immediate contact with him—contributed to such presentations of God's activity. In the later writings of Scripture, God speaks to the prophets no longer directly but through an angel (cf. Ez. 40:3; 43:6f.; 47:3–6). In many passages the question must be left open whether an activity on the part of angels created by God and distinct from him is involved, or whether a symbol of the activity of God himself is being employed. In the last analysis our certainty of the existence of angels derives from Christ. Since Christ himself is reported in the New Testament as testifying to the activity of angels, we can view both Old and New Testament passages in which God's saving activity through angels is mentioned in the light of this testimony.

The momentous vision described by the prophet Ezekiel (Ez. 1:4–29) is, of course, not a vision of an angel but a vision of God. What the prophet says about the four living creatures in this vision —without describing them in the strict sense—indicates unhindered movement, superhuman power, personal being, and association with God. The four different faces belonging to each of the living creatures are of particular symbolic power. The prophet obviously borrowed images from the Babylonian gods with their mixed forms. As recovered works of art show, there were at that time various combinations—men with the heads of eagles, bulls with the heads of men, and similar double creatures. Often lions with wings were employed as the bearers of the throne of God. There was even a quadriform Baal. In the Revelation of John four animal forms are assigned to the four living creatures (Rev. 4:7). In this symbolism man represents the mind, the lion power and majesty, the bull fertility, the eagle speed (originally the serpent appeared here as the symbol of life and death). The eagle is the guardian of the peace of God (Ex. 19:4; Deut. 32:11; Pss. 17:8; 36:7; 57:1; 61:4; 63:7; 91:4). Since Irenaeus the four living creatures have been widely viewed as representing the four gospels. In the Old Testament the angels were called messengers because of their mission (Gen. 19:1; 28:12; 32:1f.; Ps. 103:20), men because of their appearance (Gen. 18:2,16; 19:10,12), commanders of the heavenly army (Jos. 5:14) or lords of heaven because of their relation to God (1 Kgs. 22:19; cf. 1 Sam. 1:3,11; Hos. 12:4; Amos. 3:13; 6:14; Pss. 24:10; 46:7,11). In the post-exilic period angels are called "sons of God" (Job 1:6; 2.1; 38:7; Wis. 5.5), and in this the apocrypha agrees with the biblical literature. All of this shows that many popular notions have been borrowed from the surrounding cultures.

Angels are described as incorporeal beings (Tob. 12:19f.; Gen. 21.17; Ps. 78:25; Wis. 16.20); therefore they are not in themselves perceptible by the senses.

Scripture contains no speculative reflections on the manner of angelic appearances. We know that their number is exceedingly great and that they form a kind of heavenly court—completely subordinate, of course, to God's sole authority (Job 1:6–12. 2:1–7. 4:18; Ps. 89:8). They perform their divinely appointed tasks both for individual men and for the whole nation of Israel (1 Chron. 21:12f.; Tob. 3:24; Dan. 14:34f.; 2 Macc. 11:6, etc.). Whole groups of angels are mentioned as well as the names of individuals (Michael, Gabriel, Raphael).

In many ways the New Testament undertakes a demythologization of the Old Testament angel texts. Its statements about angels are fewer and more sober. But even in the New Testament they are spoken of as heavenly messengers who bring divine commissions to men. When they appear it is usually in the form of young men in glowing white garments (Mk. 16:5; Mt. 28:3; Lk. 24:4; Jn. 20:12; Acts 1:10). Again, their number is great (Mt. 26:53; Heb. 12:22; Acts 7:53; Mt. 25:31; 26:53; Lk. 2:13f.; 1 Tim. 5:21; 1 Pet. 3:22; Heb. 12:22–24). In particular, they accompany the Christ-event from its beginning to its consummation. The angel of the Lord who gives his name as Gabriel prophesies the birth and life of John the Baptist (Lk. 1:11–20). The same angel brings the message to Mary that she is to be the mother of God (Lk. 1:26–28). An angel reassures Joseph concerning what the Holy Spirit has effected in Mary (Mt. 1:20–25). An angel of the Lord announces the birth of Jesus to the shepherds and on the plain of Bethlehem a great host of angels praises God for his graciousness (Lk. 2:9–15). An angel conveys to Joseph the instruction to flee with Mary and the child to Egypt, and when the danger has passed, the new command to return (Mk. 1:13; Mt. 4:11). On the Mount of Olives, if the Son asked, the Father would send more than twelve legions of angels to free him from the afflictions which beset him— but how then would the Scriptures be fulfilled? (Mt. 26:53f.). An angel from heaven appears to Jesus in his agony and comforts him (Lk. 22:43). On Easter morning when the women on finding the tomb empty are greatly dismayed, men in glowing garments stand before them and announce to them the Resurrection of the Lord (Lk. 24:1–7). Angels are also mentioned by John (Jn. 20:12). All the angels will form the retinue of the Lord when he comes at the Last Judgment (Mk. 8:38; Mt. 25.31; Lk. 9:26). The son of Man will dispatch his angels with a loud trumpet blast, and they will gather his elect from the four winds, from one end of heaven to the other (Mt. 13:39,41,49; 24:31; Mk. 13:27).

According to the testimony of Christ, children have their angels in heaven (Mt. 18:10). Christ himself, as the Son of God, is superior to all the angelic beings both before his incarnation and after his exaltation to the right hand of God (Mk. 13:32; Eph. 1:20f.; Col. 1:16f.; 2:10; Heb. 1:4–14; 2:1–9; 1 Pet. 3:22). The Church instituted by Christ together with the angels proclaims God's plan for the salvation of men (Eph. 3:10; 1 Tim. 3:16). The angels rejoice that men are converted to God (1 Pet. 1:12; 3:22). According to the Revelation of John the angels play a comprehensive role in salvation history. Admittedly, it is more probable that the seven angels to whom the seven letters are sent are not really angels, but bishops. Still, throughout the entire book the activity of angels is repeatedly described in graphic terms.

It is not to be denied, of course, that many of the creatures portrayed in the biblical text do not prove the existence of angels. Thus one can ask whether the angel of the Annunciation is an actual angel or a metaphorical representation of the influence of God on the Virgin Mary. Nonetheless, when Christ himself testifies that the angels of children always behold the face of the Father (Mt. 18:10), or when he says on the Mount of Olives that he could ask the Father and the Father would send him legions of angels, one cannot assume that this is an adaptation to time-conditioned conceptions. It would appear to be an expression of his own conviction.

As for the development of the doctrine of angels in the post-apostolic period, it should be emphasized that the Church Fathers, in opposition to the ideas of the gnostics, defined angels as mere creatures ordered to the service of Jesus Christ and the Church. In the old covenant their task, according to the Fathers, was to prepare for the coming of Christ. In the New Testament they serve the kingdom of God founded by Christ until its consummation. From very early times the Fathers also testify to the belief that an angel of God accompanies each individual man from birth to death.

THE NATURE OR BEING OF THE ANGELS

In the patristic period, well into the fourth century, the appearances of angels were interpreted as though an angel possessed a spiritual body. Their complete incorporeality was stressed for the first time by the Greek theologian Gregory of Nyssa. Pseudo-Dionysius the Areopagite offered the first systematic doctrine of angels, in which, of course, the neo-Platonic foundations of his thought are readily discernible. He worked out the idea of the pure spirituality of the angels logically. Many Fathers speak of nine angelic choirs, and it was through Pseudo-Dionysius that this view was as widely circulated as the thesis of their division into three groups. Even earlier, Irenaeus had spoken of seven choirs of angels. In the Middle Ages it was Aquinas in particular who championed the thesis of the pure spirituality of angels, while in the Franciscan school a subtle corporeality was again accepted. It has been the conception of Aquinas which has prevailed.

THE TEACHING OF THE CHURCH

The teaching presented in Scripture and in tradition was summed up by the official Church at the Fourth Lateran Council (1215). In opposition to the dualism of the Cathari, the Council insisted that it is a principle of faith that God is the unique source of all non-divine reality, and that he has created both the spiritual and the material worlds—that is, the world of angels and that of men. In this proposition the existence of angels is viewed as part of the content of faith, but their pure spirituality has never been explicitly formulated. The First Vatican Council simply repeated the teaching of the Fourth Lateran Council.

THE PERSONHOOD OF THE ANGELS

For the theological interpretation of angels, their activity and their being, the thesis of their pure spirituality, generally accepted since Aquinas, is the point of departure. Pure spirituality naturally implies subjectivity and personality; that is, self-possession and self-transcendence. As we emphasized earlier, spiritual being manifests itself in its power of reflection. How we are to interpret the being of a creature which is pure spirit remains a mystery. In our experience only spiritual being united to matter—our own bodies—is accessible to us. For any understanding of angels we must take into account their status as finite creatures as well as their purely spiritual being; their finitude is expressed in the fact that they can reflect on themselves—and thus possess themselves—only in that they encounter other creatures, other angels. Each angel realizes his own existence by placing himself in juxtaposition to the Thou of another angel and by emerging *vis-à-vis* the other from there to "return again to himself." Thus he requires fellow creatures. For the angels being-with—intersubjectivity—is fundamental, just as it is for men. Angels of course differ from men in that their subjectivity does not realize itself in a bodily dimension. And yet, this incorporeality does not mean that the angels have no relation to matter: this is evident from the fact that they have been given the task of co-operating in salvation history, that they are associated with human history, in accordance with God's plan of salvation. Thus the self-transcendence of angels must be interpreted in a double direction: towards God and their fellow angels and towards men and matter. The carrying out of their relationship both to God and to their fellow creatures, men and angels, is characterized by that intensity and universality proper to their specially constituted knowing and willing on the one hand, and to the divine commission of salvation on the other.

The metaphysical problem involved in angelic knowledge cannot be entered into here, but their extraordinary power of penetration, which Scripture attests by numerous metaphors, should be emphasized. Their piercing and comprehensive understanding is what is meant when Scripture represents them as covered with eyes—their whole being is a beholding. Of course they do not penetrate to the depths of God which only the Spirit of God himself fathoms (1 Cor. 2:10), nor do they even know the hidden thoughts of men unless these are revealed to them by God. (This implies that there can be an intimacy between men and angels.) Their knowledge is as different from the omniscience of God as the finite is from the infinite. Their finitude implies that their knowledge can increase in the course of salvation history, and that this increase depends on the disclosures which God makes to them as well as on the progress of salvation history itself.

The angels' free and powerful will corresponds to their comprehensive knowledge. It is on account of this penetrating understanding and great power of will that they make decisions without vacillating, without deliberation and with concentrated intellectual assertion, and hence never revoke them.

The intensity of their intellectual life corresponds to their close association with God. Of course, even they are incapable of contemplating God directly unless a special grace is given to them. In fact, God presenting himself to them unveiled has summoned them to dialogue with himself. This immediate and living intercourse with God is in conformity with their participation in the salvation of Christ; that is, their insertion into the event of salvation accomplished by Christ. That the angels behold the face of God is attested for us in both the Old and the New Testament (Is. 6:2f.; Dan.

7:10; Mt. 18:10). They are taken into the inaccessible presence of God into which the seer of John's apocalypse was able to gaze only because the door of heaven was opened to him (Rev. 4:1). According to the Johannine apocalypse the angels offer perpetual praise to God (Rev. 4:5f.). Their worship is signified by the singing of the triple "Holy," the victory hymns and the psalms (Rev. 19:6; cf. Is. 6:3).

The angels' transcendence towards God whereby they fulfill their own being is described by Eric Peterson in the following manner:

The pure spirits which the gnostic encounters here, and who of their nature are ontologically orientated towards God, are not beings paralysed into some kind of dumb adoration of God. Their distinctive nature is not dictated by their standing still, but by their movement, the beating of their wings which Isaiah was the first to describe with the mighty power of his vision; and by the fact that now this beating of wings and covering of the feet with wings—so significant in the realm of mystical symbolism—corresponds to a particular form of the pouring forth in word, cry and song of the *Holy, holy, holy*. In other words: this phenomenon of pouring out in word and song is the heart of the nature of these angels. We are not saying that, in terms of human analogy, part of the angel-world is chosen for the task of always singing something before the Lord God. Indeed, that is an unbearable idea, and the desire to be doing such a thing for all eternity is plainly unthinkable. In reality we are concerned here with something totally different. We are not thinking of angels who in a completely abstract way are primarily *angels in general* who also sing: but about angels whose angelic nature consists precisely in their pouring forth, in the manner described, the praise of him who is *Holy, holy, holy*. This cry constitutes their ultimate nature: it is this effusion which makes them what they are. . . .[1]

In the time of salvation between the resurrection and the return of Jesus Christ, the angels in accordance with God's instructions assist and guard the Church, indeed, the whole of mankind and individual Christians. One should neither exaggerate nor undervalue their effectiveness. Just as they accompanied the whole life of Christ, usually unseen, so they are present in the life of the Church, but without taking away the responsibility of its members.

Since the patristic period the conviction has existed that the worship of the Church is a participation in the heavenly worship of the angels, and conversely that they share in the worship of the Church. Concerning guardian angels, we refer readers to what was said earlier on the subject of Divine Providence.

The saving activity of angels, which takes place at God's command, justifies our turning to them in confidence and trust and imploring their help in prayer. The meaning of prayer to a creature living in dialogue with God will be gone into in more detail when the nature of the Church is discussed. The Church itself calls on the angels at the death of its members as they enter into perfect communion with Christ.

As for the numerous appearances of angels recorded in Scripture, the following explanation is the best that can be attempted. They bring about understanding and love in the human person, in conformity with God's plan of salvation; or we may say that God himself produces by their means definite spiritual stirrings in man. The man so affected by the operation of God translates it, in accordance with his own mental faculties and powers of synthesis, into the picture world of his imagination, and thus expresses in an analogous way the experience produced by God. Thus the appearance of an angel—an angelic apparition—is not simply an objective, external event. Rather it is always an objectification on the part of man. It is a synthesis of objective event and creative subjective experience. The appearance of an angel must therefore be explained by analogy with the rare manifestations of the Holy.

Notes

[1] *The Angels and the Liturgy*, trans. Ronald Wall (New York: Herder and Herder, 1964), p. 44.

▶13

The Devil

HIS EXISTENCE

Like men the angels were capable of rejecting God's invitation to interior dialogue with him in unveiled intimacy. It is part of the Church's official teaching that some angels did reject this invitation. It is difficult to decide whether a specific test has to be assumed to account for this rejection: probably one must answer the question in the negative. We simply do not know anything whatever about the type or duration of any possible test or concerning the nature of their sin; revelation furnishes only hints. If every sin begins with pride (Sir. 10:12f.), then the sin of the demons must have done so. It is said of the adversary who sought to prevail with arrogant might that he exalted himself above God and all the saints (2 Thess. 2:4f.). Probably the sin consisted in the fact that Satan was so blinded by his own glory, even though it was created, that he denied his dependence on God—refused to be a creature and strove for an autonomy which is proper to God alone. As in the case of man, one will have to assume that the Devil at the moment in which he began to exist was confronted with the question of whether he willed to accept his created status or not; and that he instantly rebelled against God. Satan was probably not driven to his revolt against God primarily by the knowledge that he would have to submit to the incarnate Son of God. It was of

218

course his rebellion against God, arising from his own spiritual pride, which led to his attack on God's plan of salvation in general; and most of all at its high point in Jesus Christ. The decision of Satan, exercised with the total concentration of his great intellectual powers, will never be revoked.

In Scripture we come upon many passages which testify to the existence of evil spirits. These texts often given evidence of a close relationship with extra-biblical conceptions of demons, goblins, and assorted mischievous creatures which try to injure man and which can be restrained or appeased by various kinds of magic. Such popular notions frequently occur in Scripture, but they are not intended to testify to the existence of a Devil. Here one has to make an especially precise distinction between the content of a statement and the manner of its expression. At the same time an element of uncertainty about the boundary line between them cannot be avoided.

What Scripture actually attests about the Devil, and respectively about demons, is substantially distinguished from the profane notion of the demonic. According to the profane notion the demonic is an enigmatic, unintelligible, weird, often destructive, and impersonal power. It is an evil, impersonal divine force in the world. According to Holy Scripture, however, Satan is a personal power opposed to God. The texts which attest to such a power in the Old Testament are not many: if it also presents numerous other texts in which there is talk of demons, the intention of these texts on the whole is precisely to counteract the heathen belief in such spirits. Something of this sort is probably at issue in the Book of Tobias, which originated in the period of the Babylonian Captivity. The Israelites, living in a foreign land, were subject to numerous temptations through contact with the vain superstitions of their environment. Thus it was important that they should be restrained from embracing these superstitions and repeatedly summoned anew to faith in the gracious, protecting, living and only God. This is what is meant by the Book of Tobias.

It can probably be said that there are four major texts in the Old Testament which speak for belief in the Devil: Job 1:6ff.; Zech. 3:1ff.; Wis. 2:24; Lev. 16:7ff. The interpretation of these texts is not simple. The first text describes in poetic form how Satan attempted to prove that Job's piety was a sham. In the second Satan is at pains to thwart the pardoning of men after their sin; he is portrayed as the adversary of the merciful and compassionate—and thus also the enemy of the community, the nation and the priesthood through which the grace of God is transmitted. He learns, of course, that God's power is greater than his own. The Wisdom text is a commentary on Genesis 3. According to this it is the Devil who leads the first men astray, confusing them by means of a lie, but a lie in which he mixes truth with falsehood. That is why it succeeds. He casts suspicion on God, implying that God in a deceitful and selfish manner wants to deprive Adam and Eve of the fortunate consequences of enjoying the forbidden fruit. With cunning ambiguity he makes it appear that the eating of the fruit will only open their eyes, and he stimulates their self-esteem when he promises them godlikeness. In the last passage Azazel is mentioned: he is described as a personal being to whom the sins of the people are transferred in a symbolic rite. This is intended not simply to symbolize the removal of their sins, but that they are taken to the place where they belong—to Azazel. Azazel is probably to be identified with Satan.

In the interpretation of such passages one should not overlook the fact that what is usually attributed to the anger of God is occasionally attributed to Satan instead. Here the question arises whether Satan is a metaphor for the punishments of a righteous God, or whether he is the instrument of execution for God's sentence of judgment. In not a few places the texts favor the last interpretation.

There is in the Old Testament apparently only one Devil: Satan. This word expresses first of all a function, but it soon appears as the proper name of a fallen angel. "Satan" means much the same as adversary, enemy, the accuser before a court of justice: Satan opposes God and tries to lead men astray. In the Septuagint the word is translated by *diabolos* (slanderer, deceiver, liar, one who produces confusion). When the Old Testament speaks of disciples of the Devil it means evil men obedient to him.

A survey of the Old Testament evidence shows that belief in the

Devil does not stand at the center of the Old Testament's faith. Disaster and misfortune are not attributed to the work of an evil demon, whom one must foil by magic, but are considered as afflictions coming from the one true living God. The faith of the Old Testament is concentrated on the constantly active and gracious God who has revealed his intent to save in ever new ways since the days of Abraham and who in delivering his people from the Egyptian oppression has caused himself to be experienced in a way that is valid for ever. If his plans are thwarted, it is through the fault of men; Satan plays only a modest supporting role. Though the word Satan is seldom encountered in the Old Testament, it is of frequent occurrence in the New, especially in Matthew's gospel, the two books of Luke, and the older epistles of the apostle Paul. Christ has taken up the struggle against Satan's rule specifically in an act which signifies the breaking through of the kingdom of God —the expulsion of demons (Lk. 11:20). According to Paul, Jesus Christ has conquered the hostile powers and principalities. The New Testament speaks of an almost orderly kingdom of the Devil —though his realm is full of internal strife, it nevertheless seems to have a chief devil at its head. He is called Beelzebub or Beelzebul (Mt. 10:25; 2 Cor. 12:7; Rev. 12:7ff.; Mt. 12:24ff.). The devils are a pluralistic society, but they are as one in the struggle against God, against every appearance of the divine in history. (In every society there is some bond affording a measure of direction.) The number of devils is called legion in Scripture (Mk. 5:9). As to the proportion of good to bad angels, nothing is known about this, and the hypothesis that the number of fallen angels is greater than the number of good seems difficult to reconcile with the love and the majesty of the Creator. Nor does it do justice to the Old Testament evidence that there is only one Satan.

The Church has more than once declared that evil spirits exist. As we saw earlier on, every form of dualism was rejected by the early Church; hence we know that although there are indeed devils, they are not evil principles hostile to God or equal to him. Rather, they are fallen spirits whom God allows to produce evil in the world. The major text on evil spirits is furnished by the Fourth Lateran Council (DS 800). The council does not testify formally

to the existence of evil spirits but presupposes their existence along
with the existence of good spirits. It was vigorously asserted by this
council that everything which is not God must of its nature be
created. If there is evil in the world, this is to be attributed to the
free decisions of individual creatures. The Devil and other evil
demons were good when God created them; it is their own evil
decisions which have made them evil. They tempt man and endeavor to draw him into their own sinful revolt against God. Hence
the conciliar decree implies that the evil decision of a powerful
spirit in the world antedates the human decision for or against God.
This evil is the preliminary draft of the sin of man.

This same doctrine has been proclaimed by the Church's ordinary magisterium: there are personal forces in the world which
have been opposed to God from the beginning. Hence it is understandable that forces of hatred, negation, deceit and destruction are
constantly arising in history which contradict all rationality.

The scriptural images in which the nature of the rebellious spirits'
life is expressed are manifold—darkness, shackles, wailing and the
gnashing of teeth. In the discussion of the Last Things we will
return to this in more detail when we treat of hell.

THE DISASTROUS EFFECTS

Nevertheless the crucial thing is not an account of the metaphysics
of hell but an understanding of the disastrous effects wrought by
the evil spirits, evils radically related to the world and specifically
to salvation history (cf. Mt. 4:1–11; 2 Cor. 12:7; Lk. 22:31; 1
Thess. 3:5; Jn. 8:44; 1 Pet. 5:8; Jas. 4:7; Eph. 6:11,12). Since
the incarnation of the eternal Logos the activity of Satan in opposition to God and man has turned with special fury against Jesus.
With cunning, subtlety, deceit and finally with brutal force, Satan
seeks to destroy Jesus and his work. Jesus has come in order to
destroy the work of Satan (1 Jn. 3:8). He has not fallen into
Satan's power (Jn. 14:30). Indeed with the arrival of Jesus, Satan's
power is already overthrown (Jn. 16:11). The Devil knows that
the hour of his downfall has come (Mk. 1:23–28; 1:24,39; 3:11f.;
5:1–12; 7:24–30; Mt. 8:16; 8:28–34; 9:32f.; 15:12–28; Lk.

6:18). Jesus refuses to have his majesty and his works of power attested by unclean spirits and to let his hidden divinity emerge in this sensational way (Mk. 1:34) through the instrumentality of the Devil—who assuredly believes in God but hates him and trembles before him (Jas. 2:19).

The evil spirits attempted to make Jesus unfaithful to his mission: it was when he was preparing himself for his public activity in the desert that the Tempter approached him (Mk. 1:12f.). In the first temptation (Mt. 4:3f.; Lk. 4:3f.) Satan tried to make use of the situation in which Jesus found himself after forty days of fasting: he was hungry. Satan challenged him: If you are the Son of God, command these stones to become bread. The temptation did not lie in his suggestion that Jesus satisfy his hunger, but in his effort to persuade Jesus to use his mission to gratify his own bodily and earthly needs, to misuse it in order to help himself. Jesus refused to put his mission at the service of earthly goals. The word of God which he had to proclaim had precedence over every earthly thing. In the second temptation (Mt. 4:5-7; Lk. 4:9-13) the Devil suggested to Jesus that he perform a dramatic miracle—throw himself down from the pinnacle of the Temple. He supports his challenge with a saying of Scripture and therein proves himself to be a theologian: "He will put his angels in charge of you, and they will support you in their arms, for fear you should strike your foot against a stone"—he cites God's own words to Jesus in order to tempt him to infidelity towards God. The fascinating thing is that Satan behaves as though he were pious: he shows Jesus an easy and quick way in which the curious and sensation-hungry crowd can see and hear what it likes to see and hear, and thus be brought to faith in his Messiahship. But Jesus refuses; he says: It is written: You shall not "tempt" God. Onlookers would not be genuinely persuaded to believe in Christ by the procedure suggested by the Devil; rather, they would be overwhelmed and stupefied, and this would be a false proclamation of the word of God. It would not have led to true conversion and renewal, which can be achieved only through repentance and atonement in the context of a responsible decision of conscience. In the third temptation (Mt. 4:8-12; Lk. 4:5-8), the Devil showed Jesus

the majesty and power of this world and promised it all to him
if he would but bow down and pay Satan homage. Whereas before,
Satan played the role of a devotee, he now presents himself as lord
of the earth. This temptation is in open conflict with the mission
of Jesus; he has not come in order to establish an earthly kingdom
in splendor and majesty—his kingdom is not of this world (Jn.
18:36). The vehemence of his repulse of Satan is understandable,
for this temptation is directed against the innermost essence of his
mission. It is not a proposal that he usher in God's kingdom with
worldly power, but that he exchange it for the kingdom of this
world.

These temptations merit detailed treatment because they are also
the constant temptations of the Church. Even though Jesus overcame them at the beginning of his public life, his whole life was
still a struggle with the powers of evil. In substance, of course, their
defeat was already accomplished: Satan had fallen like a lightning
bolt from heaven (Lk. 10:17f.). The hour at which he is to be
cast out is already here (Jn. 12:31), and even the disciples through
their share in Jesus' mission can exercise power over the demons
in his name (Mk. 3:15; 6:7,13; Mt. 10:1-8). When in sending
out the Twelve to preach Jesus at the same time gives them power
over the unclean spirits, this means that there is no proclaiming of
God's kingdom without this power, just as there is, of course, no
such power without the proclamation.

The destruction of order which the Devil pursues while seeking
to turn men away from God also takes effect in man's body. Jesus
sees the evil one at work not merely in hatred, egoism and falsehood, but also in many bodily sicknesses. Not every sickness and
disaster is described as the direct effect of the Devil, but that this
is a world in which sickness and misery hold sway is ultimately to
be attributed to him. His rule over men reaches its peak in what
is called possession. There the powers of willing and acting which
belong to man are paralyzed, and he is governed by foreign powers
which seek his ruin and occasionally even drive him to self-
destruction. Jesus commands the unclean spirits and they go—they
obey one mightier than themselves. We find the most graphic de-

scription of the expulsion of a demon in Mark 5:1–20 (cf. Lk. 8:26–39; 11:21ff.; Mk. 7:24–30; Mt. 15:21–28; 9:32–34; 8:16; 12:22–37; Lk. 11:14–23; 4:41; 8:2; 16:9; 13:10–17). These expulsions of the Devil are not to be understood as the victory of one external power over another, but as the victory of goodness and love over evil and hatred. Some have sought to see in Christ's behavior an adaptation to popular views or a sign of defective medical knowledge. In point of fact, possessions frequently manifest themselves as definite diseases, and it is not really possible to draw a sharp line between sickness and possession. Nor can "possession" be established beyond a doubt by means of ordinary observation. For one who believes in Christ, however, Christ is the norm of thought and judgment. As strange as the expulsion of devils may appear to him, a Christian submits his judgment to the judgment of Christ, which is the foundation of his supernaturally transformed existence, understanding and development. Jesus' behavior cannot be understood simply as an adaptation to the demon mythology of his age; the struggle against the Devil is inextricably bound up with the life of Christ. Jesus declares repeatedly that his mission is not only to teach, to give example and to bring new life; he must destroy an evil power who is a person hostile to God. Also, it should not be overlooked that Jesus employs no magic practices but simply commands the Evil One with a word. (In contrast, a purely existential interpretation can see in the figure of the Devil only an image of the evil in man himself.)

The Devil has many assistants who do his work on earth. John gives powerful expression to this idea. The scribes and the Pharisees, along with those they have led astray, are certain to reject Jesus, because they are children of the Devil (Jn. 8:44), who sows unbelief in their hearts. He is a false prophet, the father of lies, and he so completely blinds and confuses their minds that they see a devil in Jesus and treat his words as blasphemous (Jn. 7:24; 8:48,52). Diabolic treachery reaches its climax when Satan suggests to those whom he has seduced that for the sake of God and his revelation they must put Jesus to death. Here the Devil masquerades as the guardian and defender of God's saving institutions

—the utmost in cunning and distortion which he could devise was to depict Jesus as his own servant (Mt. 12:22–32; Mk. 3:22–30; Lk. 11:14–23; Mt. 9:34). It may be that Christ is crucified by men, but behind this frightful event stands another. It is Satan— from the beginning a murderer and a liar—who suggests to Judas that he betray Jesus (Lk. 22:3; Jn. 6:72; 13:27). Those who act in the foreground are merely Satan's followers.

Jesus never allowed himself to be deflected from his mission. Nor did he ever permit himself to be driven by hate to counter-hate, by force to counter-force, or by deception and lies to cunning and craftiness; he never responded to falsehood with falsehood. Instead, the cross of Christ was the ultimate expression of love: through the cross God's rule is established and the rule of everything contrary to God is broken. The Devil, since the death of Jesus in which he seemed to triumph, is stripped of his power. For God "has forgiven us all our sins; he has cancelled the bond which pledged us to the decrees of the law. It stood against us, but he has set it aside, nailing it to the cross" (Col. 2:14). He has disarmed the powers and principalities, putting them to shame on the pillory of the cross; he has triumphed over them through Christ. Through Christ's death God willed to dethrone him who wielded the power of death—the Devil; but he also willed to save all those who through their fear of death were held in lifelong bondage (Heb. 2:14f.).

Since the death and resurrection of Jesus, the Devil and his followers are like a defeated army. Yet they can still cause considerable trouble. As long as Christ and his work live on in the Church, Satan's endeavor to destroy Christ will continue as a struggle against the Church. He may attempt to overpower the Church from within by seducing her from fidelity to her mission or persuading her to rely more on worldly means in the accomplishment of her task than on the power of the gospel itself (Rom. 1:16). He may harass her from without, seeking to obstruct her work. Both these methods are described in the New Testament (cf. 2 Cor. 12:7f.; 6:14ff.; 1 Cor. 10:20; Mt. 13:19; Mk. 4:15; Lk. 8:12; 1 Pet. 5:8; 1 Thess. 3:5; 2:18; Mt. 13:37ff.; 12:43ff.; 2 Tim. 2:26; 2 Cor. 11:13f.; Acts 5:3; 1 Cor. 7:5; 1 Tim. 5:15). The Devil seeks to sift the apostles like wheat (Lk. 22:31) and to provoke divisions and dis-

sension in the Church (Rom. 16:17; 2 Cor. 11:13ff.). The individual Christian too is exposed to the assaults and persecutions
of Satan; he has to reckon not merely with the evil grounded in
human freedom or the evil inclinations arising from within his own
being but with a personal power which wills what is evil, what is
blasphemous, as such (Eph. 6:11; 1 Pet. 5:8ff.). A man needs the
Holy Spirit's gift of discernment in order to perceive whether what
looks like an angel of light is a messenger from God or from Satan
—whether an appearance of sanctity is truth or delusion (2 Cor.
11:14); for the actions and the appearance of the saint and those
of Satan can be similar enough to be mistaken for one another.
According to the Johannine apocalypse the Devil will make a special display of power in the last days. He will exhibit such splendor,
make such an art of deception, that the temptation to apostasy will
be very great even for those of good will (1 Tim. 4:1; Rev. 12:7f.,
12f.; 19:20).

Possession represents a special form of diabolical activity. Theologians usually distinguish between three forms of possession: *circuminsessio* (an attack on all sides), *obsessio,* and *possessio.* In the
first form, *circuminsessio,* the person is besieged by Satan with all
manner of external torments. In *obsessio* the Devil makes use of a
man's organs as instruments. In *possessio* a person becomes a will-
less object, a medium of demonic activity. The actuality of any of
these forms of possession is extremely difficult to establish in any
particular case. The Church, of course, takes possession seriously,
but in the critical examination of particular cases she exercises the
greatest caution. Many illnesses manifest the symptoms from which
possession was inferred in former times. Much of what used to be
attributed to the Devil can now be accounted for naturally. Even
in the worst forms of possession the Devil cannot exercise direct
control over the human intellect or join himself to the human ego
in such a way as to form a personal unity with it. Nevertheless one
can only agree with the following remarks of Winkelhofer:

It seems as if today especially the Devil is choosing very circumspect
ways of taking possession of a man. The saints would have recognized
his presence and could perhaps, here and there, have forced him to

show himself. An element of possession is to be reckoned with in all those criminals whose acts assume international dimensions, for they seem like driven, hunted men, possessed by the unfettered logic of a self-made ideology, their guiding principle a cold hatred and ruthless contempt for man. All the restless planning with nothing in view but murder, all the restless activity, all the hidden crimes of men in high places, rendered anonymous by their positions—all these men rooted in no family or fraternal community, and in their rootlessness held in check by nothing; all these are to be feared. The probability of their being in the possession of Satan is great. For Holy Scripture, particularly the New Testament, wherever evil looms large in history it is a manifestation of the Devil.[1]

In spite of these and other warnings against the Devil, the New Testament makes it clear that the Christian need not tremble before him. Whoever believes in Christ has escaped from Satan's rule. Paul writes to the Ephesians (Eph. 2:1–5):

Time was when you were dead in your sins and wickedness, when you followed the evil ways of this present age, when you obeyed the commander of the spiritual powers of the air, the spirit now at work among God's rebel subjects. We too were of their number: we all lived our lives in sensuality, and obeyed the promptings of our own instincts and notions. In our natural condition, we like the rest lay under the dreadful judgment of God. But God rich in mercy, for the great love he bore us, brought us to life with Christ even when we were dead in our sins; it is by his grace you are saved.

(Cf. Acts 5:16; 8:7; 16:16–19; 26:18f.). One who believes in Christ does not live in fear before demons: they can do nothing against him, provided that he does not give them their opportunity (Eph. 4:27). In the final analysis even the Devil must serve as an instrument of salvation for one who believes in Christ (1 Cor. 5:5; 2 Cor. 12:7). For through his brotherly and devoted love Christ is stronger than the evil one in the world (1 Jn. 4:4). Over against all the warnings concerning the Devil stands Paul's confident expression of victory: no satanic power can separate us from

Christ (Rom. 8:38f.). Whoever believes in Christ is a son of the protecting Father in heaven, the almighty Lord of all the spirits (Mt. 24:36; 25:31ff.; Mk. 13:27; Rev. 7:1–17).

Notes

[1] A. Winkelhofer, *Satan*, pp. 125f.

Index